TROUBLESHOOTING MICROPROCESSOR-BASED SYSTEMS

TROUBLESHOOTING MICROPROCESSOR-BASED SYSTEMS

ALLAN H. ROBBINS

BRIAN LUNDEEN

PRENTICE-HALL, INC., Englewood Cliffs, N.J. 07632

Library of Congress Cataloging-in-Publication Data

Robbins, Allan.
  Troubleshooting microprocessor-based systems.

  Bibliography: p.
  Includes index.
  1. Microprocessors—Maintenance and repair.
I. Lundeen, Brian. II. Title.
TK7895.M5R63 1987   621.391'6'0288   86-25539
ISBN 0-13-931296-X

Editorial/production supervision and
   interior design: *Eileen M. O'Sullivan*
Cover design: *Wanda Lubelska*
Manufacturing buyer: *Carol Bystrom*

©1987 by Prentice-Hall, Inc.
A Division of Simon & Schuster
Englewood Cliffs, New Jersey 07632

Printed in the United States of America

10 9 8 7 6 5 4 3 2 1

0-13-931296-X   025

Prentice-Hall International (UK) Limited, *London*
Prentice-Hall of Australia Pty. Limited, *Sydney*
Prentice-Hall Canada Inc., *Toronto*
Prentice-Hall Hispanoamericana, S.A., *Mexico*
Prentice-Hall of India Private Limited, *New Delhi*
Prentice-Hall of Japan, Inc., *Tokyo*
Prentice-Hall of Southeast Asia Pte. Ltd., *Singapore*
Editora Prentice-Hall do Brasil, Ltda., *Rio de Janeiro*

CONTENTS

PREFACE

With the widespread application of microprocessor-based systems in industry, business, and elsewhere, the study of troubleshooting as a logically organized and systematic discipline is becoming of increasing importance. This book was written to help students acquire the understanding, knowledge and skills required to become competent troubleshooters. It presents basic principles of hardware troubleshooting in a systematic and orderly fashion, along with the principle tools and methodologies available for their implementation. It is designed so that any technically-oriented person, from the novice electronic/computer student to the experienced repair technician or hardware test engineer can understand and apply the principles to microprocessor-based products and systems as encountered in practice.

Some of the topics addressed by this book include:

A discussion of the hardware fault environment, focusing on the types of faults which can occur and how those faults manifest themselves.

A systematic, top-down approach to troubleshooting which the authors have found to be effective through years of troubleshooting experience. The approach shows how to begin the investigation at the highest level, then methodically narrow the search until the problem has been isolated to the lowest attainable level. With proper troubleshooting tools, component level fault identification is achieved easily with this approach.

A discussion of the various troubleshooting tools available, from traditional equipment such as oscilloscopes and logic analyzers, to recently introduced products such as dynamic in-circuit testers. More importantly, the authors show where and how to use these tools to obtain maximum results.

We assume that the reader has a basic knowledge of microprocessor architecture, elements of a microprocessor system (ROM memory, RAM memory, I/O subsystems), bus structures, decoding schemes, interfacing of memory and I/O devices to system buses, etc. It is also assumed that the reader is somewhat familiar with assembly language programming, although not an expert programmer.

Throughout the book, theory has been augmented by numerous practical examples based on selected microprocessors, most notably the Intel 8085, the Motorola 6809, and the Zilog Z80. However, the theory can be extended easily to other microprocessors. This is so, because, once you get past the processor itself, the circuitry surrounding the CPU is virtually the same, regardless of manufacturer or bus width. While this use of different processors is perhaps more confusing than staying with a single processor throughout, it represents a compromise between two conflicting demands—on the one hand to represent fairly the real world troubleshooting environment (where a variety of products from different vendors is encountered) and on the other, to keep the length of the book to a manageable size. At the level of maturity of understanding assumed on the part of the reader, this approach should represent no real problem.

We have tried to make the book useful to working professionals and students alike; thus, it may be used in a variety of courses in colleges, universities, industrial and military training programs, self study by on the job practitioners as well as by others who wish to increase their knowledge of troubleshooting principles, modern tools, and techniques.

ACKNOWLEDGMENTS

This book has its origins in a course developed at the Industrial Applications of Microelectronics Centre in Winnipeg. The authors would like to thank Dr. W. Kinsner, Director of Research at the Centre, for suggesting the development of this course and the Centre for providing the resources to undertake it. We would also like to thank Red River Community College (where we are currently employed) for the opportunity to extend the ideas and develop them further.

The authors would like to thank the many firms who supplied data and photographs for this book. These include Hewlett-Packard Company, John Fluke Manufacturing Company Inc, Motorola Semiconductor Products Inc, Intel Corporation, Zilog Corporation, Creative Microprocessor Systems and Applied Microsystems Corporation. Our special thanks goes out to Andrew Tung of Tektronix Canada Inc. for his extra effort on our behalf, as well as to Greg Burnell and Rick Williamson of Prentice-Hall for their helpful advice. Finally, we would like to thank the following reviewers—Dr. Gerald W. Cockerell of Indiana State University, Brian R. Anderson, Karl R. Brown and Jerome S. Schatten of Vancouver Community College, Loren Boyle of the British Columbia Institute of Technology and Dominic Eng of the Southern Alberta Institute of Technology—whose valuable comments increased the quality of this book immeasurably.

Allan H. Robbins

Brian Lundeen

TROUBLESHOOTING MICROPROCESSOR-BASED SYSTEMS

1

INTRODUCTION TO TROUBLESHOOTING MICROPROCESSOR-BASED SYSTEMS

As microprocessor-based systems have evolved in complexity, a companion need for new tools and test methods has arisen. In response to this need, new approaches have been developed. Now the troubleshooter, whether in the design/development, production, or maintenance/service environment, has a range of powerful tools from which to choose. This chapter introduces the main ideas and the various troubleshooting tools to be discussed in this book. However, much troubleshooting in real life can be done using simple tools and simple techniques. Therefore, part of this chapter is used to describe how traditional tools and methods (the oscilloscope, for example) can be used to diagnose many commonly encountered faults.

1-1 NATURE OF THE TROUBLESHOOTING ENVIRONMENT

Except for gross failures such as power supply or clock malfunctions, the operational status of microprocessor systems is not readily determined by traditional means [1]. Microprocessors are characterized by complex bus structures, intricate timing relationships, and software-dependent operation. Such characteristics tend to obscure fault sources and complicate the diagnostic effort. Because the system operates under software control, there is no longer a simple relationship between hardware elements and logic signals. It is thus difficult to localize faults by operating symptom [2].

Troubleshooting difficulties are further complicated by the fact that it may not be known at the outset whether the problem is hardware based or software based (or even worse, a combination of the two). In some cases, it is obvious; in others it is not. For the latter, there may be no easy way of telling since hardware faults sometimes masquerade as software faults, and vice versa. For example, the incorrect operation of an I/O port does not necessarily mean that the port itself is defective—the problem may be due to a software error or to a fault in some other portion of the system hardware [3].

A third factor concerns the question of electrical versus logic faults. Systems that are logically correct may fail due to electrical problems such as marginal rise and fall time, excessive noise, and so on. Such failures can happen even in a system whose design is logically correct and where no component failures have occurred (Section 2–11.)

The concerns noted above present the troubleshooter with a number of testing and diagnostic problems not encountered in traditional designs. Paradoxically, however, some of those characteristics of microprocessor systems that tend to make them so difficult to test using conventional tools have in fact been turned to advantage in the design of some microprocessor service tools. Microprocessor systems have highly systematic, bus-oriented architectures, and except for single-chip designs, these buses are accessible as universal stimulus and monitoring points. In practice a particularly convenient access port to these buses is the processor socket. This entry point gives the troubleshooter access to and control over the entire system, permitting him or her to exercise and observe its inner workings. Variations on this concept yield such diverse testers as outlined in Section 1–4.

1–2 EVOLUTION OF MICROPROCESSOR TROUBLESHOOTING TOOLS

Over the years, a number of tools and methodologies have evolved. The earliest of these were the so-called "nodal" testers. These migrated to the microprocessor environment from the earlier digital environment. Such testers include logic probes, clips, comparators, pulsers, current tracers, and of course, the oscilloscope. These tools are still in use today. However, they have little diagnostic capability and are thus of chief value when it is known generally where the fault in a system lies.[1] The other, more difficult task of ascertaining which portion of the suspect system is actually malfunctioning and the companion problem of localizing problems to the node level cannot be handled easily by these tools. Such problems call for system-level tools. Such tools implement testing in a broader sense than do the nodal testers. Some of them contain a great deal of diagnostic capability, permitting efficient localization of faults to the nodal level. It is at this point that nodal testers such as pulsers and current tracers can be effectively brought back into the picture. By combining the two classes of test instruments, an efficient, systematic test strategy is possible.[2]

---

[1]Except for the oscilloscope. As we shall see, it permits a limited amount of general system investigation.

[2]Some commercial implementations incorporate both system-level and node-level capabilities in a single test instrument.

1-3 SYSTEM-LEVEL TOOLS AND TEST APPROACHES

First consider system-level tools and methodologies. Currently, there are three principal approaches in use. Two are hardware based and the third is software based.

1. *Microprocessor Principle testers.* Microprocessor (μP) principle testers employ computer principles as their basis of operation. Since they work in fundamentally the same fashion as microcomputers, they are able to take advantage of the computer nature of the systems that they are designed to test.

2. *Signature analysis testers.* Signature analyzers (SAs) employ a variation of the time-honored technique of signal tracing, borrowed from the field of analog electronics but updated for the digital environment. A controlled signal is injected into the system under test and traced, using appropriate instrumentation until the monitored signal no longer matches the expected signal. When this occurs, a fault has been uncovered.

3. *Logic analyzers.* Logic analyzers are oscilloscope-like devices—in fact, logic analyzers were first conceived as "digital scopes." Basically, they are signal data flow monitors that gather and store information and present it to the user on a CRT screen for analysis. They permit the user to observe externally the data flow activity occurring internally in the system under observation. They can be used to track program execution and provide the user with a history of computer operation prior to and following a fault. Note, however, that in spite of the fact that logic analyzers are software oriented, they can be used to troubleshoot both hardware and software faults.

As we shall see, each of these approaches has its advantages and disadvantages and preferred areas of application. Sometimes several strategies are combined in practice. Let us now examine each in more detail.

1-4 PROCESSOR-SOCKET μP PRINCIPLE TESTERS

Let us now consider processor-socket μP principle testers. These work in fundamentally the same fashion as computers and are sometimes referred to as "μP emulator" testers. Because these testers access the basic system elements via the target system bus, they are able to exercise and test bus devices directly, checking for correct functional operation, failures in functional blocks, and so on. In fact, some of the tools in this category can best be described as "service computers"—portable, easy-to-use microprocessor-based service instruments that let the user "reach" into the suspect system and test its internal workings (buses, decode logic, memory circuitry, I/O ports, etc.), as well as reach beyond to test the external side of I/O logic. The basic setup is illustrated in Figure 1-1.

Now, instead of a simple passive processor plugged into its socket, the unit under test (UUT) is driven by an active, user-directed diagnostic tool that permits the operator to take charge of the troubleshooting process, and systematically test and verify the

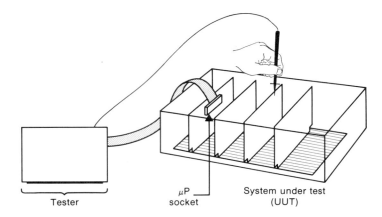

Tester   μP   System under test
                               socket   (UUT)

Figure 1-1: Test Set-up. Tester stimulates system. Probe permits fault tracing.

operation of system elements, as well as track down and isolate faults. The actual details of how this is done and the capabilities of individual testers vary from vendor to vendor. We will look at several types, including dynamic and static implementations. Although the dynamic types are the most useful, a simple, inexpensive version with limited but useful capabilities can be constructed by the user for a few hundred dollars worth of parts. Such a tester is described in detail in Chapter 6.

One of the advantages of this type of tester is that they are inherently capable of troubleshooting systems, even if no part of the system under test is working. Thus they are usable, even at the prototype stage.

The Fluke 9010A MicroSystem Troubleshooter

Perhaps the best known example of this type of tester is the John Fluke Co. 9010A MicroSystem Troubleshooter shown in Figure 1-2. It is a portable, easy-to-use instrument with powerful and elegant features. Note the console keyboard and alphanumeric display. These are used interactively by the operator during troubleshooting sessions. Personality pods tailor the general-purpose mainframe to specific processors. Both single-processor and multiprocessor systems can be handled. The 9010A is inherently capable of accommodating 8-, 16-, and 32-bit machines. A wide selection of pods covering the major popular processors is available. It is intended for use in the design/development, production, and maintenance/service environments.

The 9010A implements directly a systematic, top-down testing strategy. Built-in global functional tests permit localization of problems to major functional blocks such as the bus, ROM, RAM, or I/O. A second level of tests implements more focused testing, permitting the user to access and test individual memory and I/O locations. Other tests implement a circuit-tracing capability, easily permitting the user to pinpoint problems to the failed circuit node. More details on processor socket testers are presented in Chapter 5.

Figure 1–2:   The Fluke 9010A MicroSystem Troubleshooter. Photo courtesy of John Fluke Mfg Co Inc.

1–5 SIGNATURE ANALYZERS

Signature analysis provides an easy-to-use approach to troubleshooting that requires little knowledge on the part of the user at the routine test and service level. This means that in the depot, service center, or production environment, relatively unskilled workers can be employed to perform initial testing and product screening, with the more difficult problems passed to more experienced and knowledgeable personnel for solution. It has the disadvantage, however, of a substantial cost overhead associated with the gathering, documenting, and upkeep of signatures. For this reason, signature analysis is most suitably applied in the high-product-volume environment. It is not well suited to the low-volume environment, where only a few systems of any given design are produced.

To understand the SA troubleshooting methodology, consider again the classic analog troubleshooting approach. Typically, a known, controlled test signal is injected into the system and traced, using appropriate instrumentation (an oscilloscope, for example). To aid in the diagnostic effort, annotated schematics are frequently employed. These show the correct waveforms at key nodal points in a properly functioning system. The operator probes the system, comparing scope readings against system documentation. When a waveform is found that does not match, a fault has been uncovered. Tracing from here, the troubleshooter explores the circuit until the faulty element has been isolated.

Signature analysis applies the same principle to digital troubleshooting. However, while analog signals can be visually validated by observing their characteristics, such as shape, voltage, frequency, and so on, digital signals cannot. In digital systems, all signals look basically the same, and thus visual inspection is inadequate. However, since visual inspection is used primarily to determine whether the signal is correct, we do not really need to see waveforms at all if we can determine their correctness in some other fashion. This is what a signature analyzer does for us.

Figure 1-3 shows a typical signature analyzer. It is a device similar to a multimeter. The probe is used to investigate signals at suspect nodes. The tester determines the correctness of signals by compressing the data stream at the node under test into a unique numerical value that represents the signal at the node. This numerical value is referred to as its "signature".[3] These signatures are the counterparts of the known good waveforms of the analog environment, and like them, may be documented on logic schematics (Figure 1-4). Each node in any given system has its own characteristic signature—in essence, a "fingerprint" that identifies that particular node. The number 64F1 indicated on the meter in Figure 1-4(a) is what a typical signature looks like. Note, however, that this number itself has no meaning. It simply tells us whether the node is behaving correctly or incorrectly. The operator probes the system in the suspect area, comparing signatures against those documented. When a mismatch is encountered, a fault has been uncovered. Tracing from here, the troubleshooter explores the circuit as in the analog case until the faulty component has been isolated.

One of the shortcomings of the SA approach is that a data bank of known good signatures is required before testing can be done. Since these must be gathered from a properly working system, SA cannot be used to debug prototypes that have never worked, or systems for which signatures are not known. However, a number of manufacturers (such as Hewlett-Packard) include signature information in selected service manuals for use by service personnel.

Node probing as described above is just one aspect of the overall SA approach. Practical implementations always include a means of system stimulation which, together with probing, constitutes the SA approach. Details are described in Chapter 7.

The Hewlett-Packard 5006 Signature Analyzer

Signature analyzer test gear ranges from simple, multimeter-like devices to sophisticated computer-controlled systems. At the low end are the manual instruments. With these, the user must manually verify signatures by comparing instrument readings

---

[3]The technique used for data compression is surprisingly simple and easily understood; see Chapter 7.

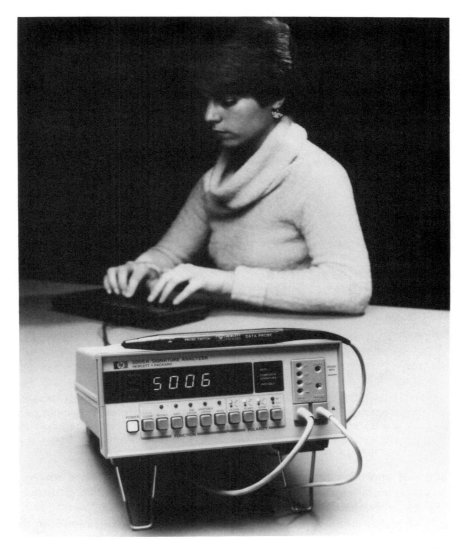

Figure 1-3: The Hewlett-Packard 5006A Signature Analyzer. Photo courtesy of Hewlett-Packard Company.

against system documentation. The process is slow, tedious, and error prone. More sophisticated versions include features such as composite signature and automatic signature verification.

A typical tester is the Hewlett-Packard 5006 analyzer shown in Figure 1–3. It features an HP-IL (Hewlett-Packard Interface Loop) that permits it to be used in an automatic test environment. Alternatively, an IEEE–488 interface may be selected.

The signature analysis approach is basically passive in nature—signatures are simply gathered and compared. This is in contrast to the μP socket-tester approach, where operator involvement is more interactive. This means that the control and

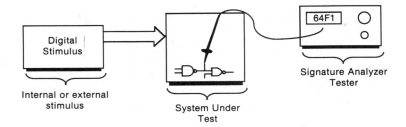

(a) Test Set-up

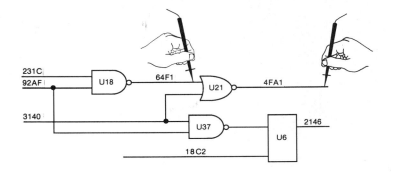

(b) Signal tracing using annotated schematic

Figure 1–4:   Digital system troubleshooting using Signature Analysis. Note the similarity to traditional analog signal tracing. In (a), the system under test is stimulated and the circuit probed. Annotated logic schematics as in (b) show signatures in a properly working system. Service Tech compares measured signatures against known good signatures. A mismatch indicates a faulted node.

stimulus approach generally provides the operator with greater control over the troubleshooting process, permitting real-time interaction between the operator and the test environment.

Another area where signature analysis is finding application is in the area of self-test of VLSI chips. Signature analysis techniques permit incorporation of self-test mechanisms on the chip to permit the user to verify the chips functionality to a high level of confidence.[4]

1-6 LOGIC ANALYZERS

Logic analyzers migrated to the service environment from the design/development environment. However, in spite of their name, logic analyzers are not really analyzers at all—they are passive observation tools much like oscilloscopes— the user has to

---

[4]At the writing of this book, few chips have such built-in test capability.

Figure 1–5: Troubleshooting using a logic analyzer. Here, the analyzer is being used in the time domain mode. Photo courtesy of Tektronix Inc. Copyright © 1986 Tektronix Inc. All rights reserved.

do the analysis. Still in the hands of a skilled operator, a logic analyzer is a powerful troubleshooting tool. Figure 1–5 illustrates a typical analyzer.

A logic analyzer is to the digital world what a storage oscilloscope is to the analog world. Basically, it is just a digital memory that captures and stores data in digital form [5]. Connected to the bus of the system under test via mechanical probes, data are captured and stored for operator analysis. Typical modern analyzers permit capture and storage of up to 64 simultaneous signals. Signals of interest include addresses, data, and control. Data are clocked into the memory in real time so that testing can occur at full speed.

For analysis, the captured data are played back on the screen. Generally speaking, logic analyzers have two basic display modes:

1. *Data-domain mode.* In this mode, the analyzer displays the captured data as a history of computer operation, permitting the user to track program execu-

tion directly on the screen. This is illustrated in Figure 1-6. By comparing the actual program execution (as depicted on the screen) against that expected (as indicated on the program documentation), the user can watch for devient system behavior. In this manner, the troubleshooter can check for flaws in software, and indirectly, for faults in hardware as well.

2. *Time-domain mode.* In this mode, the analyzer displays the captured data as a set of multichannel timing waveforms as depicted earlier (Figure 1-5). This mode is especially useful for investigating hardware-related phenomena such as race conditions, noise spikes, and signal glitches. Typically, 10 or more channels may be displayed simultaneously. This allows investigation of simultaneous data on data buses, address buses, control buses, and so on.

Logic analyzers and their use are considered in detail in Chapters 8 and 9.

1-7 NODAL TESTERS

As noted, nodal testers were the earliest service aids available to the troubleshooter. Figure 1-7 shows a trio of hand-held test tools. Let us briefly consider each of these in turn. (Chapter 10 provides more complete usage details.)

Logic Probes

Logic probes are simple to use, hand-held devices that indicate the logic state (high or low) of the probed node by means of a set of built-in indicator lamps. Typically,

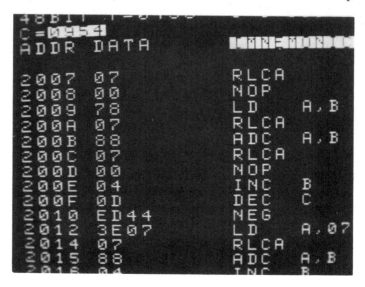

Figure 1-6: Logic Analyzer data domain display shows actual execution history. Example shown is a dis-assembled trace.

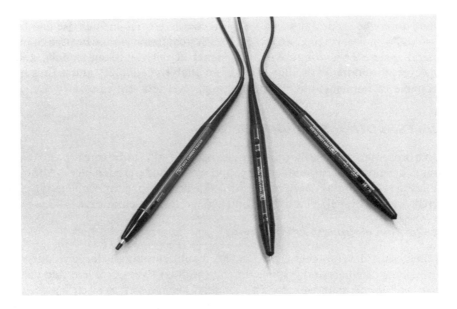

Figure 1-7:   A trio of hand-held nodal testers. Illustrated are a logic probe, a logic pulser and a current tracer.

two lamps are provided: a red lamp to indicate logic high and a green lamp to indicate logic low. Some also provide a means of indicating floating (tri-state) conditions.

Logic probes are useful for tracing logic levels, identifying stuck nodes, or determining whether a node has activity on it. Many probes contain pulse stretcher circuits so that even very short pulses can be observed.

Logic Pulsers

Logic pulsers are also hand-held service tools. They are used to stimulate nodes with short, powerful pulses. The node's response to this stimulation is simultaneously monitored (using a device such as a current tracer, logic probe, or oscilloscope). Pulsers are useful for identifying stuck nodes, as well as for providing the stimulus needed for current tracer usage.

Current Tracers

Current tracers are hand-held current-detecting devices that are used to trace current flow in logic and microprocessor circuits. They find use in locating shorted components, foil shorts and solder bridges on PC cards, and so on.

Oscilloscopes

The oscilloscope is a multipurpose instrument—it functions as a nodal tester, a signal analysis tester, and (to a limited degree), a system-level tester. As a nodal tester, it may be used in place of a logic probe for investigating logic levels; as a signal analysis tester, it may be used to observe electrical characteristics such as rise and fall times, pulse width, noise, ringing, and so on; as a system tester, it may be used to investigate general system behavior looking for signal activity, missing signals, and so on. However, the common oscilloscope has no analysis capability and is thus inherently incapable of implementing efficient system-level test strategies.

1-8 TROUBLESHOOTING ENVIRONMENTS

Microprocessor troubleshooting environments fall into three basic catagories: design/development, manufacturing, and service and maintenance.[5] Although there is considerable overlap, each has its own characteristic set of problem types and preferred (or traditional) sets of test and service instrumentation.

Design/Development Environment

In the design/development environment, troubleshooting is largely concerned with getting new products and systems up and running. Every problem that can possibly occur will be encountered here. This includes logic as well as electrical design errors, errors in construction (wire wrapping or PC board layout), board defects (improperly etched boards or faulty plate-through holes), power supply problems (blown fuses, improper or missing voltages, excessive ripple), faulty or misinserted electronic components (integrated circuits, resistors, capacitors, diodes, etc.), improperly seated boards, bent pins, cold solder joints, faulty sockets, loose or broken wires, improper cable configurations, misset option and configuration switches, missing jumpers, as well as software errors.

For many years, the primary hardware fault analysis tools used here have been the logic analyzer and the oscilloscope. Part of the reason for the widespread use of the logic analyzer in this role is historical (for many years, there was little else available) and part is its tremendous capability (it is the only tool available that permits software as well as hardware troubleshooting plus system integration). However, for purely hardware troubleshooting, it is no longer necessarily the best choice—μP socket testers can be a much better choice in many instances. Signature analyzers, on the other hand, are of no value, as they cannot be used to debug hardware during the development stage when signatures are not yet available.

Manufacturing Environment

In the manufacturing environment, troubleshooting is largely concerned with getting those new products and systems up and running that failed the manufacturing process. (Manufacturing is interpreted here in a broad sense to mean the assembly

---

[5]*Maintenance departments* here are taken to mean troubleshooting and service areas (as found in large companies, educational institutions, the military, etc.) that maintain their own installed base of electronic equipment and systems. Equipment from many manufacturers (including in-house designs) is encountered here. *Service depots* are taken to mean shops that repair or replace customer equipment. These can vary from simple board swap operations to component-level troubleshooting and repair centers.

of previously designed products or systems, whether it be in a factory or in a one-person shop.) As above, almost any type of problem that can occur will occur (with the exception of design-related faults that have presumably been worked out during the design/development phase).

The type of troubleshooting gear encountered here also varies widely. In large factories, automatic test equipment (ATE) systems may be found. For small and medium-sized production levels, μP socket testers are very useful. Signature analyzers are another good alternative for certain types of production testing. As always, the oscilloscope and multimeter are useful tools. For very small shops (or personal use), the static stimulus tester of Chapter 6 provides an excellent alternative.

Maintenance and Service Environment

In the maintenance and service environment, troubleshooting is concerned largely with fixing products or systems that have previously worked. Design- and production-related problems such as misinstalled components, wiring errors, bent pins, board defects, and so on, generally need not be considered (unless, of course, field changes have been made). Experience has shown that a large percentage of maintenance and service problems are associated with components or connections that have failed. (A recent study [7] has shown that over 80 percent of field problems in mature computer products are due to electrical adjustment errors or mechanical problems rather than component or board failures.)

The troubleshooting equipment encountered here also varies widely. In maintenance departments, quite sophisticated test gear may be met, including μP socket testers, logic analyzers, and signature analyzers. Service centers, on the other hand, are unlikely to utilize logic analyzers.

For service centers troubleshooting large volumes of a particular product, signature analysis is a good choice, as relatively unskilled personnel can be employed to perform initial testing and product screening, with the more difficult problems passed to more experienced personnel for solution.

1-9 GETTING STARTED

When faced with a malfunctioning or inoperative system, where do you begin? Since troubleshooting is both an art and a science, there is generally no single, unique way to attack any given problem. There is, however, a general order of progression that it makes sense to follow, as certain steps and procedures naturally follow after others. Remember to always correct obvious faults first.

An approach that has been found useful by the authors for troubleshooting small computer products in the general service environment is outlined below. It recognizes that a large percentage of problems can be identified to the node level by visual inspection, mechanical probing, and self-test. The order is quite satisfactory if you have no tools other than an oscilloscope and a multimeter. If you have a powerful microsystem tester (such as the Fluke 9010A), it should be pressed into action anywhere after step 3. If you are using static stimulus testing or signature analysis, you should wait until about step 5 or 6. However, this is a judgment call and depends on what is uncovered during preceding test steps. Note that the use of such tools will generally make step 7 unnecessary.

1. Perform a visual inspection.
2. Reseat the boards and cables. (The power should be off.)
3. Check the power supplies.
4. Run the system self-test (if available and working). If the self-test indicates the general area of fault, try ''board swapping'' if spare boards are available. If the fault cannot be localized using the self-test (or a self-test is not available), try minimizing the system, and if it works, build it up a little at a time until the fault reappears.
5. When the problem is isolated to a particular board or section of a board, begin your investigation as below (or return to the manufacturer).
6. If you have a kernel problem, try a CPU swap, as it will generally be socketed. In general, if the board contains VLSI devices which are socketed, try substitution if parts are available. Observe handling precautions.
7. If this does not work, start gross signal checking, looking for clocks, bus activity, and control signals.

Let us now expand on each of the above.

Visual Inspection

Check for blown fuses and replace if necessary. Look for loose and broken wires, improperly seated connectors, loose or broken wires, misset switches, missing jumpers, and so on. Check for obviously damaged components (i.e., components burned or discolored due to overheating). Check both at the component and at the printed circuit board, since overheating is sometimes not visible on the components but shows up as brownish burned areas on the PC card instead.

Reseating Boards and Components

Edge connectors are a common source of problems. Power-down the system and remove the PC boards. Examine the edge connectors for contamination and clean them if necessary. Reseat any loose components (such as socketed ICs). Reseat the boards and power-up.

Power Supply Checks

Check the power supply for missing voltages and voltages out of spec. A digital multimeter may be necessary, as voltage specifications are quite tight; logic supplies, for example, must be within ± 5 percent of 5 V. Do not forget that many systems use multiple supplies and all must be checked. Make such checks on the circuit boards at their points of usage, not just at the terminals of the power supplies. (Breaks can occur in interconnection paths due to loose or broken wires, poor solder joints, and so on.) Check power supply quality (noise and ripple) using an oscilloscope. If problems are found, correct them. (Power supply servicing is discussed in detail in many electronic servicing texts; see Ref. 8.)

Self-Testing

The equipment may contain self-test routines that let the system test itself. Note, however, that for these to be used, at least the kernel of the system must be functional and able to execute code.

ROM-based self-test diagnostics.   Routines may be supplied in ROM. These generally provide a quick check of ROM and RAM and a simple accessibility test of programmable devices. Front-panel switches and indicators are often used to invoke test sequences and to display pass/fail results.

Disk-based diagnostics.   For systems that include disks (such as personal computers), diagnostics may be supplied on diskettes that are loaded into the computer's memory for execution. Obviously, a very considerable portion of the system must be operational to use them. Typically, disk diagnostics include quite comprehensive memory tests as well as tests of keyboard logic, serial ports, and parallel ports, and tests to verify the read and write capabilities of the disk subsystem. Such comprehensive diagnostics permit failures to be isolated to major subsystems and sometimes to the component. (Diagnostic testing is detailed in Chapter 4.)

Board Swapping

Board swapping involves the substitution of a known good board for a suspect one. If all power supply voltages have been verified in a previous step, board swapping should be possible without a great deal of hazard to the good board. Do not forget to powerdown before removing and inserting boards. Swapping can also be applied to whole subsystems. For example, if you suspect a problem in a power supply or a disk drive, swapping can be used to provide quick confirmation.

   If previous tests offer little information as to the nature of the problem, or if spare boards are unavailable, you might check to see if the minimum system configuration works. In multiboard systems, remove all boards not required for minimal system boot-up. Disconnect external equipment, such as printers, monitors, and so on. If the problem goes away, reconnect one item at a time until the failure reappears.

   In these procedures, remember that faults between various boards and subsystems can be interactive. Although the board (or subsystem) that causes the system to crash during this rebuilding process is probably the one that contains the fault, it may not be—there may be interaction between several boards (or subsystems), and the last one installed before the crash may simply have interacted with the faulty board (or subsystem) to pull the system down.

When a faulty board (or subsystem) has been identified, we still face the problem of how to find the actual part or component failure. However, we have at least isolated the problem to a single board (or subsystem), which, if necessary, can be returned to the factory or serviced according to the strategies of later chapters.

The problem with board swapping as a service strategy is the cost in terms of spare boards inventory. As pointed out in Ref. 7, the field spare boards inventory for some companies amounts to 5 percent of their total assets and the total estimated worldwide cost of this inventory in 1982 amounted to about $9 billion. In addition, many of the "bad" boards removed from products during servicing and sent for repair are actually good. (The same source estimated that between 25 and 30 percent of the boards fit in this category. Other sources put the estimate much higher [2].)

VLSI Component Swapping

VLSI devices are very difficult to troubleshoot even with sophisticated tools because of their complexity.[6] In many systems, these devices are socketed for easy replacement. If so, and if spare components are available, try swapping VLSI devices in the suspect area. It takes very little time to do this and can save a great deal of investigative time and effort. However, caution is required, as VLSI devices are very susceptible to damage from static electricity. Even if the device is not destroyed outright, static may cause problems that result in progressive degradation and ultimate failure, perhaps weeks or months in the future. Swapping should therefore be done with a great deal of care and in a static-free environment. This should include a grounded, antistatic table mat and wrist strap, at the very least [9].

Gross Signal Checks

Gross signal checks can be performed using a common oscilloscope. Check for clocks (there may be more than one). Verify logic levels, rise and fall times, and frequency. (Consult vendor data sheets for appropriate specifications.) Ensure that clock signals appear correctly on the buses, not just at the output of the clock circuits.

Oscilloscopes may also be used to investigate general system behavior. However, since they are inherently incapable of synchronizing to the complex signals present in microprocessor systems, they cannot provide an accurate picture of such activity and are thus basically useful only for searching for things that are periodic or obviously wrong. They do, however, provide the troubleshooter with a general indication of the state of the system's health.

Check for the presence of signals on the various buses (address, data, and control) and verify that they look reasonably correct—that is, have signal activity on them if they should. (Some lines may not have activity on them because none is called for. For example, if the system ROM is located at the low end of memory and activity is centered on its program, there may very well be no activity on high-order address lines even if there are no faults.) Generally, there should be activity on data bus lines,

---

[6]However, future trends point to the inclusion of more self-test features on large VLSI chips.

however, as any CPU activity at all should result in data movement between the CPU and the ROM. If no such activity is present, try to find out what is hanging up the CPU. Likely suspects include CPU control inputs (reset, halt, etc.), as well as faulty clocks and power supply voltages. (However, the latter two should have been checked in an earlier step.)

If general activity is present, check for the presence of decoded outputs, such as chip selects, output enables, and so on, at kernel elements such as ROM and RAM memories as well as I/O ports. Note that it may be very difficult to trigger on these signals since they are very narrow and occur infrequently (low repetition rate). If the signals are detectable and look good, the corresponding circuitry is probably good also. You may also be able to get some indication of whether other logic and control signals look good as well. Through such testing, it is sometimes possible to get the basic hardware kernel (CPU, ROM, RAM, and bus system) up and working.

Scope loops.   Since ordinary oscilloscopes trigger properly only on repetitive signals, it is sometimes advantageous to create repetitive signals for the purpose of signal observation and tracing by means of a "scope loop," a short program segment that repeats itself continuously. If these test routines are to be programmed in EPROM, you will need a programmer. In addition, to be able to swap easily in the test EPROM, the system ROM needs to be socketed.

As an example, consider Figure 1-8. By reading from or writing to a particular device, a repetitive device access signal is created. If the signal appears correct, the

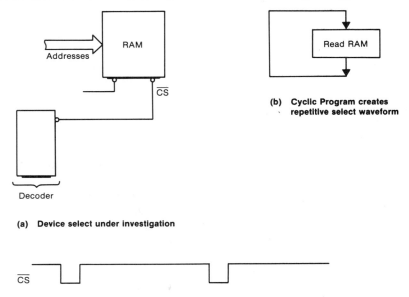

(a) **Device select under investigation**

(b) **Cyclic Program creates repetitive select waveform**

(c) **Repetitive waveform can be observed on oscilloscope**

Figure 1-8:   A 'scope loop can facilitate limited circuit tracing by providing a repetitive signal to trigger the 'scope on.

device select logic is probably okay. If not, backtrace to the output of the driving circuit and explore the signals there. In this manner, a basic signal tracing capability can be implemented. (The basic strategy of signal tracing is discussed in Chapter 3.)

While testing in this manner may lead to a solution, it may not. The problem here is that the oscilloscope is the wrong tool for the job. For problems that do not yield to it, you will need more appropriate tools and strategies. Such topics are discussed in Chapter 3 and subsequent chapters.

Another problem that sometimes occurs is noise on the ground system. Using the oscilloscope, check for noise at ground pins of ICs. There are several reasons why such noise may occur. One is a floating ground caused by a break in the ground connection (Section 2–13) or an improperly designed ground system (Chapter 11).

1–10 HARDWARE VERSUS SOFTWARE PROBLEMS

The strategy described in Section 1-9 is appropriate to the troubleshooting environment indicated. For others, however, it is incomplete. For example, in the design/development environment, software errors may also be present that prevent the system from working as intended. Thus it may not be apparent at the outset whether the problem is hardware or software related.[7] The question is an important one and difficult one that has no simple, definitive answer. We will, however, offer a few guidelines.

Fully Debugged Products

Products and systems that have worked fine up to the time of the failure (such as those encountered in the service center environment) have probably failed because of a hardware problem.[8]

Systems under Development

In the design/development environment, you are likely to encounter both hardware and software problems during the development process. One thing that you should not attempt to do here is to use untested hardware to test untested software, as there is generally no easy way to tell which is at fault. The best approach is to thoroughly debug the hardware first (using the methods described in this book), then test the software when you have a stable hardware vehicle to work on.

---

[7]The only tool described in this book that even addresses the problem is the logic analyzer. All other tools are exclusively hardware oriented and assume that the fault we are looking for is of a hardware nature.

[8]There is, of course, the chance that an obscure software bug is at fault, even in the best debugged of systems.

Failures That Come and Go

Failures that come and go may be due to either hardware or software. For example, consider a system that functions correctly, then "crashes" but appears to recover correctly on restart. The problem here may be due to a hardware intermittent (perhaps caused by heat or vibration; Chapter 2), or it may be due to software (perhaps the program has not been thoroughly debugged and an execution path through the untested portion of the software[9] has occurred). Such cases are very difficult to diagnose and a great deal of interactive trial-and-error testing may be necessary.

1-11 SUMMARY

The type of effort that goes into solving a problem depends on the nature of the problem and the circumstances. It has been suggested that in the service environment, probably 75 percent of the problems can be identified to the nodal level by visual inspection and mechanical probing. Of the remaining 25 percent, nearly half will yield to the oscilloscope; this then leaves 10 to 15 percent to deal with. In the design/development stage the figures will be quite different, since systems here are still under development and have probably not worked yet. The bottom line is ultimately economics. As noted in Ref. 10, the use of an appropriate troubleshooting tool enables close to 100 percent fault detection in time periods ranging from fractions of an hour to hours, compared to much lower detection percentages from a human troubleshooter armed only with an oscilloscope and days of effort.

Even with an appropriate set of tools, however, serious troubleshooting demands knowledge and skill. The remaining chapters address this need.

REFERENCES

1. KINSNER, WITOLD, and DENNIS JOHNSON, Signature Analysis, *MICROS Journal,* September 1980.

2. HARDOS, BARNEY, What's New in Testing Techniques, *MICROS Journal*, September 1980.

3. *Guide to Testing Microprocessor Based Systems and Boards*, Millenium Systems, Inc.

4. *9010A Micro-System Troubleshooter Operator Manual*, John Fluke Manufacturing Co., Everett, WA.

5. PINE, KEN, *A Logic Analyzer Primer*, Dolch Logic Instruments, San Jose, CA.

6. *The IC Troubleshooters*, Application Note 163–2, Hewlett-Packard Co., Palo Alto, CA.

7. COMERFORD, RICHARD W., Automation Promises to Lighten the Field-Service Load, *Electronics*, April 7, 1982.

[9]Software can be so enormously complex that it is sometimes impossible to test every possible combination that might occur. Therefore, "fully debugged" software may still have a number of errors.

8. PEROZZO, JAMES, *Practical Electronic Troubleshooting*, Delmar Publishers, Inc., Albany, NY, 1985.

9. *Static Zap Makes Scrap*, Hewlett-Packard Bench Brief, March/May 1983.

10. CANNON, DON L., *Understanding Digital Troubleshooting*, Texas Instruments, Inc., Information Publishing Center, Dallas, TX 1983.

11. *A Designer's Guide to Signature Analysis*, Application Note 222, Hewlett-Packard Co., Palo Alto, CA.

12. *Signature Verification*, Application Note, Data I/O Corporation, Redmond, WA.

13. PAYNTER, ROBERT T., Microcomputer Operation, Troubleshooting, and Repair, Prentice-Hall, Englewood, Cliffs, N.J.

2

UNDERSTANDING THE TROUBLESHOOTING ENVIRONMENT: HARDWARE FAULTS

Microprocessor systems malfunction for a variety of reasons. Faults occur at the system level, at the board level, and at the component level and may encompass mechanical as well as electrical failures. In this chapter we examine typical hardware faults, their characteristics and symptoms, and their impact on system and circuit behaviour. We will not discuss troubleshooting strategies here, however, as this is left for subsequent chapters. The order of presentation of material in this chapter is therefore not to be taken as a suggested or preferred sequence for testing.

2-1 PARTITIONING THE SYSTEM FOR FAULT ANALYSIS AND TEST

To ease the analysis and test problem, systems may be logically partitioned into small independent blocks. As indicated in Figure 2-1, microprocessor systems have natural boundary points for such partitioning.

Power supply	RAM
Clock	I/O subsystems
CPU	Other bus devices
Bus system	Peripheral controllers
Memory subsystems	Other subsystem controllers
ROM and EPROM	External logic

Figure 2-1: Partitioning for fault diagnosis. No one tool is suitable for diagnosing troubles in all segments.

No single tool or strategy is suitable for analyzing or testing all blocks. Although conventional tools such as multimeters, oscilloscopes, and frequency counters are adequate for testing power supply and clock circuits, they are generally not very effective for troubleshooting the remaining parts of the system.

2-2 POWER SUPPLY CONSIDERATIONS

Power supplies are one of the most failure-prone portions of systems but one of the easiest to test and repair. (Troubleshooting and repair procedures are well documented in electronic repair manuals such as Ref. 1 and will not be repeated here.) Do not forget, however, that many systems utilize multiple power supplies, and failure of any one can render the system inoperational—thus all must be checked. Problems such as blown fuses are a common occurrence, but they can be found by inspection. In the troubleshooting process, this is one of the first tasks that should be undertaken (see Section 1-9).

Other problems include failed regulators, out-of-spec voltages, excess ripple, and so on. Failed regulators usually result in voltages that are grossly in error. Out-of-spec voltages or excessive ripple are not as obvious but are still easy to find. Remember to check voltages at the points of usage, not just at the terminals of the power supplies, as breaks or voltage drops in the interconnection path may result in voltages that are good at the power supply terminals but faulty or missing entirely where needed.

Another power supply consideration that needs attention is decoupling of integrated circuits. When loads are switched, voltage spikes are created on power buses. If severe enough, these can cause a system to malfunction, usually intermittently. To smooth out these spikes, small "decoupling" capacitors are required between V_{cc} and ground. This topic is discussed in detail in Chapter 11.

2-3 CLOCK CONSIDERATIONS

Faulty clocks can also cause problems. Symptoms here range from a fully stopped system to a fouled but "running" system—that is, a system that appears to be running correctly but that, in fact, is not. (It may, instead, be caught up in some meaningless or undefined execution sequence. However, one has to be careful in jumping to conclusions here, as faulty software is a more likely cause of a hung system.)

In some systems, frequency extremes may be quite critical—for example, some processors and their associated family elements, such as peripheral controllers, are sensitive to speed, and even a slight departure from specifications may upset their operation. Both upper and lower frequency limits may be of concern and should be checked.

Considerable variation in clock circuits exists in practice. Designs may range from *RC*-controlled oscillators to crystal-controlled oscillators. Clock circuits may be built into the logic of the processor itself or be implemented externally. External clocks may be user designed or may make use of one of the special clock circuits developed by microprocessor vendors. To complicate matters, some old processors require unusual clock signals that are not TTL compatible, with voltage swings that vary widely and with rise and fall times that are critical. Clock failures may therefore be quite varied, ranging from no clock at all to waveforms that do not meet the required clock specifications (frequency, logic levels, rise and fall times). Even crystal-controlled oscillators are not immune to frequency problems, as crystal oscillators may fail to self-start on power-up (or may self-start on some occasions only). In addition, they may "jump modes" and begin operating on a harmonic of the fundamental crystal frequency [2]. Fortunately, these problems are rare. They are easy to check using conventional tools such as oscilloscopes and frequency counters.

2-4 CPU-RELATED CONSIDERATIONS

CPU-related problems are another concern. Since none of the common troubleshooting tools adequately tests CPU logic, the usual approach to CPU verification is a CPU swap. If the system works with the new CPU but not with the old one, the old CPU is deemed defective.

When faced with a malfunctioning system, there is the temptation to try a CPU swap immediately. However, the failure rate of microprocessors (and other LSI devices) is relatively low and most problems are not due to such failures. (This is why in the strategy of Section 1-9 the CPU swap was not performed until the more likely causes were eliminated). Still, the substitution of a known good chip for a suspect one (if it is socketed) is a valid troubleshooting tactic. Even its mere removal and replacement may clear up the problem, as intermittent and erratic behavior can be caused by dirty or ill-made contacts. Reseating a device firmly in its socket may also clear up problems.

Aside from CPU chips themselves, there are several other processor-related problems that need consideration. In particular, a CPU typically has a number of control inputs that, with faulty signals present, can hang up the processor or otherwise foul its operation. Typically, such inputs include the Reset line, interrupt inputs, DMA request inputs, clock stretching inputs, and so on. Below are highlighted some potential problems and their symptoms.

Reset

A reset circuit is required to start processor operation in a known (initialized) state. Often, reset circuits also initialize companion LSI devices, such as I/O ports. Failure of the reset signal to perform its task can result in the processor and/or its associated devices starting off in an undefined state—for example, with internal register bits not properly set or cleared, I/O lines not properly defined, interrupt flag bits not properly enabled or disabled, and so on.

Reset circuits generally depend on an *RC* charging circuit. The function of this circuit is to maintain a logic low voltage at the CPU reset pin for a specified minimum time after power has been applied to permit the clock to start and the CPU initialization process to take place. (Typically, this requires between 10 and 100 ms, depending on the processor.) If there is inadequate reset time, the processor may not reset properly, in which case unpredictable results follow—for example, the processor may not start at all, or it may start and appear to run fine for a time, then "crash," or it may lock up in some undefined and meaningless execution sequence, and so on. In any event, an improperly reset processor's operation cannot be relied upon.

Another problem sometimes occurs even with circuits that have adequate reset time. For short power outages the capacitor may not discharge sufficiently for the circuit to generate a clean reset. (The problem may also occur during manual reset if the system is powered OFF, then back ON too quickly.) Adding a diode across the charging resistor will sometimes solve this problem by permitting the capacitor to discharge more rapidly on loss of power. Reset waveforms can be checked using storage oscilloscopes to determine whether specifications are met. Watch for reset waveforms that are too short, too noisy, or too slow in transition.

Interrupt Inputs

Interrupt inputs may originate from a variety of sources, including keyboards, printers, and dynamic RAM refresh circuits, as well as assorted real-world devices. When a device or subsystem wants interrupt servicing, it asserts the interrupt request input on the CPU (to which it is connected) and waits for the processor to take over.

There are basically three types of problems that can be encountered in this environment. First, peripheral logic may be faulty, so that no interrupt is generated. Second, logic between the peripheral and the CPU may be faulty. Third, the CPU interrupt logic itself may be defective. For the first case, no interrupt request will reach the processor. For the second case, there are two possibilities. If the fault simply blocks the request, again the request will not be seen by the processor. Alternatively, if the fault holds the interrupt request input stuck in its active state, (assuming it is level sensitive) the CPU will be constantly interrupted. In this case, symptoms may range from a fully stalled system to a system that struggles along slowly as the processor attempts to execute its application software while spending most of its time servicing this "phantom" request. Faults in internal CPU interrupt logic can also block interrupt requests as well as create phantom interrupt requests that have symptoms similar to the second case above. Interrupt logic may be checked as discussed in later chapters.

Other CPU Control Inputs

Additional problems result when faults occur on other control inputs. Specific symptoms depend on the victim control input as well as the processor under consideration. For example, consider the memory ready (MRDY) control input on the 6809. An active low on this control pin stretches the system clocks in integer multiples of one-quarter($\frac{1}{4}$)bus cycle. This feature is provided so that the processor can communicate with slow peripherals. Normally, MRDY is asserted only when a slow peripheral transaction is required. If a fault occurs on this line, however, MRDY may be asserted when it should not be, causing the processor to execute many (if not all) of its operations at the slowed clock speed. This shows up as a greatly reduced average execution rate.

2-5 BUS SUBSYSTEM AND SIGNAL-LINE CONSIDERATIONS

Bus subsystems and other signal carrying lines malfunction for reasons such as conductor opens, shorts, loading caused by faulty components, excessive capacitance created by long conductor runs or too many IC loads, bus contention, and others.

Open-Circuit Faults

Incomplete paths in the bus system may be created by faulty gates or buffers blocking signal transmission, by improperly enabled gates and buffers in the signal path (also blocking signal transmission), or by mechanically related problems such as foil breaks, as detailed in Section 2-10. Such faults may result in the affected line floating or, alternatively becoming stuck in a permanent high or low state, depending on circuit details. In any case, these types of faults will not permit correct passage of signals.

Short-Circuit Faults

Shorts may be caused by solder bridges, faulty components (i.e., ICs with an input or output node internally shorted to Vcc, ground or some other node; Section 2-9), loose components that intermittently or permanently touch against other components, and so on. As with the open-circuit case, such faults will not permit the correct transmission of signals.

Bus Contention

Contention or bus conflicts occurs when two or more devices attempt to drive a bus line simultaneously, as illustrated in Figure 2-2. There are two basic possibilities— either the device connected to the bus has failed or logic driving the device's tri-state output has failed. Although the result of contention can be seen on an oscilloscope, the oscilloscope unfortunately provides no information as to the source of the fault. If the fault is due to a faulty control input to the device [i.e., a bad output enable ($\overline{OE}$)], testers such as those described in Chapters 5 to 7 can easily pinpoint the problem. Another useful tool is the current tracer. It may be used to determine which bus devices are actually in conflict as discussed in Chapter 10.

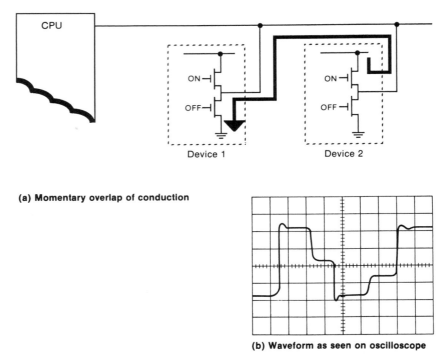

(a) Momentary overlap of conduction

(b) Waveform as seen on oscilloscope

Figure 2–2:   Two devices in contention. The result is an invalid state that is neither high nor low as in (b).

2-6 MEMORY SUBSYSTEM CONSIDERATIONS

Modern high-density memory is subject to a variety of failure modes. Anything from a single faulty bit of stored data to a total system "crash" can occur. Problems are difficult to identify by operating symptom, since there is often no obvious link between the actual failure and the symptom observed.

RAM Memory

RAM may be used for simple data storage or for stack storage, or the application program may reside in and operate out of it. The effect of a failure depends on what duty is assigned to the faulty RAM. If the defective area is used solely for the storage and retrieval of data, the fault may simply foul the data while permitting the application program to operate normally (even though it is working with corrupt data). RAM failures in the stack area, however, may produce more immediate and spectacular consequences, such as a total system crash. (This could happen, for example, if a subroutine return address on the stack gets destroyed.) Similarly, if the application program is executed out of the defective RAM, instruction sequences can be destroyed, again creating a system crash. In the latter two cases, even a single bit error can be disastrous.

Dynamic RAM.   To maintain their data, dynamic RAMs (DRAMs) must be refreshed periodically. Maintaining the charge on their internal storage cells requires substantial peak currents (between 50 and 200 mA for 256K DRAMs, for example). This abruptly changing current demand can create voltage "glitches" (noise) on the V_{cc} power bus. If these glitches are severe enough, they will cause random loss of data (soft errors). Proper capacitive decoupling of memory chips (as discussed in Chapter 11) is essential to control the magnitude of these voltage swings to avoid data-loss errors [3].

ROM Memory

The effect of failures here is similar to the last RAM case cited above.

Probably the most odious type of fault is that whose effect is barely perceptible and of such a nature that it permits the system to operate nearly normally (e.g., the first fault discussed above). Such faults are devious and can result in creeping degradation, slow corruption of data, and so on. The problem is particularly dangerous, as its effect may go unnoticed for some time, lulling the user into believing that nothing is wrong. In some cases, its effect is to arm the system gradually for a crash, which then occurs without warning and for no apparent reason, as its cause has long since been buried in the processor's past execution history. Thorough memory testing (as discussed in Chapter 4) can be used to find RAM and ROM faults.

2-7 SUPPORT LOGIC CONSIDERATIONS

Beside the processor and other LSI devices, systems generally contain support devices. Some typical problems are highlighted below.

Decoder Circuits

Decoding circuits generally use standard off-the-shelf combinational logic devices or programmable logic devices such as PALs or small high-speed ROMs (Figure 2-3). In Figure 2-3(a), the decoder has failed with its output stuck in the inactive state. In this case, the target device is never selected. In part (b), the decoder has failed with its output stuck in the active state. In this case, the device is constantly selected. However, the results here can be misleading, as the device may appear to work correctly some of the time. For example, consider a RAM with a stuck select. When the CPU reads from or writes to this RAM, it responds correctly. However, since it is constantly selected, it will also respond to reads and writes intended for other

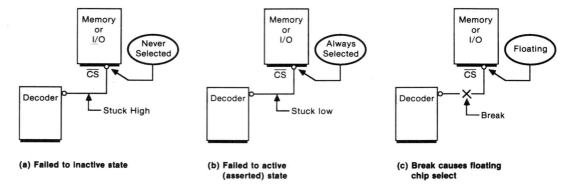

(a) Failed to inactive state

(b) Failed to active (asserted) state

(c) Break causes floating chip select

Figure 2–3: For failure (a), device cannot be accessed; For failure (b), device is permanently selected and may cause bus conflicts; For failure (c), intermittents may result.

devices. This produces contention during reads and results in the RAM accepting data that are not intended for it during writes. For the case shown in part (c), $\overline{CS}$ floats, making device operation unpredictable—see Question 2–3.

Transceivers

There are several transceiver-related problems that may occur, some caused by failure of the transceiver itself and some caused by failure of the logic that controls the transceiver. For example, if the direction control input DIR (Figure 2–4) is stuck in the down-line read state, the transceiver is constantly enabled, and data from upline reads will be corrupted by the floating data bus on the down-line side. On the other hand, if DIR is stuck in its down-line write state, reads of down-line devices are not possible. Now consider the enable input G. If G is stuck in its inactive state, both sides of the transceiver will go to the high-inpedance state and transactions with down-line devices can never occur (read or write). Failures in the transceiver itself may result in several of these same problems as well.

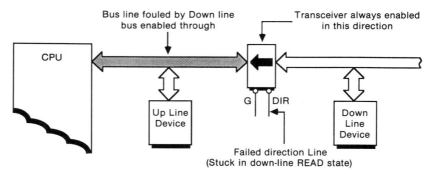

Figure 2–4: Illustrating problems due to faults in transceiver and transceiver control logic.

2-8 I/O SUBSYSTEM CONSIDERATIONS

I/O subsystems are subject to many of the problems described above, with the added complication that faults may also occur in the interface between the I/O port and the outside world. For example, peripheral side I/O lines may go through hostile environments where they are subject to user-handling hazards, including accidental damage. In addition, peripheral side lines drive power devices such as relays, solenoids, motors, and other high-current and high-voltage devices—see Question 2-10. As a consequence, components in this environment may have a higher-than-average failure rate.

Displays

Display failures include burned-out segments, faulty storage latches, and so on. In addition, multiplexed displays often share circuitry in common with multiplexed keypads, and a fault in the common circuitry may be manifested in both the display and the keyboard operation.

Keyboards

Mechanical switches may stick or they may bounce. Stuck switches are "hard" failures and are relatively easy to identify. Sometimes they can be returned to successful operation merely by unjamming them. Bouncy switches, on the other hand, can cause more subtle problems. Although all mechanical switches bounce to some extent, a faulty switch may bounce longer than normal. Debounce schemes (whether hardware based or software based) are designed to handle the bounce times of normal switches; if a switch bounces for an unusually long time, it may still be bouncing when the debounce logic has timed out. If this occurs, bounces that occur after the bounce time-out are seen as additional switch operations, thus making a single switch operation appear as many.

2-9 INTEGRATED-CIRCUIT FAILURES AND OTHER COMPONENT FAILURES

The problems considered above are mostly system related. Let us now turn our attention to device- and circuit-related problems. We will begin by examining device failure types and their effect on circuit performance. A knowledge of common faults and their symptoms can be useful in helping the troubleshooter identify failed devices.

Most digital ICs fail catastrophically. Faults include open lead bonds on inputs and outputs, internal shorts to V_{cc} or ground, internal shorts to other nodes, and failure of internal IC logic circuitry. About 75 percent of digital IC failures are caused by opens on either the input or the output [4].

Open-Lead-Bond Failures

Inside each IC are thin wires that connect the device's internal circuits to its external package pins. The effect of a lead-bond break here is to isolate this internal circuitry. Breaks may occur at inputs or outputs.

Output-lead-bond failures.   The effect of an output lead-bond failure depends on the circuit configuration to which the failed output is attached. Since the output pin is no longer connected internally, its state is completely independent of input drive conditions and depends wholly on the external circuitry to which it is connected.

To illustrate, consider the circuit of Figure 2–5. Here the failed device is driving a pair of TTL (or LSTTL) devices, one an AND gate and the other an OR gate. For the two cases, the results are quite distinct. First, consider the AND device. Since an open input to a TTL device rises to approximately 1.5 V, it usually has the same

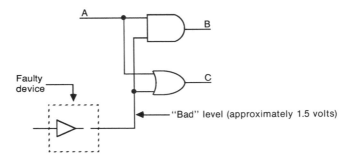

(a) Example: Driving TTL devices. Faulty device is depicted as a buffer here.

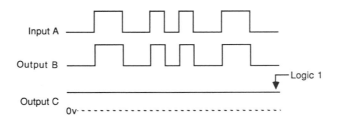

(b) Sample waveforms

Figure 2–5: Faulty device driving TTL devices. Since the floating input looks like a logic high to TTL, the AND gate is unconditionally enabled, passing the signal through without qualification. For the OR gate, the static "high" on the floating input clamps the output high.

effect on circuit operation as that of a static logic high [5]—thus, in this case, it permanently enables the AND gate, passing input A directly through. For the OR gate, however, the floating input blocks the gate and the output clamps high, independent of its A input. Thus in both cases, the outputs are logically incorrect in terms of the intended circuit operation.

Input-lead-bond failures: For devices with input-lead-bond failures, the input signal will be correct up to and including the device pin. However, on the internal side of the device pin, the signal ends at the open and is thus blocked from reaching the device's internal logic. In this case, the input to the affected circuit floats, and one or more of its outputs will usually malfunction. Symptoms include the affected output sticking high, low, or behaving erratically. Any of these cases can result in contention if the device is driving a bus.

Shorted-Lead Failures

Component failures can short nodes high, low, or together. The effect of some shorted components is highlighted below.

Output pin shorted to ground.   A short on an output pin will pull all devices driven by the device low. Such a short will disable AND logic but enable OR logic. Exact details are left as an exercise for the reader—see Question 2-6.

Input pin shorted to ground.   If the fault is a solid, low-resistance short, the node will be pulled solidly low. The effect on AND and OR logic is illustrated in Figure 2-6(a) and (b). Such a fault in TTL may be caused by a defective input protection diode. In this case, the fault may not yield a true zero-volts level, but rather a level a few hundred millivolts above ground—the forward drop of the diode, as shown in Figure 2-6(c).

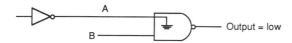

(a) AND gate is disabled by ground

(b) OR gate is enabled by ground short

Figure 2-6: Shorted input failure.
Effect of solid low shown.

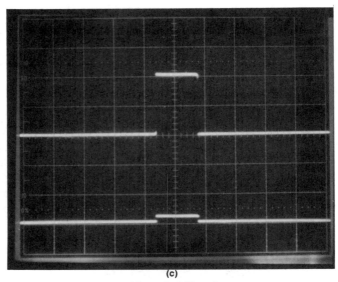

(c)

Figure 2–6 (Cont.)

Nodes shorted together.   When two nodes are shorted, the effect depends on the nature of the two nodes, the nature of the logic devices, and the circuit to which the device is connected. To illustrate, consider a pair of TTL gates with their outputs shorted together as illustrated in Figure 2–7. Here the shorted node will be

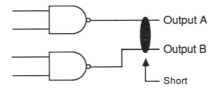

(a) **Fault**

Output B	Output A	When Shorted
0	0	Low
0	1	Low
1	0	Low
1	1	High

(b) **Table shows outputs A and B as they would be if not shorted.**

Figure 2–7:   TTL outputs shorted. Note that either output low will pull the other low.

low if either output A or output B is driven low by its respective input signals. The only time that the shorted node can go high is when both output A and output B are driven high by their respective inputs. Thus the connection behaves as a logical AND of the two outputs. It is sometimes referred to as a phantom AND.

Faults in Bus Structures

In practice, many devices connect to buses as indicated in Figure 2–8. Troubleshooting is compounded by the fact that any device may be at fault. For example, a bus stuck low may be shorted to ground at the output of one of the drivers or at the input of one of the listeners; similarly for a line stuck high. In either case, the effect is to render the line inoperational. If the fault is due to a driver circuit, it may be because the device is faulty, or it may be because the driver is enabled to its active state by a faulty logic signal driving it. Since all points on the bus are at the same voltage, simple voltage-measuring devices such as voltmeters, oscilloscopes, and logic probes cannot indicate which device is causing the bus to be stuck. Identifying the faulty component can be accomplished by using current tracers or other techniques as described in Chapter 10.

There are many other potential faults, of which these are just a sample. A knowledge of device characteristics is useful in understanding the effects of such faults. Since our intent here is not to catalog all possible faults, we will leave the topic now and move on to other considerations. However, we will meet some of these and other fault types again in the troubleshooting examples of later chapters.

Memory Chip Failures

When memory chips fail, either a bit shows up as a zero when it should be a 1 or a 1 when it should be 0. The first case is termed a "bit drop" and the second a "bit pick."

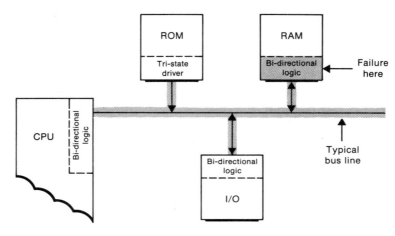

Figure 2–8: A single faulty device can foul the complete bus.

Modern high-density memory is subject to a variety of failures ranging from stuck bits to pattern sensitivity. Stuck bits due to cell opens and shorts are often caused by manufacturing defects such as mask misalignment or imperfect metallization [6]. Stuck bits are termed ''hard'' errors, as they can be reproduced at will. Hard errors are relatively easy to find. Errors that cannot always be reproduced are called ''soft'' errors. Failures of both types are common but depend somewhat on the type of RAM in use. For example, for wide word configurations (such as ''x 8 bit'' devices), hard bit failures are caused principally by the failure of a complete chip, while for designs using ''x 1 bit'' devices, a single soft error is the most common, followed by a single hard error. As you would expect, soft errors are much more difficult to find than hard errors.

Because of the geometrical layout and high density of modern chips, interaction due to capacitive coupling and resistive leakage can occur. This means that data written to or read from one location may affect the contents of other locations. The memory may even be pattern sensitive—that is, some combination of bits written at some time to some memory cells may cause other bits in other cells to change. Only certain combinations of bit patterns or the sequence in which the patterns occur may cause the problem. A memory bit may even be sensitive to its neighbors and pick only if all the bits surrounding it are one. As you can imagine, such faults are enormously difficult to test for exhaustively.

In addition to these difficulties, soft errors may be temperature sensitive. For example, some problems occur only if the memory is hot, whereas others show up only if the memory is cold. Problems that occur only when the memory is cold tend to go away after the system has been in operation for awhile and has had time to warm up. Problems that occur when the memory is hot do not show up until the system has been in operation long enough to get warm. To check thoroughly for such problems, testing should be done under both conditions.

Dynamic RAM.   While static RAMs are typically organized in byte-wide configurations, dynamic RAMs (DRAMs) are typically organized in one-bit-wide configurations (e.g., 64K by 1 bit). This means that an 8-bit-wide DRAM system would have its 8-bit word spread across eight DRAM chips operated in parallel instead of being totally contained in one IC. With such an organization, complete failure of one DRAM IC would show up as one bad bit position throughout the whole map of the memory. In contrast, complete failure of a byte-wide RAM would affect every bit position throughout the map of the failed chip.

Memory test strategies are discussed in Chapter 4.

2-10 MECHANICAL PROBLEMS

Mechanical problems include open circuits caused by breaks in the conductor foil, bad solder joints, solder bridges, improperly seated components, components with bent or missing pins, contaminated or otherwise defective connectors, broken wires, misoriented or misconnected components, broken leads, missing jumpers, faulty plate through-holes, and so on. Some of these faults result in opens, others in shorts to V_{cc} or ground, and others may result in nodes floating or pulled to some intermediate voltage level. Do not forget that shorts and opens can also be caused by such seemingly innocuous components as resistors and capacitors that have failed.

2-11 DESIGN DEFICIENCIES

In addition to circuit and component failures, malfunctions can be caused by marginal design, design deficiencies, or just plain bad design (design errors). However, such problems can foul the operation of a system just as surely as can failed components. Although it may be argued that these problems are the designer's concern rather than the troubleshooter's, the fact remains that when a system goes down, it winds up on the bench of the service person who is then expected to determine the cause of the malfunction. At the outset, there may be no indication of whether the problem is a true fault or a design-related malfunction. Thus it is important that the troubleshooter have some understanding of the nature of the problem and its symptoms. Some design deficiencies that may be encountered are highlighted below.

Excessive Capacitive Loading

Microprocessor components are designed to drive specified maximum load capacitances at full rated speed over specified temperature and voltage ranges. For loadings beyond the specified limits, performance suffers. Excessive capacitive loading manifests itself as slow rise and fall times and generally reduced timing margins.

Microprocessors are typically able to drive several TTL loads plus about 100 pF of capacitance. This equates to about 8 or 10 MOS bus loads plus associated line capacitance. One possible consequence of working beyond specified limits is that a system may operate satisfactorily at room temperature, but become marginal and erratic at temperature extremes.

If performance is marginal due to a design deficiency, a reworking of the circuit may be necessary to correct the problem. Buffers and bus transceivers may, for instance, be required to handle the drive currents. Alternatively, if the problem is excessive capacitive loading and it is not necessary to operate at full-rated speed, simply lowering the clock frequency may cure the problem. (This can be done if there are no speed-related software routines or hardware circuits and it is physically possible to slow the clock.) For systems that use RC-based clocks, changing speed can usually be accomplished by changing a resistor or a capacitor. For systems that use crystals, a lower-speed crystal would be required.

Sometimes the cause of marginal performance is subtle and easily overlooked. Such a case is illustrated in Figure 2–9. Here device A is driving a back plane to which many boards are connected. The capacitance driven here includes the capacitance of the line from the driver to the edge of the board, the capacitance of the backplane bus, the capacitance of the connector, the sum of the capacitances of the lines on each board leading from the edge connector to the various driven devices, plus the

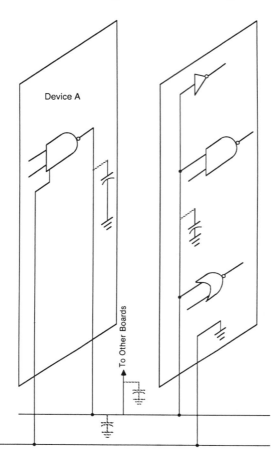

Figure 2-9: A poorly designed system.

capacitance of all devices connected to the driven line. The total capacitance can be quite substantial.

There are several courses of action that one may take when faced with such a situation. One is to slow the clock speed as noted above if this is practical. Another is to use drivers with greater capacitive drive capability. Alternatively, it may be necessary to correct the deficiencies inherent in the design. This is illustrated in Figure 2-10. Here we have installed a buffer on each driven card near the edge connector. This does two things—it shortens the length of conductor run on each board as well as reduces to one the number of IC devices driven per board, thus lowering the amount of device input capacitance seen by the driver. (Each device input represents typically 15 pF of capacitance.) In addition, moving the driver closer to the edge of its board shortens the conductor run there also, further reducing the capacitance. The modifications above can probably be accommodated reasonably easily at the prototype stage. However, the reworking of existing PC cards to the extent noted above is a non-trivial task. Obviously, such precautions should be built into the design in the first place.

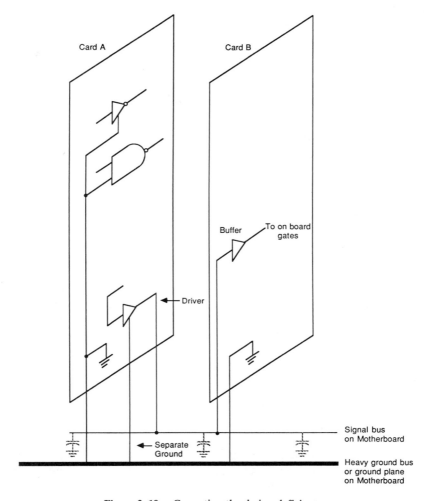

Figure 2-10:   Correcting the design deficiency.

Boards from Different Vendors

Another design-related problem that is easily missed occurs when boards from different vendors are intermixed [7]. Some clock systems have very tight margins and the insertion of as little as a 10-ns delay in a signal path may disrupt system operation. Ten or so nanoseconds represents one worst-case TTL buffer delay. Assume now that the system consists of a processor board from vendor A installed in a backplane driving a memory or peripheral board from vendor B. Most likely, the processor board will buffer the clock onto the back plane and the memory or peripheral board may also buffer the clock as it comes off the back plane. This places two buffer delays in the clock path and the system will probably not operate reliably under adverse conditions. (It may work quite well under lab conditions because most parts actually perform better than their worst-case specifications indicate.) Thus boards from multiple vendors, although designated as "compatible" to some standard, cannot always be relied upon to work correctly when linked together. This again is a design deficiency, this time caused by delay paths that have not been coordinated. The troubleshooter must always be alert to such unusual and unexpected problems.

Specification deficiencies.   In the manufacturing process, parts such as ICs are statistically sampled rather than 100 percent tested. This means that a certain percentage of new parts can be expected to be faulty or at least deficient in some specification. When installed in a system, therefore, some portions of the system may be marginal or outright faulty due to these "bad" components. The problem is compounded since semiconductor-device operation is temperature dependent and the marginal portion of the design may work at room temperature but become intermittent and erratic at other temperatures, or even fail outright. Should such a condition be encountered, stress testing as described below may be needed to identify the marginal elements.

The effect of even a modest failure rate on incoming parts can be quite surprising. As discussed in Ref. 8, devices with an acceptable quality level (AQL) of 1 percent can have up to 1 percent of devices bad, and when 100 such components are installed in a system, the chances of at least one component being bad is 63 percent. Even if the percentage of defective ICs is reduced to 0.1 percent, the chances of a bad IC in the system is still 10 percent.

2-12 STRESS TESTING

Hard (solid) failures are generally relatively easy to find. Soft failures, on the other hand, are much more difficult. Soft failures are generally caused by marginal or intermittent conditions and thus may come and go, depending on temperature and other parameter changes. Stress testing will sometimes temporarily cause these types of problems to improve or deteriorate (which is also helpful), or cause them to fail outright, in which case they can be identified and corrected. Useful means of aggravation include vibration (tapping boards, for example) as well as heating and cooling.

Vibration

As long as care is taken to avoid physical damage, flexing, twisting, pulling, and so on, can be used to check for integrity of connections, cables, and similar parts [5]. Connections through sockets, edge connectors, and so on, should be immune to any reasonable amount of such aggravation. Tapping PC cards may also reveal intermittent connections. If the operation of the system (or the troubleshooting test gear) is affected by such activity, an intermittent connection should be suspected. Check proper seating of PC cards, proper seating of socketed ICs, and so on. Sometimes removing PC boards and cleaning their "fingers" with a pencil eraser[1] or circuit board contact cleaner will restore contact integrity. If connector contacts are slightly sprung, pressing the component or board in firmly may restore contact, thus helping to identify the problem area. If reliable contact integrity cannot be restored, the connector should be replaced.

Thermal Checking

Applying heat, then cold, will sometimes cause an intermittent component to fail permanently, thus making it easier to locate. Note, however, that thermal stresses can be very high and discretion should be used to avoid damage to good components. Heat may be applied with a heat gun (or hair dryer); cooling may be accomplished with an aerosol spray can of appropriate coolant. Avoid spraying devices that may be damaged by the spray—for example, electrolytic capacitors.

Thermal stressing causes boards and components to expand and contract. This may cause some intermittents to open and others to close. Note, however, that while heating and cooling are applied locally, the resulting expansion and contraction affects the whole board in varying degrees, and problems far removed from the actual application of the heat or cold may be affected. This tends to obscure the location of the fault.

When a device fails, it may draw an abnormally large current, causing discoloration. It may also run considerably hotter than other devices of the same type. Such parts may be located visually or by touch. Be careful, however—defective devices sometimes get so hot that they can burn quite painfully.

2-13 SOME ILLUSTRATIVE EXAMPLES

With this as background, let us now consider several illustrative examples. Although simple, they illustrate what can happen in real life. Here we will only describe the problem and its symptoms; methods of testing for these conditions are detailed in later chapters.

Example 2-1

The problem is a break in the conductor path between address pin A13 of the CPU and the corresponding input to the 74LS138 decoder, as illustrated in Figure 2-11. The problem showed up initially as an inability to access RAM, although the ROM worked perfectly. When we see the problem in front of us like this, it is apparent why this is so. Since the 74LS138 is a TTL-type device, an open input appears to it like a logic high. This means that when we try to access the RAM by outputting 0 0 0 on address lines A13, A14, and A15, respectively, inputs A, B, and C of the decoder see 1 0 0, respectively,

---

[1]Repeated use of an eraser may cause damage. Use care.

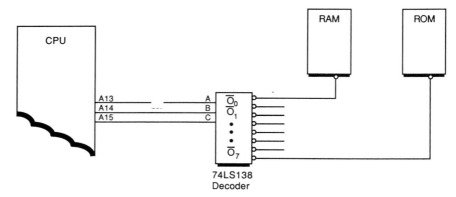

Figure 2–11:   Odd numbered outputs select correctly. Even numbered outputs cannot be selected.

instead. This means that output $\overline{O_1}$, is asserted rather than $\overline{O_0}$, and consequently, the RAM is not selected. However, when we read from the ROM, we output 1 1 1 on A13, A14, and A15, and thus, even with the fault, input A sees its correct logic level. Consequently, $\overline{O_7}$ is asserted and the ROM is selected correctly. This fault is easily located using appropriate test gear, as described in later chapters.

Example 2–2

The problem is again a break, this time in address line A0 between RAM and the CPU. During operation, it was apparent that something was fouling data. A little thought will show why. Because of the break, address input A0 of the RAM floats and hence may look to its internal decode logic as a logic 0 or a logic 1. To see the effect of this, assume that pin A0 at the RAM looks low when a transaction (read or write) with RAM is in progress. If the RAM location under consideration is even numbered (e.g., address 0000), A0 will be low at the RAM as it should be, and the transaction will take place correctly. However, if the RAM location of interest is odd numbered (e.g., address 0001), the RAM will see logic 0 at pin A0 instead of logic 1, and the RAM location will not be correctly accessed (e.g., location 0000 will again be accessed instead of location 0001). Only even-numbered addresses will be accessed correctly under these conditions. Similarly, if A0 looks high, only odd-numbered locations are accessible.

Example 2–3

The problem here is a solder bridge shorting two outputs of the decoder, as illustrated in Figure 2–12. The symptoms here were that the two input ports were interacting. For example, a bit input from port A would always read correctly if the corresponding bit from port B was identical; similarly for port B. An examination of the circuit shows why. Because of the short, both ports are selected whenever either is accessed by the CPU. This means that both devices drive the bus simultaneously and thus contention results.

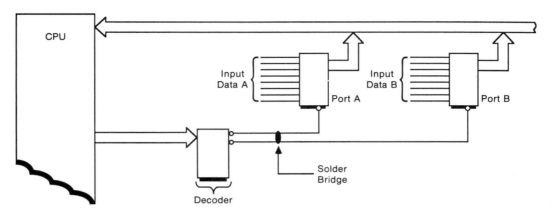

Figure 2-12:   When either port is selected, bus contention results.

Example 2-4

The problem here is a defective solder joint at the ground pin of a RAM, as illustrated in Figure 2-13(a). In this case, the floating chip fouled the bus lines and rendered the system inoperational. In this instance, the floating ground was found using an oscilloscope. Figure 2-13(b) shows a photograph of the voltage measured at the ground pin of the RAM. This measurement was taken on the device pin on the component side of the board. The voltage on the ground pad of the printed circuit board was correct (i.e., solidly low). This pointed to a break. Closer inspection revealed a defective solder joint that was making no connection.

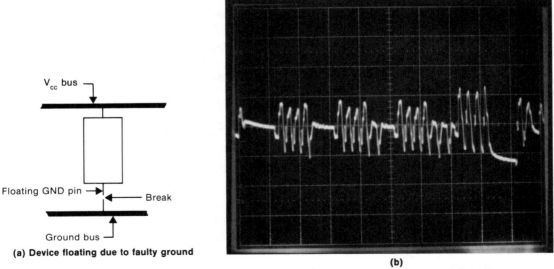

Figure 2-13:   A floating ground fault. Note the voltage at the device ground pin in (b).

2-14 SUMMARY

This chapter has attempted to provide some insight into the microprocessor system fault environment. With an awareness of fault types, their symptoms, and their impact on system and circuit behavior, the troubleshooter should be better equipped to recognize and identify problems that are found in the real-world troubleshooting environment.

REFERENCES

1. PEROZZO, JAMES, *Practical Electronics Troubleshooting*, Delmar Publishers, Inc., Albany, NY. 1985.

2. SLATER, MICHAEL, and BARRY BRONSON, *Practical Microprocessors*, Hewlett-Packard Co., Palo Alto, CA.

3. MARTIN, ARCH, *Decoupling 256K DRAMs*, AVX Corporation, Myrtle Beach, SC.

4. Application Note 163–2, *The IC Troubleshooters*, Hewlett-Packard Co., Palo Alto, CA.

5. NAMGOSTAR, M., *Digital Equipment Troubleshooting*, Reston Publishing Co., Inc., Reston, VA, 1977.

6. Application Note 00041, Micro Control Co., Minneapolis, MN.

7. ZUMCHAK, EUGENE M., *Microcomputer Design and Troubleshooting*, The Blacksburg Group, Inc., Blacksburg, VA, 1982.

8. BLAKESLEE, THOMAS R., *Digital Design with Standard MSI and LSI*, John Wiley & Sons, Inc., New York, 1975.

9. *Guide to Testing Microprocessor Based Systems and Boards*, Application Note, Millenium Systems, Inc.

10. GASPERINI, RICHARD E., *Digital Troubleshooting*, Hayden Book Co., Inc., Hasbrouck Heights, NJ, 1975.

11. CANNON, DON, *Understanding Digital Troubleshooting*, Texas Instruments, Inc., Information Publishing Center, Dallas, TX, 1983.

12. 6800 Flex™ Diagnostics, Technical Systems Consultants, Inc., West Lafayette, Indiana.

13. FICHTENBAUM, MATHEW L., Circuit Layouts Minimize Noise in Digital Systems, Electronics, August 19, 1976.

REVIEW QUESTIONS

2–1. A single bit error in the data storage area of RAM may cause graceful degradation, but a single bit error in the STACK area of RAM will almost certainly lead to a system crash. Explain the difference.

2–2. Assume that a device failure results in contention on the data bus at the instant an instruction is being fetched from ROM. This could cause a system crash. Why?

™FLEX is a trademark of Technical Systems Consultants, Inc.

2-3. For the circuit of Figure 2-3(c), discuss some of the symptoms that might occur.

2-4. In the circuit of Figure 2-4, if the tranceiver direction control input DIR is stuck opposite to that shown, which of the following can occur correctly?

(1) Up line reads   (3) Down line reads

(2) Up line writes   (4) Down line writes

2-5 Repeat question 2-4 if DIR is correct but the enable signal G is stuck so that the transceiver is constantly disabled (i.e., in its tri-state condition).

2-6 Assuming that the fault in Figure 2-5 is a short to ground on the output of the faulty device (instead of the open shown), sketch the outputs for B and C.

2-7 Consider decoder U5 of Figure B-7 in Appendix B. If outputs 0 to 3 select correctly but outputs 4 to 7 do not, which of the following is the probable fault?

(1) An internal open on input C

(2) An internal short to ground on input C

(3) An internal short to V_{cc} on input A

Explain your choice of answer.

2-8 Same decoder as in Question 2-7. If outputs 2, 3, 6, and 7 select correctly but all others do not, which of the following is the probable fault?

(1) An internal open on input C

(2) An internal open on input B

(3) An internal short to ground on
    Input A

Explain your choice of answer.

2-9 If none of the devices connected to decoder U5 of Figure B-7 respond to read and write commands, which of the following is the most likely cause?

(1) Eight faulty devices   (4) Faulty $\overline{RD}$ and $\overline{WR}$ inputs

(2) A faulty OR gate   (5) (2), (3) or (4) above

(3) A faulty decoder

Explain your choice of answer.

2-10 The relay driver in the circuit of Figure 5-27 fails and must be replaced each time the application program issues a command to deenergize the relay. Which of the following is the the most likely cause of the failure?

(1) A faulty (open) diode   (4) A bad solder joint at the diode

(2) A faulty driver   (5) A diode installed backwards

(3) A poor software programmer   (6) (1), (4) or (5)

Explain your choice of answer.

3

MICROPROCESSOR HARDWARE TROUBLESHOOTING PRINCIPLES

Tools currently available permit implementation of an organized, systematic approach to troubleshooting that brings order and discipline to the fault-finding process.

The basic strategy is depicted symbolically in Figure 3-1. As indicated, it is top-down in nature. In this chapter we describe basic principles; in Chapters 4 to 7 we provide implementation details. Chapter 4 covers functional testing; this corresponds to level 1 in the basic strategy. Chapters 5 to 7 describe dynamic stimulus/response testing, static stimulus testing, and signature analysis testing, respectively. These are used to mechanize level 2 circuit tracing. In conjunction with functional testing, any one of these may be used to implement the first two levels of the strategy illustrated.

Although usually considered separately, the three test methods noted above are not as disjoint as they appear—in fact, they can all be viewed as simply different ways of performing the same basic task—that of tracing faults in a malfunctioning system to the circuit node level. Thus, in principle, they all fit within a common framework, permitting development of a unified approach to fault finding that is quite general in application and independent of the actual set of tools used to implement the testing.[1] Such an approach greatly simplifies the learning process as initially, we need not concern ourselves with specific details of specific test tools, but can, instead, focus on basic principles and concepts. With this approach, the user can more easily grasp the underlying principles without being distracted by implementation details.

[1] We require only that functional testing and node-level circuit tracing be mechanized.

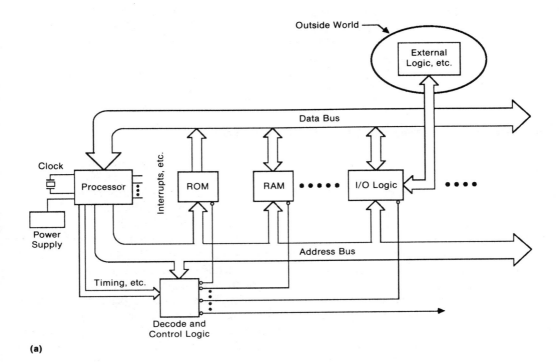

(a)

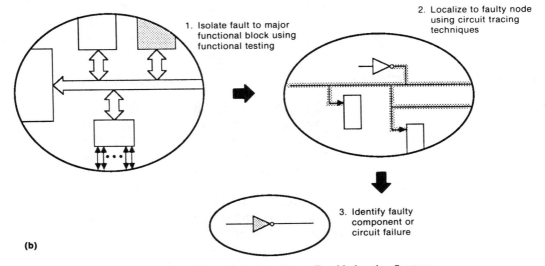

(b)

Figure 3-1:   Top-Down Troubleshooting Strategy.

Once basic principles are in hand, of course, practical details must be considered, since differences in detail are important at the application level. For example, the order of progression of testing may vary from tester to tester, depending on its capabilities. In addition, if functional testing is implemented internally (rather than via an external tester), the order may be different again. The third level of testing (Figure 3–1) is very conventional and is discussed in Chapter 10.

3–1 ORGANIZING THE TROUBLESHOOTING TASK

To provide order and discipline, troubleshooting may be organized in a top-down fashion, as depicted symbolically in Figure 3–1. Such an organization permits a systematic progression of testing; the first stage establishes the broad bounds of the suspected fault area, the second stage narrows the search to the circuit-node level, and the final stage determines the actual failed circuit element itself.

In this scheme, testing starts at the system level. This permits the troubleshooter initially to ignore all low-level detail and concentrate solely on the "big picture." When working at this level, we are not concerned about specific logic circuit details, individual gates, and so on. Instead, we view the system as a group of interconnected functional blocks. This greatly simplifies the problem and permits us to concentrate on the task at hand—that of determining in which block the problem actually lies.

As testing continues and the problem and its solution come into focus, we shift our attention more and more from the general to the specific. Thus, as we pass from the general system level to the detailed subsystem level to the detailed circuit level, we increasingly ignore the overall picture and focus instead on specific logic blocks and electronic circuits. In this manner we always work to keep the magnitude of the problem and its detail at a size that our minds are able to comprehend.

3–2 SYSTEM PARTITIONING

To aid in this process, the well-known method of system partitioning is used. With this method, the system is subdivided into a group of small subsections, each of which can be treated individually. Once the system has been partitioned in this manner, we concentrate on each block as a separate problem and essentially ignore the rest of the system. This approach reduces large, complex problems into a series of smaller, more manageable ones.

In practice, partitioning microprocessor-based systems is a relatively straightforward task. They are characterized by a few well-defined subsections with natural boundary points. Major blocks are summarized below.

CPU
Bus system

Memory system
  RAM system
  ROM system
I/O system

Some of these may be subdivided further; for example, under I/O, we may have

Display systems
Keypad and keyboard systems
Parallel I/O
  Input ports
  Output ports
Serial I/O
Analog in (A/D)
Analog out (D/A)

More complex systems employing multiple processors with several levels of local and global buses, bus arbitrators, system controllers, and so on, may be encountered in practice. Although more complex in detail, such configurations are simply extensions of the basic design and are thus included within the framework of this chapter.

3-3 FAULT BRACKETING

Fault bracketing is an important stage in the process described above. It is a process whereby testing is used to establish the limits of the suspected fault area. Often, a simple test or set of tests can eliminate large portions of the system under test from the suspect list and help narrow the area that needs detailed investigation. Such tests may be used to establish the integrity of major system blocks, small groups of components, or even individual circuit elements. As the checks are made, the area between the brackets becomes smaller and smaller until the fault itself is ultimately isolated. The large-scale functional tests of Chapter 4 perform this task at the global level; the circuit-testing techniques of Chapters 5 to 7 perform this task at the local level. Ultimately, of course, both levels of testing must be used in concert.

Fault Bracketing: General

Let us now consider the application of this technique. It is valid for microprocessor-based designs as well as non-microprocessor-based designs. Let us illustrate by considering the general logic circuit depicted in Figure 3-2. Assume that a fault exists

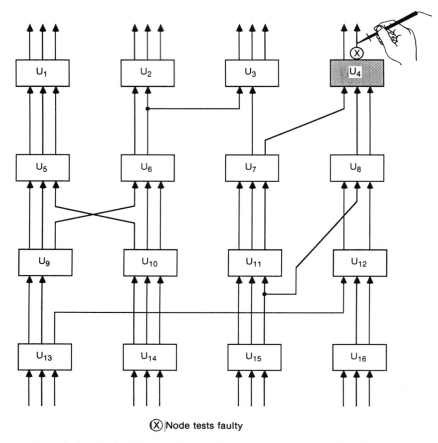

(X)|Node tests faulty

Figure 3-2:   Testing detects a faulty node at the output of U_4. This makes U_4 our initial focus of suspicion.

and that it manifests itself as a set of faulty nodes. As noted above, we can use any of the methods of Chapters 5 to 7 to investigate this circuit.

Assume that our testing detects a faulty output on U_4. Assuming that nothing on the output of U_4 is causing the problem, we conclude that either U_4 is defective or that one or more of its inputs is faulty. Testing further, we determine that one of its inputs is bad. This is indicated in Figure 3-3. Back tracing from here takes us to U_8. Again, we suspect either a component failure or a bad input. In this case, we find a bad input as indicated in Figure 3-4. Further back tracing leads to U_{12}. Here we find a faulty output. Further investigation shows a bad input, this time traceable to U_{13} (Figure 3-5). U_{13} is now our focus of suspicion. Again, we test inputs. Here we find that they are all good. This suggests that U_{13} is defective. However, this is not necessarily so—while all its inputs are good and its output is bad, it is

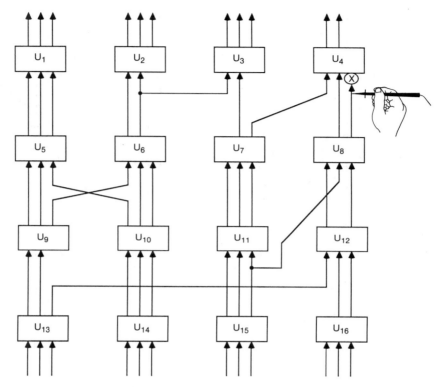

Figure 3-3:   Further probing yields a faulty input. This suggests that U_4 may not be at fault. Therefore, we continue testing.

not necessarily U_{13} that is at fault. Looking a little more closely, we see that there are three possible causes of the faulty output

1. U_{13} is indeed bad.
2. The trace between U_{12} and U_{13} is defective.
3. There is a fault in the input circuitry of U_{12}.

This is indicated in Figure 3-6. Note that although we have not yet identified the actual circuit failure, we have succeeded in bracketing the fault, as we set out to do. Unfortunately, however, this is as far as node-level circuit tracing can take us. The next step is to break open the node in some fashion and isolate the problem. This procedure is discussed in Chapter 10.

In the example above, we detected a problem at the output of U_4. The question arises: Do we randomly probe until a fault is found, then work from there, or is there a more systematic approach? The answer depends on the situation. In the descrip-

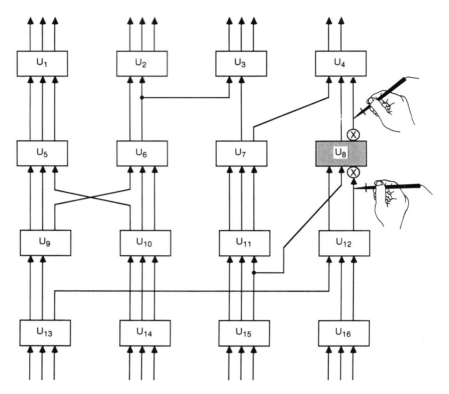

Figure 3–4:   Backtracking takes us to U_8. Since a bad output is detected, it becomes our focus of suspicion. However, further testing reveals a bad input, this time traceable to U_{12}.

tion to follow, preliminary functional testing is used to narrow down the source of the error enough for circuit tracing to begin. In other cases, a procedure known as "half-splitting" is useful. With half-splitting, the troubleshooter selects a point approximately midway through the circuit to begin testing. If the selected point tests okay, the next trial test point is selected roughly halfway between there and the input of the circuit. This process of probing at the halfway points continues until a faulty node is found. A new test point roughly halfway between the faulty node and the last good test can now be selected. In this way, the fault can be bracketed. It should be noted, however, that half-splitting is not as useful with microprocessor-based circuitry as it is with analog circuitry or random logic designs. The approach described below is more appropriate to the microprocessor environment.

Fault Bracketing: LSI Devices

Microprocessor systems contain a variety of complex LSI components (such as memory chips) whose internal circuit details are unknown and whose internal nodes are inaccessible to the troubleshooter. This presents the user with the task of trying

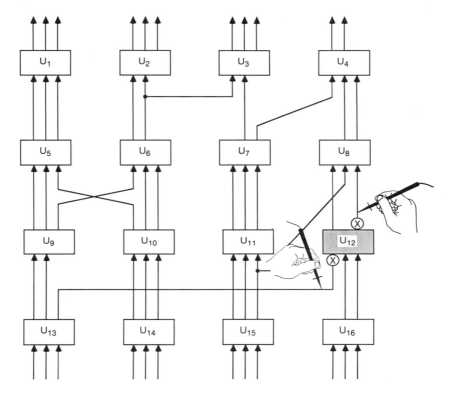

Figure 3-5: Our focus of suspicion now shifts to U_{12}. However, further testing reveals a bad input, traceable to U_{13}.

to determine by external observation, whether there are faults within components that cannot be seen into. Any testing done here necessarily involves accessing the device's internal electronics via its external circuitry. This compounds the testing problem, since we have no assurance that this external circuitry is itself free from faults unless it also is tested.

Functional testing.   Fortunately, in practice, many devices can be checked easily using relatively simple functional tests. To illustrate, consider a RAM memory subsystem. RAM can be checked functionally by writing known data to each location, then reading it back for verification. If the data retrieved match those stored initially, the operator can assume that the RAM and its associated circuitry are free from errors.[2] ROM and many other devices can be tested similarly.

[2]At least to the level of confidence built into the test. While the level of confidence is usually high for ROM, it may be quite low for RAM, depending on the sophistication of the test chosen. See Chapter 4 for details.

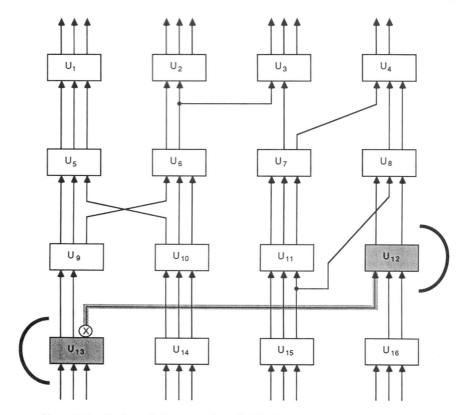

Figure 3-6: U_{13} has a faulty output but all of its inputs test okay. This appears to indicate that U_{13} is faulty. However, it may not be. . .the problem could be due to U_{12}, U_{13} or the trace between them. We have however, bracketed the fault.

Let us now generalize the approach. Consider the subsystem of Figure 3-7. A test of this subsystem could fail for either or both of the following reasons:

1. The device itself is faulty.
2. There is a problem in some associated external circuit.

Since problems may be internal or external and since we have no means of testing the internal circuitry directly, a two-step testing sequence is necessary. First, the device is checked for correct functional operation using an appropriate test of the type described above. If the test passes, it verifies not only the device, but also its bus and interface connections, including much of the combinational logic, between the device and the processor.

If the test fails, however, we do not know which of the two possible causes noted above is responsible. The second set of tests must therefore permit us to determine whether the failure of the first test is due to a faulty device or due to a fault

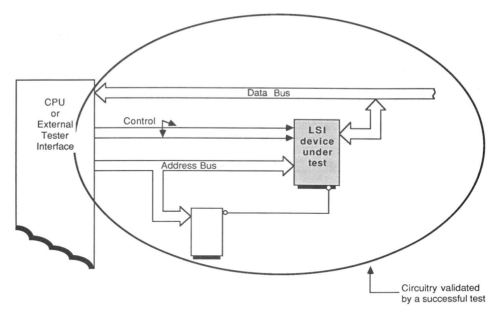

Figure 3-7: A successful test verifies not only the device itself but also all of its associated bus, interface and control electronics.

in some external circuit. The second set of tests we will choose are circuit-level tests that permit us to validate independently the device's interface logic. Using circuit stimulus and tracing techniques,[3] check at the device's package pins. If no faults show during these tests, it can only be concluded that it is the device itself that has failed. This is depicted in Figure 3-8.

If a failed node is detected, however, it means that a fault probably exists externally, that is, in the subsystem's support circuitry. (It may not, however, as certain internal faults can also result in faulty node behavior. Most likely, however, the fault is external.)

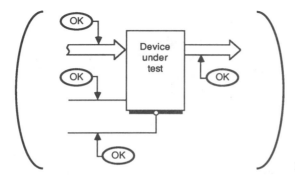

Figure 3-8: Bracketing a failed device.

[3]Any of the methods of Chapters 5 to 7 may be used for this purpose.

Assuming an external fault, fault tracing of the type depicted in Figures 3-2 to 3-6 is called for. If this tracing reveals a problem, it must be isolated (as described in Chapter 10) and corrected. If however, no faults are found, return to the device and check further, as it is time to suspect an internal fault. At this point, the methods of Chapter 10 will prove useful.

3-4 APPLICATION TO MICROPROCESSOR SYSTEM TESTING

Now let us turn our attention to the microprocessor environment explicitly. To apply the procedures described above intelligently to microprocessor system troubleshooting, it is useful to examine its application to specific subsystems. Let us start with the bus system.

Bus Subsystem

Generally, bus lines can have five types of faults [2]:

1. They can be shorted high.
2. They can be shorted low.
3. They can be shorted to adjacent signal lines.
4. They can be open due to a missing jumper, broken trace, defective plate-through hole, and so on.
5. They can be connected to a faulty IC.

For the latter fault, either the driving device or the driven device can be the cause of the problem. Failures here can be traced using the methods described above and illustrated by Figures 3-2 to 3-6. Note also that these fault types apply to all signal lines, not just bus lines.

RAM Memory Subsystem

RAM memory subsystems are subject to a variety of faults, both external and internal. A typical RAM is illustrated in Figure 3-9. For this system to be fault free requires that:

1. The address inputs to the RAM are correct.
2. The read/write ($R/\overline{W}$) to the RAM is correct.
3. The chip select input to the RAM is correct.
4. The data bus interface to the RAM is correct.
5. The RAM functions correctly (i.e., data can be stored and retrieved correctly).

The read/write capability of the RAM can be checked by writing known data to each location and reading it back for verification. If the test passes, the RAM and its associated interface and control logic, bus connections, and so on, as indicated in Figure 3-9(a), have been validated and no further tests are generally necessary. If the test fails, however, it does not necessarily mean a bad RAM, since some circuit failure external to the RAM may be causing the problem. This is illustrated in Figure 3-9(b), where a fault has been detected on the chip select line. In such a case, circuit-tracing techniques as illustrated in Figures 3-2 to 3-6 must be used to follow the problem back to its source. If no faults are found as in Figure 3-9(c), we must conclude that it is the RAM chip itself that is at fault and that it should be replaced. When making these tests, it is a good idea to make them right at the pins of the device so as to preclude possible problems caused by faulty sockets or bad solder joints.

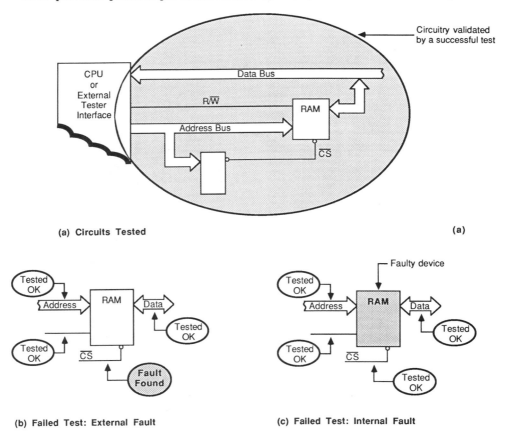

(a) **Circuits Tested**

(b) **Failed Test: External Fault**

(c) **Failed Test: Internal Fault**

Figure 3-9: RAM memory subsystem. A successful test validates the RAM and its associated decode and control logic, buses, etc. b) Failed test. Here, a fault is detected in the chip select logic input. c) Failed test. Since no external faults have been found, a defective RAM is indicated.

ROM Memory Subsystems

ROM subsystems are handled similarly. Figure 3-10 illustrates a typical circuit. For this system to be fault free requires that:

1. The address inputs to the ROM are correct.
2. The read input to the ROM is correct.
3. The chip select input to the ROM is correct.
4. The data bus interface to the ROM is correct.
5. The contents of the ROM itself are correct.

ROM contents can be checked via checksum or CRC verification, as described in Chapter 4. If the test passes, it verifies not only the ROM chip itself, but also

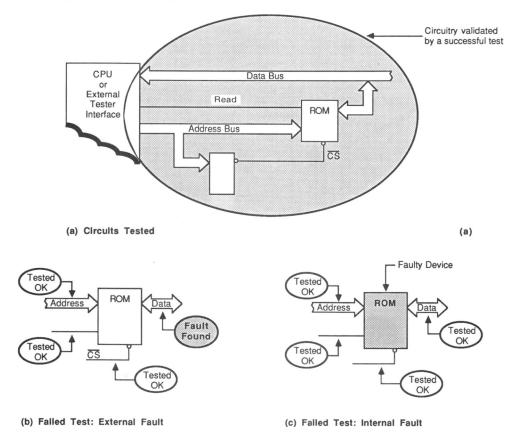

(a) **Circuits Tested**   (a)

(b) **Failed Test: External Fault**   (c) **Failed Test: Internal Fault**

Figure 3-10: ROM memory subsystem test. A successful test validates the ROM and its associated decode and control logic, buses, etc. b) Failed test. Here, a fault is detected in the data bus interface. c) Failed test. Here, since no external faults have been found, a defective ROM is indicated.

all bus, decode, and control logic between it and the CPU, as indicated in Figure 3-10(a). If the test fails, however, it does not necessarily mean a bad ROM—as with the RAM case, it could mean that some circuit failure external to the chip itself may be causing the problem. This is illustrated in Figure 3-10(b). If such a fault is detected, circuit-tracing techniques as discussed in Figures 3-2 to 3-6 must be used to follow the problem back to its source. If no faults are found as in Figure 3-10(c), we must conclude that it is the ROM chip itself that is at fault.

I/O Subsystems

I/O subsystems are handled similarly. Problems to be expected here are similar to those described previously, with the added complication that faults may also occur in the interface between the device and the outside world. Of concern to us therefore are the following:

1. The address inputs to the port
2. The read/write input to the port
3. The chip select input
4. The data bus interface
5. The interface to the external world
6. The I/O device itself

Testing proceeds here basically as outlined above, beginning with a functional test. If the test passes, this, as usual, verifies the port and its associated logic and the interface to the outside world. If it fails, however, device pins should be checked next. If no faults are found, we must conclude, as usual, that it is the device itself that is at fault. As always, if a fault is found, use circuit-tracing techniques to follow the fault to its source. In this case, however, since problems can occur on both the bus side and the peripheral (outside world) side of the port, you may have to check both.

It should be noted that there is generally a great deal of circuitry common to the various subsystems considered above. A fault in the common circuitry will show up in all affected subsystems until corrected. Conversely, repairing a problem in the common circuitry may restore all subsystems to correct operation.

Interrupt Systems

Now consider interrupt systems. Although there are almost as many variations as there are processors on the market, generally speaking, only three types of faults are encountered [2]:

1. An interrupt line may be stuck in its active state causing the processor to be in a state of constant interruption.
2. Interrupt requests may not be reaching the processor, due to incorrect logic conditions in the enabling circuitry.
3. External conditions necessary to enable an interrupt may not be occurring.

The first fault could be due to a problem on the interrupt signal line due to any of the reasons considered previously, including a fault inside the CPU that is holding the line clamped. All others are also faults of a type considered previously— bad signal lines or faulty components in the path between the source of the interrupt and the CPU. Signal tracing can be used to eliminate some of these from consideration.

The problem could also be due to software or improper initialization of software-configurable devices. In many systems, for example, interrupt requests pass through programmable I/O ports. Such devices may contain enable/disable logic that intercepts the interrupt request. If this logic is incorrectly initialized, the request may be blocked and thus will not be passed to the processor. Testing for this type of fault is discussed in Chapter 5, Section 5.11.

3-5 IMPLEMENTING THE GENERAL APPROACH

With this as background, we can now illustrate the application of the general methodology. As depicted in Figure 3-1, the process encompasses three major steps:

1. Large-scale tests are used to globally isolate faults to major subsections.
2. Circuit-tracing techniques are used to localize faults to the node level.
3. "Node-busting" techniques are used to pinpoint faults to the actual failed circuit component level.

These major steps can be furthur expanded in detail. Specifically, testing proceeds as follows:

1. The first major subsection to be tested is selected and the applicable functional (global) test is performed.
2. If the test passes, the subsection is designated tested and we move on to the next subsection.
3. If the test fails, we use circuit-testing techniques to trace the problem to the faulty node level.
4. When the faulty node has been identified, node-busting techniques are used to pinpoint the actual failed circuit element.
5. The problem is repaired.

Testing is continued in this manner until all faults have been found and corrected. Finally, a final system check is performed to verify that no further problems remain.

Order of Testing

The question arises as to which subsystem should be checked first and what should be the order of testing that follows thereafter. The answer here depends on the methodology chosen, the test setup in use, and the capabilities of the test equipment.

Some general guidelines can be offered. Generally, the bus subsystem is checked first. If it has faults, little else can be expected to work. Often ROM comes next, since it is easy to check, followed by RAM, then I/O. After this, it is difficult to generalize. However, this is not always the order. For example, the Fluke 9010A manual [3] recommends BUS, RAM, then ROM, followed by I/O (for very good reasons, discussed in Chapter 5). Signature analysis has several variations, depending on whether SA is built in or whether it is implemented via an external tester. For the built-in case, it may be necessary to perform some level 2 testing and fault correction to get the kernel up and working before level 1 testing can even be undertaken. Such details are discussed in Chapter 7.

3-6 SOME ILLUSTRATIVE EXAMPLES

To illustrate the general methodology, let us consider a few practical examples. In the first two cases, we will specify the problem in advance and show how the general methodology leads directly to the fault. In the third example, we will specify only the symptoms of the problem and deduce from observation and test what the problem is. This, of course, is the way problems are encountered in practice. All examples are taken from actual experience.

Test Setup

In keeping with the general nature of this chapter, assume an external tester (see Figure 1-1). Such a setup encompasses the methods of Chapters 5 to 7. (This restriction to an external tester will be relaxed later to permit testing using built-in facilities, as in traditional signature analysis implementations.) For purposes of illustration, assume that the recommended testing sequence is ROM followed by RAM followed by I/O. (In later examples in the following chapters, we utilize the sequence that is optimum for the particular methodology and test setup being illustrated.) Assume also that the tester has a console with a readout that reports errors to the operator as well as a probe that permits circuit tracing. (Although not all testers have such readouts, all provide the same information to the operator in one way or another.)

We will begin with an 8085-based single-board computer with its application program in ROM, a hex keypad and hex display for operator interaction, a bank of eight status LEDs, a bank of eight switch inputs, and a parallel I/O port. (A complete logic schematic for this system is shown in Figure B-7.)

Example 3-1

As a first example, let the fault be a defective plate-through hole on address line A13 between the output of the address buffer U_2 and the input to the address decoder U_5. (The portion of the circuit of interest for this example is shown as Figure 3-11.)

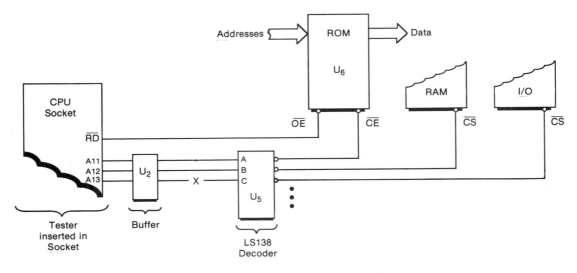

Figure 3–11: Portion of faulty system for Example 3-1.

Troubleshooting the Fault

Step 1. In keeping with the general strategy of this chapter, we select the first major subsection to be tested and perform the applicable global test. As noted above, this will be the ROM test. In this case, it will fail since one of the address lines linking the ROM circuitry to the CPU has a fault—thus the tester will report a ROM failure to the operator.

Step 2. Because the test indicated a problem in the ROM subsystem, we begin circuit investigation at the ROM, as indicated in Figure 3-12. The following are the potential reasons why the ROM test failed.

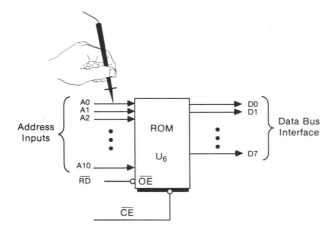

Figure 3–12: Failed ROM test. To locate the source of the failure, systematically test the ROM pins to determine whether the ROM chip is defective or whether the problem is in its external circuitry.

1. The ROM is not being accessed properly.
   (a) Could be a bad address input.
   (b) Could be a bad read strobe $\overline{RD}$.
   (c) Could be a bad chip enable input.
2. There is a fault on the data bus, causing data on it to be garbled.
3. The ROM itself is defective.

Using the circuit probing capability of the tester, we begin a systematic investigation of the ROM pins. In this case, the address lines and the $\overline{RD}$ input check, but a fault is detected when we test the chip enable input $\overline{CE}$.

   Step 3. Now use the circuit-tracing feature of the tester to investigate the $\overline{CE}$ circuit failure.

1. Backtracing from $\overline{CE}$ takes us to U_5 (the address decoder). Here we find a faulty output, as indicated in Figure 3-13.

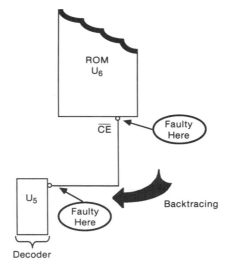

Figure 3-13: Testing reveals a faulty chip enable. Backtracing, we trace the fault to the decoder output.

2. Now test the inputs to U_5. Address inputs A11 and A12 test okay, but A13 indicates a fault.
3. Backtracing on A13 takes us to address buffer U_2 (Figure 3-14).

Note that the output of U_2 pin A13 is correct but that the input to U_5 pin A13 is faulty. This suggests a problem somewhere between U_2 and U_5. Further probing shows that the signal is good from U_2 to the plate-through hole but that on the opposite side of the hole, the signal is not correct. Thus we have pinpointed the fault.

   Since we have found the fault, there is no need to look further. However, did we just "luck out" when we opted to test the ROM circuitry first? The answer is no. If we had opted to test the RAM circuitry instead, systematic investigation would have

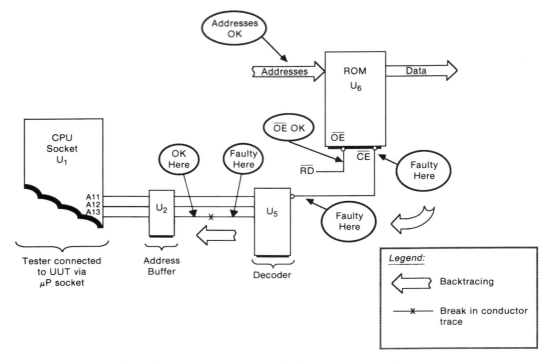

Figure 3–14: Further testing reveals a faulty input to U_5. Backtracing takes us to U_2, the address buffer. Its outputs test okay. . .thus, the fault has been bracketed to the trace between U_2 and U_5.

lead us to the same fault with about the same degree of effort. This is left as an exercise for the reader (Question 3-1).

Example 3-2

System of Figure B-7 as before. Assume a faulty RAM chip U_8. As before, use the strategy depicted in Figure 3-1.

Troubleshooting the Fault

> *Step 1.* Begin with the ROM test. In this case, it passes.
> *Step 2.* Select the next major subsystem, in this case RAM. The test fails.
> *Step 3.* Based on the failure of the RAM test, we can draw up the following list of possible problems

1. The RAM is not being accessed properly.
   (a) Could be a bad address input.
   (b) Could be a bad read/write control input $\overline{WE}$.
   (c) Could be a bad $\overline{OE}$ input.
   (d) Could be a bad chip select input.

2. There is a fault on the data bus, resulting in failed read/write operations.
3. The RAM itself is defective.

As before, we begin by systematically investigating bus and other signal connections at the RAM pins. In this case, they all check (Figure 3-15). Since the RAM has been bracketed by tested, good circuitry, the only conclusion is that the RAM itself is faulty and should be replaced.

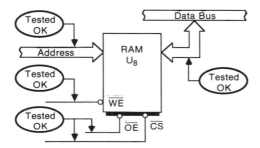

Figure 3-15:   RAM test. All external circuitry checks good.

Example 3-3

The system this time is 6809 based similar to that depicted in Figure A-6. (An additional RAM (RAM 2) connected to decoder output $\overline{O_6}$ has been added.) In this case, let us not specify the fault in advance. (This is, of course, the situation encountered in practice.) Again, we proceed by systematic testing. The troubleshooting log is summarized below. Let the UUT be a single-board computer that has just been put together in wire-wrap form and thus may include wiring errors.

Troubleshooting Log

Step 1. Try the ROM test. It passes.
Step 2. Try the RAM test (RAM 1). It passes.
Step 3. Try the RAM test (RAM 2). It fails.
Step 4. Investigate the RAM 2 interface signals. In this case a fault is detected on chip select line $\overline{CS}$ (Figure 3-16). Backtracking on $\overline{CS}$, a faulty output is found at the address decoder U_{11}. Checking inputs shows that A13 and A14 are incorrect.
Step 5. Backtracing to the CPU, we find that address outputs A13 and A14 are correct. Following the wires, we find that during the wire-wrapping process, A13 and A14 have been crossed, as indicated (Figure 3-16). Rewrapping the wires correctly restores the system to full operation.

One may wonder why the crossed address lines did not affect the ROM test and the test of RAM 1. The reason is actually quite simple, as a little thought will show. This is left as an exercise for the reader (Question 3-2).

Although the examples above may seem trivial, this is misleading. Such faults foul the operation of a system just as surely as more obscure faults do, and when one has no idea of what is wrong, they are just as intimidating. However, we introduce more satisfying faults in later chapters.

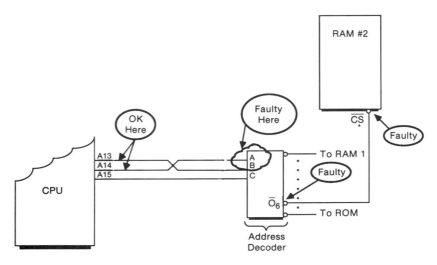

Figure 3–16: During wire wrapping, A13 and A14 have been crossed.

3-7 IMPLEMENTING THE TEST STRATEGY

As noted, implementing the general strategy requires two basic sets of tests. These tests must

1. Functionally verify major system blocks or alternatively designate them as faulty.
2. Check the integrity of circuit nodes and if they are found faulty, permit tracing of faults to their source.

Functional Testing

Functional testing as illustrated above was mechanized by means of an external tester. In terms of the general strategy, this is not necessary. Functional testing is generally mechanized by software, and this software can reside either in an external tester or in the UUT itself. To be sure, there are some practical questions regarding how such testing can be performed if the kernel of the UUT is inoperative and thus unable to execute test code. However, this is a question of detail, not of principle. In practice (as we shall see in Chapters 6 and 7), means are available to test the kernel and get it up and running independently of the functional tests. Once this is done, functional test software may be employed to test the rest of the system. Thus, in principle, it does not matter whether the test software resides in an external tester or in memory inside the unit under test. In practical terms, however, the external tester approach has the advantage that it removes the impact of kernel failures from the environment of the test.

Commercial Test Gear

Some of the commercial test instruments on the market that may be used to implement testing and troubleshooting as described here are the Fluke 9010A, the Applied Microsystems ET-2000 tester/troubleshooter, and the Creative Microprocessor Systems SST (Static Stimulus Tester). The Fluke 9010A, for example, incorporates in a single instrument both level 1 and level 2 capability, with all required tests built in and invoked automatically by single-keystroke operation. A synchronized probe mechanizes circuit-level fault tracing. In addition, signature analysis capability is provided. With its programming capability, guided fault testing can be implemented. (Troubleshooting using the Fluke 9010A is described in Chapter 5.)

The Applied Microsystems ET-2000 also incorporates functional testing and circuit tracing capability in a single test instrument. Tests are called up by single-keystroke operation. In addition, it implements a portion of level 3 troubleshooting, as it can locate shorts and opens in circuits. Its circuit-tracing capability is implemented by a bus line stimulus/monitoring algorithm that automatically identifies the bus line by name using standard logic diagram terminology. It, too, includes a signature analysis capability.

The μP version of the Static Stimulus Tester of Creative Microprocessor Systems incorporates functional testing of RAM, ROM, and I/O ports directly using built-in tests. For node verification and circuit tracing, it makes use of a simple logic probe (or oscilloscope). This is possible because the tester holds the unit under test in a stopped state while fault tracing is in progress. A manual version is also available. (Troubleshooting using the manual version is discussed in detail in Chapter 6.)

Historically, one of the earliest tools to implement functional testing and circuit-level fault tracing was the MicroSystem Analyzer (μSA) from Millenium Systems, Inc.[4] Although not as convenient as some of the tools noted above, it was, nonetheless, a powerful and capable performer. Functional tests had to be developed by the user, cast in EPROM, then installed in a debug ROM socket located on its front panel. Circuit-level fault tracing was implemented via built-in signature analysis.

3-8 SUMMARY

In this chapter we have described a generalized strategy for troubleshooting microprocessor-based systems. The strategy basically provides a mental construct to guide the troubleshooter systematically through the task from the system to the node to the component level in a logical sequence. The construct is much like a flowchart in that it shows the flow of ideas in a manner that is independent of both the system under test and the tools used to implement the testing. In the following four chapters, we will consider implementation details.

[4]Although Millenium Systems corporation is no longer active, there are still μSA systems active in the field at the time of writing this book.

REFERENCES

1. Blakeslee, Thomas R., *Digital Design with Standard MSI and LSI*, John Wiley & Sons, Inc., New York, 1975.
2. *Guide to Testing Microprocessor Based Systems and Boards*, Millenium Systems, Inc.
3. *9010A Micro-System Troubleshooter Operator Manual*, John Fluke Manufacturing Co., Inc., Everett, WA.
4. *Signature Analysis Seminar*, Hewlett-Packard Co., Palo Alto, CA.
5. *Hands-On Troubleshooting Microprocessor Systems* (Course Notes), Integrated Computer Systems, Santa Monica, CA.

REVIEW QUESTIONS

For these questions, assume an external tester with built-in functional tests plus a node-level circuit tracing capability. Test in the order ROM, RAM, parallel port, then serial port unless directed otherwise.

3-1. Consider Example 3-1. If we had elected to perform the RAM test before the ROM test, systematic investigation would have led to the fault with about the same degree of effort. In the troubleshooting log format of Example 3-1, outline a set of steps that would lead to finding this fault.

3-2. Consider Example 3-3. Why did the crossed wires not affect the ROM, and RAM 1, tests?

3-3. Consider the circuit of Figure A-6. Assume a faulty NAND U_{10}. In the troubleshooting log format, outline a set of steps that would lead to finding this fault.

3-4. Repeat Question 3-3 if the fault is a cold-solder joint at the PIA (parallel I/O port) socket, resulting in an open circuit on data line D3.

3-5. Consider the circuit of Figure B-7. Assume that gate U_4 fails and outputs a faulty logic signal to input E3 of the 74LS138 decoder. In the troubleshooting log format, outline a set of steps that would lead to finding this fault.

3-6. Repeat Question 3-5 if the demultiplexing latch U_3 fails.

3-7. Consider the circuit of Figure C-5 (Appendix C). Assume that gate U_8 fails. In the troubleshooting log format, outline a set of steps that would lead to finding this fault.

3-8. Repeat Question 3-7 if $U_{9(c)}$ fails.

4

FUNCTIONAL TESTING

Microprocessor systems are composed of functional subsystems. Testing for correct functional operation of any given block is generally performed by software. Software routines whose specific duty it is to test hardware blocks are referred to as "diagnostics." Diagnostics may range from relatively simple routines whose only purpose is to verify the correct operation of the module or subsystem under test to complex software routines whose task it is to pinpoint system faults directly. The former are referred to as functional diagnostics, while the latter are referred to as fault-locating diagnostics. The prime use of functional diagnostics is in the field service, prototype testing, production testing, and depot service environments. It is this class of test software that we will deal with here. Fault-locating diagnostics, on the other hand, are more complex and are used primarily in the manufacturing environment, where they are usually associated with expensive automated test equipment (ATE) systems.[1]

There are many possible subsystems to be tested and thus many specific tests that may be required. A comprehensive discussion of all such tests is beyond the scope of this book. Accordingly, we will present the main ideas behind the tests only and illustrate using some of the more common elements that are likely to be encountered in practice. Specifically, we will describe and illustrate routines to validate memory (ROM and RAM), I/O ports (parallel and serial), display subsystems (status annunciators and numeric displays), keypad and switch input subsystems, analog I/O subsystems (A/D converters, D/A converters), and so on. The principles described are quite general, however, and the ideas can be extended to other blocks as the need arises. However, comprehensive tests for many of these blocks may not be as easy to devise as the examples illustrated in this chapter might suggest—thus some measure

[1]Fault-locating software is beyond the scope of this book and will not be considered.

of ingenuity will probably be needed to devise test strategies for the more difficult ones.[2]

As noted in Chapter 3, it does not matter in principle where the test software resides—in an external tester or in the memory of the unit under test. Thus, initially, we will make no distinction. The question is an important one to be sure, as the form of the tester and the test setup in use have considerable impact on operational procedures and other practical details. It will thus be considered in due course (Section 4-12). For the moment, however, we will assume simply that a means exists to execute the test software and, in turn, advise the operator of test results.

A clear distinction should be made between application programs and test programs. Test programs are just what their name implies—programs designed to check specific portions of the unit under test. Their sole purpose is testing—they make no attempt to run the system in its application environment. It should be noted that these tests are useful whether the strategy of Chapter 3 is followed or not.

4-1 GENERAL PRINCIPLES OF FUNCTIONAL TESTING

Functional testing is used to verify the operation of a subsystem or designate it as faulty. The basic strategy consists of selecting a block from the system to be tested, stimulating it via software, monitoring the result, then by comparing the observed response against that expected, determine whether the test passed or failed [1]. This is indicated in Figure 4-1.

In practice, this strategy is relatively easy to implement for many system elements. For example, to test read/write memory, we need only write selected bit patterns to memory, read them back, then verify that the patterns read back match the patterns stored (Figure 4-3). ROM is tested similarly (Figure 4-2). Here, however, ROM patterns are known in advance and do not have to be written by the tester. For displays, patterns may be written to the readouts and confirmed visually by the operator. Other tests are performed in a similar manner.

Standard Tests versus Customized Tests

Standard functional tests for common devices (such as RAM and ROM) are well known and readily available from various sources (books, magazines, etc.). For other subsystems, however, the required tests are somewhat more unique and may have to be customized. For these, a few guidelines are in order. When devising your own routines, you should design them to test small, well-defined sections, one at a time [2]. (This is why we logically partitioned the system as we did in Chapter 2.) Each test should be structured to test an independent block if possible. You should be particularly careful to limit interactions between the block being tested and other system blocks that have not yet been tested. In addition, test programs should generally be made so simple that they need no debugging. This is to avoid the uncertainty created

---

[2]Some subsystems have their own specialized equipment and techniques—for example, disk systems.

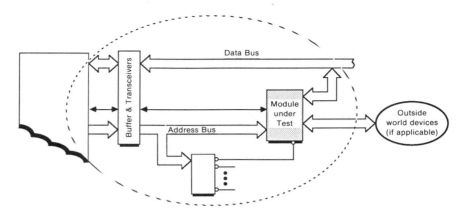

(a) Subsystem Under Test

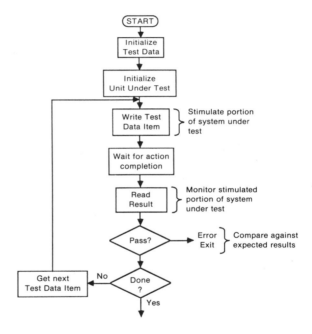

(b) Logic of test

Figure 4-1: Functional testing. A successful test verifies all logic within the dotted lines. Conversely, a failed test means the problem can be due to any circuit within the dotted lines or the fault may be propagated in from outside.

by having untested software attempt to test untested hardware. However, if the routines are to be used many times over, it may well be worth the effort to enhance them with additional features once you have a thoroughly debugged piece of hardware available to validate the expanded test software on. Let us now turn our attention to testing specific modules and subsystems.

4-2 MEMORY TESTING

Memory testing is straightforward and conforms exactly to the test strategy depicted in Figure 4-1. Variations exist to handle most categories of known faults. Many of these routines provide much more than simple go/no-go verification, however—for example, many contain considerable diagnostic resolution, permitting identification not only of the failed bit (or bits) but also the address where the failure occurred. ROM and RAM tests are somewhat different and will be described separately.

4-3 ROM AND EPROM TESTING

ROM and EPROM testing is exceptionally easy. Since the contents are known in advance, all that the user has to do is verify that all locations can be read from and that none of the original ROM content has changed. In principle, this can be done by manually stepping through each device location by location and comparing its content against the original documentation. In practice, this is impractical, and a more efficient strategy based on data compression is generally used. Using a data compression algorithm, the complete ROM content is reduced to a single numerical value. This number is referred to as its "signature."[3] Now, instead of having to cycle manually through the ROM to verify its content, we need only verify that its signature is correct.

To test using the signature verification method, a known good signature for each ROM is needed. In practice, these are obtained by compressing the data from known good ROMs. These good signatures are then documented. During testing of a malfunctioning system, the signature for each suspect ROM is regenerated using the same procedure as was used to generate the original good signature. If the two signatures match, the ROM test passes. As noted in Chapter 3, in addition to checking ROM contents, this test inherently exercises all circuitry associated with the ROM, including address and control lines, decoding circuitry, and the data bus interface. Thus a successful test not only verifies the ROM, it also verifies all its associated circuitry as well.

Generating a Simple Signature

In practice, there are several variations in the method of computing a ROM signature. The simplest approach is to compress the ROM contents into a "checksum" by summing its contents using exclusive-OR summation. To generate such a checksum, start at the first location in ROM and successively add each word in turn until the complete ROM contents have been summed. Exclusive-OR addition is used instead of simple arithmetic addition, as it provides a higher level of uniqueness. Figure 4-2(a) shows a flowchart for checksum generation. This is the logic used to generate the

[3]A ROM's signature depends totally on its content—even changing a single bit will completely change the signature.

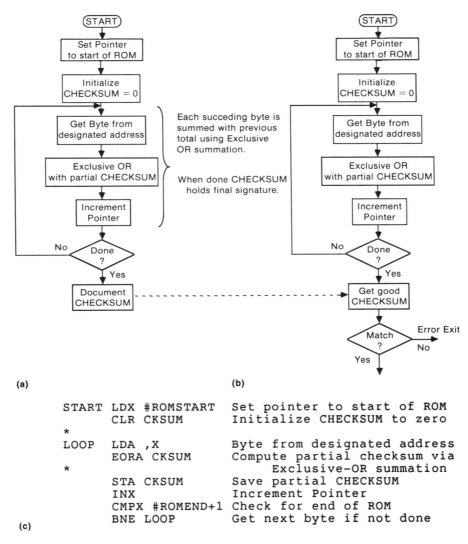

Figure 4-2: ROM test using Checksum for Signature. (a) Logic for generating Checksum for known good system. (b) Logic for testing ROM in suspect system. (c) Checksum generation using 6809.

original "good" or "gold" signature. Logic for testing a suspect system is shown in part (b). Note that exactly the same algorithm is used except for the comparison to the gold signature.[4] A 6809 program segment is shown in part (c) to illustrate the process of generating the good signature. The software is simple to write and versions

[4]The gold signature is the signature of the unfaulted ROM.

for other processors can be prepared easily as well. Unfortunately, the simple checksum approach is not totally reliable. Although it detects all single-bit errors and many multiple-bit errors, there are combinations of errors that it could miss. However, the program is short, easy to write, and is useful for those in need of a quick and simple test.

An improved version of the ROM test makes use of a CRC check character.[5] This character is generated by a division process, rather than by the addition process described above. The CRC technique is inherently more reliable than the checksum technique and provides a much higher level of security.

CRC techniques are also used for signature analysis testing. In this case, however, data compression is usually performed by hardware rather than by software. Details of this method are contained in Chapter 7. Reference 3 discusses the mathematical basis of the algorithm used by Hewlett-Packard and others.

4-4 RAM TESTING

In principle, RAM testing is also simple—the diagnostic need only write known test patterns to memory, read them back, then report errors if a mismatch occurs. Comprehensive testing using all possible patterns would ensure that all patterns could be written to all locations and read back without affecting the contents of any other location. Such comprehensive testing is impractical, however, as it takes an enormous amount of time to test even moderate-size memories. Instead, modern testing strategies use groups of tests, each concentrating on finding a subset of possible faults [4]. Such testing is designed to provide a high level of confidence but cannot guarantee 100 percent certainty. For this reason, RAM test credibility is not as high as that of ROM. If the RAM test fails, we know that something is wrong. If the RAM passes a reasonably comprehensive battery of tests, it is probably okay. Let us look at some sample tests.

Simple go/no-go test.   A fast way to test for gross failures is to write 0s to all locations, then read them back to ensure that no bits are stuck high, then write 1s to all locations, then read them back to verify that no bits are stuck low. Logic for this test is shown in Figure 4-3. Although the test is simple and quick, it can only be relied on to catch hard errors. Sometimes it is used simply to verify the memory hardware interface.

Simple checkerboard test.   A similar test is the checkerboard test. It is probably the most common of all RAM tests. Here, alternating 1s and 0s are written to memory in a checkerboard fashion, as indicated in column 1, then read back and verified. The pattern is then inversed as shown in column 2 and the test repeated.

---

[5]CRC stands for "cyclic redundancy check."

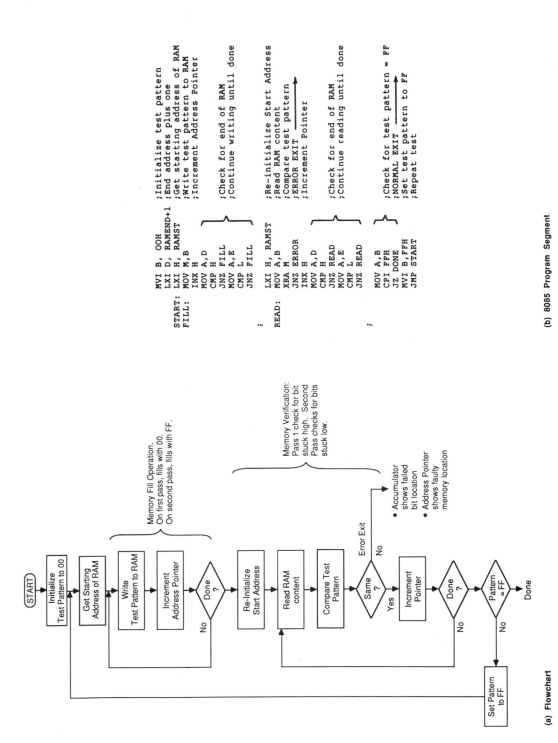

Figure 4-3: RAM test using simple zero/one check. Detects and identifies bits stuck high and bits stuck low.

(b) 8085 Program Segment

```
START:  MVI B, OOH          ;Initialize test pattern
        LXI D, RAMEND+1      ;End address plus one
FILL:   LXI H, RAMST         ;Get starting address of RAM
        MOV M,B              ;Write test pattern to RAM
        INX H                ;Increment Address Pointer
        MOV A,D
        CMP H                ;Check for end of RAM
        JNZ FILL             ;Continue writing until done
        MOV A,E
        CMP L
        JNZ FILL
;
READ:   LXI H, RAMST         ;Re-initialize Start Address
        MOV A,B              ;Read RAM content
        XRA M                ;Compare test pattern
        JNZ ERROR            ;ERROR EXIT
        INX H                ;Increment Pointer
        MOV A,D
        CMP H                ;Check for end of RAM
        JNZ READ             ;Continue reading until done
        MOV A,E
        CMP L
        JNZ READ
;
        MOV A,B              ;Check for test pattern = FF
        CPI FFH              ;NORMAL EXIT
        JZ DONE
        MVI B,FFH            ;Set test pattern to FF
        JMP START            ;Repeat test
```

(a) Flowchart

73

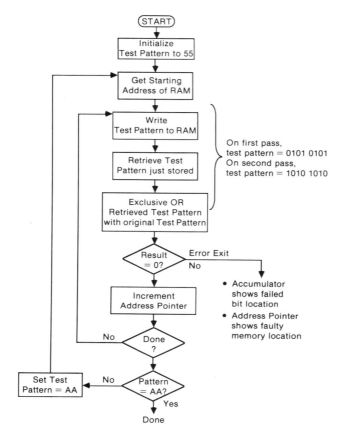

On first pass,
test pattern = 0101 0101
On second pass,
test pattern = 1010 1010

• Accumulator
  shows failed
  bit location
• Address Pointer
  shows faulty
  memory location

Figure 4–4: Simple checkerboard test.
This version tests stored data
immediately after it is written. Other
versions use logic similar to Figure 4–3
where the RAM is first filled with a
background of alternating ones and
zeros, then inversed.

	First Test	*Second Test*	
	0 1 0 1 0 1 0 1	1 0 1 0 1 0 1 0	
	0 1 0 1 0 1 0 1	1 0 1 0 1 0 1 0	
	0 1 0 1 0 1 0 1	1 0 1 0 1 0 1 0	
	0 1 0 1 0 1 0 1	1 0 1 0 1 0 1 0	
	0 1 0 1 0 1 0 1	1 0 1 0 1 0 1 0	
	0 1 0 1 0 1 0 1	1 0 1 0 1 0 1 0	
	etc.	etc.	

Increasing Addresses

During the verification phase, exclusive-OR comparison of the patterns is used. This results in a bit map in the accumulator showing the failing bit positions.

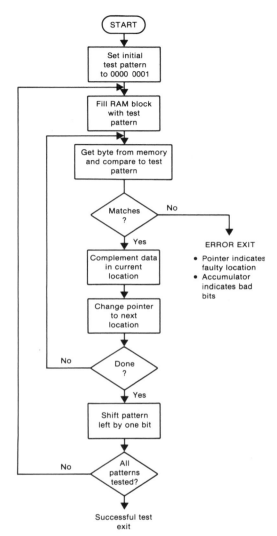

Figure 4-5: A quick march RAM test.

Several variations of this test have been devised. The version shown in Figure 4-4 tests each location as it is written. Two passes are made, first with the pattern 01010101, then with 10101010. An alternate version (Problem 4-1) uses slightly more complex logic but implements a better test algorithm.

These tests, like the previous one, check for hard errors plus failure of decode logic and other support circuits. They are sometimes used with a delay between memory fill and memory read to test for data retention. They do not catch many pattern-sensitive memory failures.

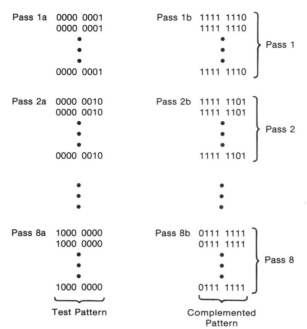

Pass 1a 0000 0001   Pass 1b 1111 1110 ⎫
         0000 0001   1111 1110 ⎪
           •   •   ⎬ Pass 1
           •   •   ⎪
           •   •   ⎪
         0000 0001   1111 1110 ⎭

Pass 2a 0000 0010   Pass 2b 1111 1101 ⎫
         0000 0010   1111 1101 ⎪
           •   •   ⎬ Pass 2
           •   •   ⎪
           •   •   ⎪
         0000 0010   1111 1101 ⎭

           •   •
           •   •
           •   •

Pass 8a 1000 0000   Pass 8b 0111 1111 ⎫
         1000 0000   0111 1111 ⎪
           •   •   ⎬ Pass 8
           •   •   ⎪
           •   •   ⎪
         1000 0000   0111 1111 ⎭

        Test Pattern   Complemented
                                      Pattern

Figure 4–6: Test progression for quick
march test of Figure 4–5.

Galloping Pattern Testing

To search for pattern-sensitive and other soft errors, a group of "galloping pattern" tests have been devised. Many variations have been developed, including "walking 1s and 0s," "marching 1s and 0s," and so on. We will describe a simple march test.

Simple march test.   This test checks for address sensitivity as well as some cell interaction. Basically, it tests whether each location is capable of storing 1s and 0s and whether writing to any given location disturbs data residing at other locations. The flowchart of Figure 4–5 outlines the logic of the test.[6] The program makes two passes through the RAM address range for each bit—thus, for an 8-bit processor, $2 \times 8 = 16$ passes are required. Test patterns are produced by shifting a single logic 1 bit through the accumulator as indicated in Figure 4–6. The first pass for each pattern stores the selected pattern in all locations; on the second pass for that pattern, each location is read and checked to see if anything has changed. If the data check okay, the location is marked to show that it has been tested. This is done by complementing its contents. If there is interaction between cells, it will be detected when the test reaches the address affected. An alternate version of this test based on checkerboard patterns is detailed by Coffron in Ref. 13.

[6]James Laurino [5] outlined the quick-march test on which this example is based.

Random patterns.   Random pattern testing is sometimes used to test for pattern sensitivity. In such a test, a series of pseudorandom numbers is generated by software, written to memory, retrieved, then checked for errors. The process is repeated over and over in the hope that pattern-sensitive errors will be uncovered.

These are but a few of the possible memory test techniques available.[7] As before, if the tests pass, they verify not only the memory, but also all associated address bus, data bus, and decode and control logic associated with the subsystem.

Length of Time to Test

Time limitations are an important factor in memory testing. For some schemes, testing time goes up proportional to the number of memory locations N to be tested (N test), while others go up proportional to the square of the number of locations to be tested (N^2 test). This can have enormous impact on the duration of the test for large memories and should be considered when planning a test strategy. For very large memories, test duration using N^2 testing can stretch into months. This obviously is not very practical in a servicing environment. However, in a design environment, there are cases where comprehensive testing is required to verify that the design works under adverse conditions.

4–5 I/O SUBSYSTEM TESTING (PARALLEL AND SERIAL)

Testing I/O subsystems is also simple in principle and follows the general strategy of Figure 4–1. For the output case, test patterns may be written to output devices, then checked by the operator to verify correct response; for the input case, signals may be applied at input ports and read to ensure that they load in correctly. The same principle applies whether we are dealing with general-purpose I/O ports, analog ports, display systems, switch and keypad inputs, and so on. Details vary for each case, of course. Let us begin by considering general-purpose parallel I/O ports.

4–6 PARALLEL I/O PORT TESTING

Output ports and input ports can be verified independently or tested together. Testing together may be faster, but if there is a fault in one of the devices, they will have to be broken apart to determine which is at fault. For LSI devices such as the Motorola PIA, Intel PPI, and others, this determination may not be necessary, however, because if either section has a fault, generally the complete device must be replaced.

---

[7] For further discussion of memory tests, see Ref. 4, 6, and 13.

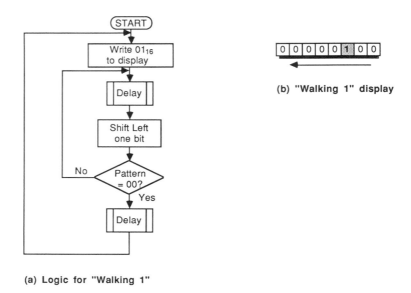

(b) "Walking 1" display

(a) Logic for "Walking 1"

Figure 4-7: Testing port using a "Walking 1" bit.

Testing Parallel Output Ports

Verifying correct operation of parallel output ports is relatively straightforward. A simple test can be implemented by writing patterns to their output for observation. The ability to correctly output both a 0 and 1 to each bit position must be verified. If the port has indicators for observation, suitable patterns are a slowly rotating 1, a slowly rotating 0, and so on. These patterns are a good choice because they can be confirmed easily by observation.

A "walking 1" test is illustrated below (Figure 4-7). Here a 1 is walked across the display in a cyclically repeating fashion. A short delay between shifts holds the pattern long enough for the operator to observe. If the port does not have indicators, use a logic probe or an oscilloscope to check the logic levels on each pin. In this case, you will have to output static patterns to permit probing.

The tests described above are simple go/no-go tests that provide a high level of confidence but do not test for all possible faults (such as multiple-bit interactions). More thorough testing can be achieved using all possible combinations of patterns. One convenient way to do this is to use a binary counting sequence. Such a test is described in the example of Figure 4-9.

Testing Parallel Input Ports

Verifying input ports is also easy if some means exists to input known signals. (Switches provide a convenient method.) We also need to verify whether the data are read in correctly. With a capable external tester, this is straightforward, as the tester itself will provide a console display. On the other hand, if your test setup consists of the UUT with test software in memory, you will have to devise some method of turning the data around and outputing them. Fortunately, most systems include a display or output port that can be used for this purpose. Make sure that you use a previously verified device for this task.

The logic of the test software is straightforward and is indicated in Figure 4-8. The test program reads the inputs and writes to the outputs for confirmation. Again, all bits should be tested to ensure that the ports can handle both logic 0 and logic 1 correctly.

Loop-Back Testing

An alternative to individually testing input and output ports is to use the loop-back technique and test them together. This is indicated in Figure 4-9. Here a pattern is

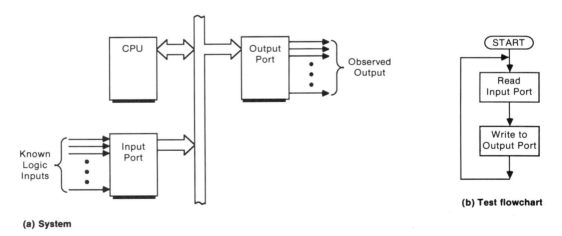

(b) Test flowchart

(a) System

Figure 4-8: Testing an input port. Ensure that output port is known to be good.

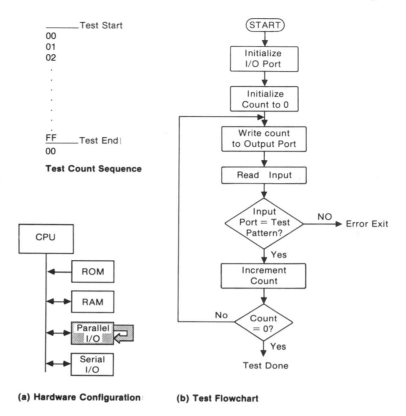

Figure 4–9:   Parallel Loopback test.

written to the output, read back, then compared. If a match occurs, the next pattern is output. If the test fails, the operator is advised. Simple go/no-go versions can be used, or with a little extra effort, the software can be written to identify the bit (or bits) that are in error. As usual, the test must check the ability of each bit to output and input a 1 and a 0. This can be done in a variety of ways. The program shown outputs a binary counting sequence to test all possible combinations of 1s and 0s. Alternative versions rotate a 1 or a 0 or some other pattern [2].

Example 4–1: Testing the Motorola PIA as a Simple I/O Port

As described in Appendix A, the Motorola PIA (peripheral interface adapter) is a typical (dual) LSI I/O port. In this example, it is used as a simple I/O port, with port B for output and port A for input. A program implementing the logic of Figure 4–9 is illustrated in Figure 4–10. As each byte is output, it is read back and compared. If a mismatch occurs, a branch to the error exit is made.

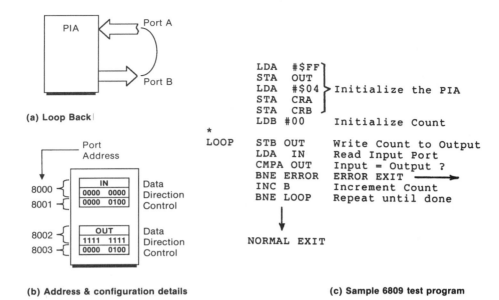

(a) Loop Back

(b) Address & configuration details

```
        LDA   #$FF ⎤
        STA   OUT   |
        LDA   #$04   ⎬ Initialize the PIA
        STA   CRA   |
        STA   CRB  ⎦
        LDB   #00      Initialize Count
*
LOOP    STB   OUT      Write Count to Output
        LDA   IN       Read Input Port
        CMPA  OUT      Input = Output ?
        BNE   ERROR    ERROR EXIT ⟶
        INC   B        Increment Count
        BNE   LOOP     Repeat until done
                  │
                  ↓
        NORMAL EXIT
```

(c) Sample 6809 test program

Figure 4-10: Parallel loopback test for Motorola PIA using counting sequence. (Assumes PIA initially cleared on Reset).

Testing Port Control Lines

In addition to simple I/O, many LSI ports include interrupt inputs, handshake control lines, and so on. We need to be able to test these as well. For ease of testing, they may be looped back as indicated in Figure 4-11. A thorough test requires that all modes be tested. In any given application, however, it is usually only necessary to test those modes that are actually used. This saves test time. Because of the many variations possible for any given port and the volume of detail, we will only illustrate the principle.

Example 4-2: The Motorola PIA Control Input CA1 and Output CA2

As noted in Appendix A, the PIA designates its control lines as CA1 and CA2 for side A and CB1 and CB2 for side B. Here we will illustrate for side A only. Consider input CA1. An active transition on this line sets an internal flag in A side port logic. (The active edge can be defined as either low to high or high to low through software initialization of the port.)

Control line CA2 in this example is defined as output. Via software, CA2 can be programmed to go from low to high or from high to low. CA2 is looped back to CA1 as in Figure 4-11(b) and the test program is devised to toggle CA2. For a thorough test of the flag logic, both edges are checked. As indicated in the flow chart, the active edge of CA1 is initially set for a low-to-high transition and CA2 is toggled high. The flag is then tested to see if it sets. If it does, the active edge of CA1 is changed and CA2 is toggled low. Again, the flag is tested to see if it set. If (in either case) it did not set, a branch is made to an error exit and the user advised that the test failed. Test logic is shown in flowchart form only, but is easily coded. Testing of other general-purpose LSI I/O ports, such as the Intel PPI, Z80 PIO, and so on, may be performed similarly.

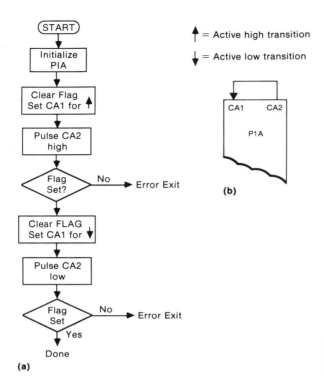

Figure 4-11: Logic to test CA1, CA2 and FLAG of PIA. Identical logic can be used to test B side.

4-7 SERIAL I/O PORT TESTING

Serial ports may be synchronous or asynchronous with selectable baud rates, parity, character length, and so on. This leaves a lot to be tested, and thorough testing requires a set of routines that can completely and exhaustively exercise all operational logic. As noted previously, this is seldom necessary in practice, as testing can usually be limited to those features of interest in the particular application under consideration.

Serial ports can also be tested according to the strategy of Figure 4-1. For example, asynchronous ports may be tested by connecting them to a CRT terminal through an RS-232 link, then verifying that characters can be input from the keyboard and output to the CRT display. Basic test logic is indicated in Figure 4-12(b). The serial port contains an input flag and an output flag. When the user presses a key, CRT keyboard logic encodes the data and transmits them in serial form to the receive port. When a character is received, port logic sets a flag. This flag is interrogated by software to determine whether the character has been received. When the flag becomes set, software reads the input character from the port. Before this character can be output to the CRT display logic, software must test to see that the transmit port is ready to receive the new character for transmission to the CRT. It does this by testing the transmit port flag. Logic for this test is indicated in Figure 4–12(c). If the test passes, it verifies the serial port, the RS-232 link, all decode and control logic, and so on, in the CPU/port interface. If it fails, you may wish to break the test down into two independent tests, one for input and one for output and test the two interfaces separately.

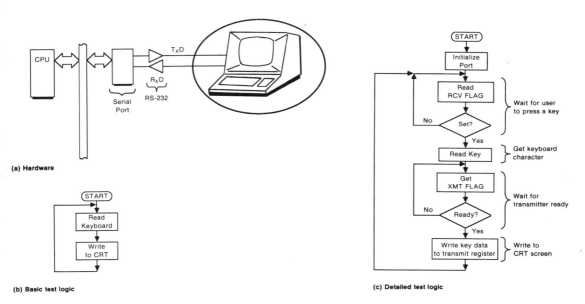

(a) Hardware

(b) Basic test logic

(c) Detailed test logic

Figure 4–12:   Simple test of serial I/O port. User presses key. Processor reads key and echoes it on the CRT screen. Operator verifies visually.

Serial Testing Using Loop-Back Technique

Serial ports can also be tested using loop-back techniques (Figure 4–13). Data transmitted by the output are read by the input and compared. If a mismatch occurs, the operator is alerted. The example illustrates a test using flag polling. For interrupt-driven devices, program logic would have to be modified.

4-8 TESTING DISPLAYS

Display systems can be verified visually. Test software need only output a known test pattern for the user to observe. Some examples are described below.

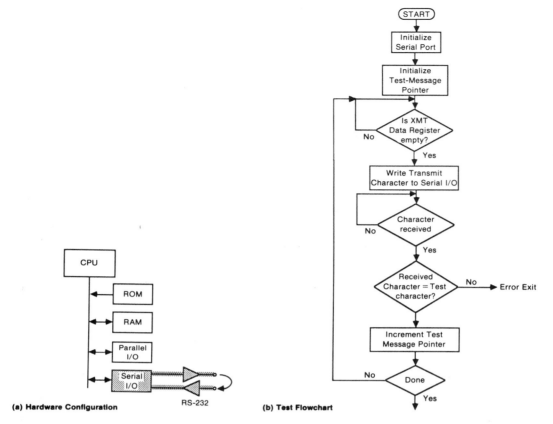

(a) Hardware Configuration   RS-232   (b) Test Flowchart

Figure 4–13: Serial Loopback test.

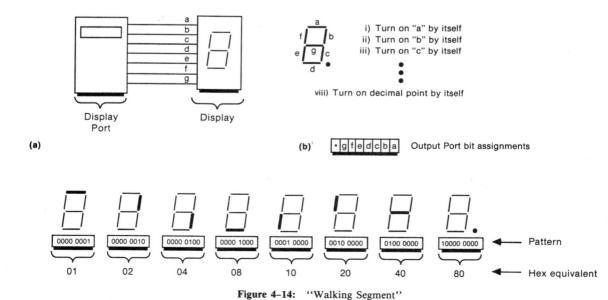

i) Turn on "a" by itself
ii) Turn on "b" by itself
iii) Turn on "c" by itself

viii) Turn on decimal point by itself

(a)

(b) Output Port bit assignments

Pattern

Hex equivalent

Figure 4–14: "Walking Segment" display test.

84

Verifying LED Arrays

Testing again follows the general strategy of Figure 4-1. Variations that are useful include walking patterns and slow binary counts, as illustrated previously in Figure 4-7. Walk patterns provide a fast verification, while binary counts check more thoroughly by verifying all possible combinations.

Verifying Numerical Displays

Numerical displays can also be checked visually. The example below illustrates testing of a seven-segment readout (Figure 4-14). Test software writes a pattern to the display to illuminate one segment at a time, walking it from position to position. A short delay between shifts holds the pattern long enough to be observed. Depending on circuit details in any given system, a 1 or a 0 may light a segment. For the example indicated, we have assumed a 1.

   The logic of the program is straightforward. A flowchart and a program listing for the 8085 are shown in Figure 4-15. Other processors are handled similarly. In a multidigit display, the test is repeated for each character. Such a test is described in detail in Chapter 5.

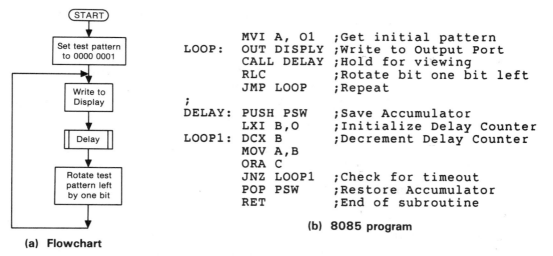

(a) **Flowchart**

(b) **8085 program**

Figure 4-15: Logic and sample program for "Walking Segment" test.

4-9 KEYPADS AND SWITCH INTERFACE TESTING

Keypad, keyboard, and switch operation may be verified by user interaction. The operator presses keys while test software monitors and displays the results. To illustrate, consider the encoded keypad of Figure 4-16. When a key is operated, its binary equivalent is generated by the keyboard encoder and presented to the processor, together with a flag indicating that new key data are available. Keypad status

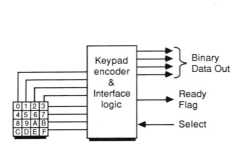

(a) Keypad subsystem

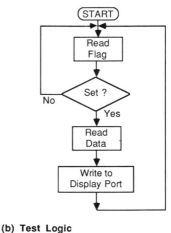

(b) Test Logic

| 0 | 0 | 0 | 0 | 0 | 1 | 0 | 1 | Display Port

(c) Example: Key 5 pressed

Figure 4-16: Basic keypad subsystem test strategy.

may be tested as indicated in the flowchart. When new data are available, they are read, then displayed on a suitable indicator.

If you are using an external tester, results may be displayed directly on its console. For self test configurations, a previously verified display or output port may be used.

Unencoded keypads may be tested similarly. See problem 4–5.

4-10 ANALOG I/O SUBSYSTEM TESTING

Analog inputs and outputs may also be tested independently or together. As with previous tests, the loop-back technique can save time, although if a fault is uncovered, the units will have to be broken apart to determine which device (D/A or A/D) is at fault.

A/D and D/A converters need to be checked for both accuracy and monotonicity.[8] Accuracy tests can be performed statically, using a known voltage to drive the A/D converter and a precision digital multimeter to measure the output of the D/A converter. Usually, three values, representing minimum, midrange, and maximum are checked. A monotonicity test (described below) may be used to verify that no bits are bad; simply testing at a few values can easily miss this problem.

[8]Monotonicity means that the converters should maintain an incremental increasing (or decreasing) output for an increasing (or decreasing) input—see Figure 4-17(b).

Testing D/A Converters

As noted, an accuracy test can be performed by outputting values to the D/A register and verifying its output using a digital multimeter. Check at minimum, midrange, and maximum. The monotonicity test can be implemented by ramping the contents of the D/A register and observing the analog output on an oscilloscope. If no bits are faulty, the output will change linearly as shown in Figure 4–17(b). If there are stuck bits, the waveform will have dropouts or spikes as indicated in part (c).

Testing A/D Converters

The accuracy test can be performed by connecting a known source to the analog input, initiating a conversion, reading in the converted value, then by comparing this value to that expected, verify whether the conversion is correct. Again, check at minimum, midrange, and maximum.

Testing Analog Subsystems Using the Loop-Back Technique

Testing an A/D converter by itself for monotonicity is difficult. However, if a compatible D/A converter is available on the system, they can be looped and tested together. Test software outputs values to the D/A converter, reads the A/D port

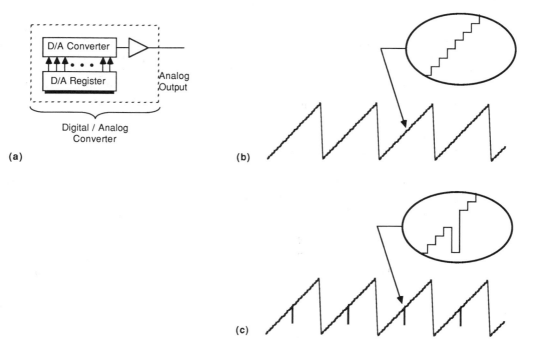

Figure 4–17: Monotonicity test of a D/A converter.

after conversion, then compares the values. By ramping the D/A as in Figure 4–17, the operator can visually verify monotonicity for the D/A, while the program can compare the input A/D value against the output D/A value and check for agreement. This test therefore checks for A/D monotonicity. In this scheme it may be necessary to mask the LSB because of the tolerances of the D/A and A/D conversion processes. As with other tests, it is assumed that there is some way to report errors to the operator. For those with an external tester, this reporting will be via its operator's console. For self test configurations, use pretested displays or output ports to report pass/fail, as noted earlier.

4–11 CPU TESTING

The CPU is seldom tested directly. The reason for this is that comprehensive testing of CPU logic is a difficult and time-consuming task. As noted in Ref. 6, the only way to test a CPU thoroughly is to operate it functionally and verify the correct execution of each instruction as well as the correct behavior of interrupt logic, DMA logic, and so on. Such a thorough check takes an enormous amount of time, and consequently, this type of testing is seldom implemented in practice. Instead, some commercial testers verify the CPU indirectly by substitution. If the unit under test works with the tester substituted for the CPU but fails with the CPU, the CPU is deemed defective and should be replaced. If the system still does not work with the tester in place, troubleshooting of the suspect system is in order.

There are some exceptions to this general comment. A few processors, for example, contain built-in self-test capabilities that permit the user to perform go/no-go testing of the CPU directly. To implement such testing, the CPU is removed from the unit under test and inserted into a special test jig. On power-up, the CPU executes a set of built-in self-test routines. The MC6804 from Motorola features this capability. With the evolution of VLSI, it is expected that this trend will accelerate and many VLSI devices will ultimately be able to test themselves on board.

4–12 PLACEMENT OF FUNCTIONAL TEST PROGRAMS

As noted previously, it does not matter in principle where we locate test diagnostics as long as we provide a means of executing them, a means of validating test results, and a means of reporting errors to the operator. In practice, test software may be located:

1. In an external tester
2. In the unit under test
   (a) In the application ROM
   (b) In a debug ROM
3. In the UUT RAM (loaded from disk at run time)

Each of these approaches has its advantages and disadvantages. Let us consider each in turn.

External Testers

A capable external tester represents the most convenient and flexible troubleshooting configuration. Such testers remove the impact of kernel failure by moving the diagnostic software outside the unit under test. Typical testers interface to the unit under test via an umbilical cable inserted into the system's microprocessor socket, as depicted previously (Figure 1-1). In contrast to other schemes, this approach works even if the target system is completely inoperative and unable to execute even the most primitive software. In addition, some testers permit interactive operator involvement via a fully featured operator's console. This permits the operator to take complete charge of the troubleshooting session. The disadvantage of the exernal tester approach is that the capital cost is high (although costs can often be quickly recovered through increased service throughput), not all processors are supported, and a separate personality pod is required for each processor.

An example tester.   The Fluke 9010A tester (Figure 1-2) fits this category. It includes within a single test instrument the following general-purpose functional test routines:

Built-in bus test

Built-in RAM tests

Built-in ROM test

Built-in I/O test

An assortment of other useful tests

This unit easily implements all the tests described in this chapter. It is especially convenient to use since none of the standard tests have to be programmed by the user— they are factory designed in and are called up during troubleshooting by single-keystroke selection. Custom tests are also easily mechanized. In addition, the console features an alphanumeric display for operator interaction and feedback. (Troubleshooting with this unit is described in Chapter 5.)

Other commercially available testers with built-in functional test capability include the ET-2000 from Applied Microsystems Corporation, the B2000 from Polar Electronics Limited and the SST (μP based version) from Creative Microprocessor Systems. (These units are also highlighted in Chapter 5.)

ROM-Based Diagnostics

Testing may be implemented using ROM-based diagnostic firmware installed in the unit under test. Test routines may be designed into the product at design time and occupy space in the application ROM or they may be supplied in the form of a debug ROM that is substituted for the application ROM during testing.

Application ROM resident diagnostics.   This configuration has the advantage of requiring no additional hardware, but the disadvantage that its capabilities may be limited due to the lack of space available in the application ROM. In addition, to be useful, at least part of the UUT must be operational in order to execute the test firmware. This is not always the case and the user may be thrust into the position of not being able to run the test diagnostics at the very time when they are needed most—when the system has a problem. Obviously, they will not be able to run if the kernel itself is inoperative. However, if the problem is outside the kernel, resident diagnostics can be a very effective, low-cost troubleshooting aid.

In most applications, it is up to the designer or the user to develop the required test routines. These may be devised according to the principles and examples of this chapter. In many designs, some of the required tests fall out of the application software development effort, and only a small amount of additional work is required to adapt them for testing purposes. It is basically a matter of ensuring that the job gets done. In the crush to get products to market, it sometimes does not.

Plug-in ROM diagnostics.   Diagnostics based on plug-in ROMs are an extension of the foregoing idea. During testing, the debug ROM is either installed in an unused ROM socket, or the application ROM is removed and the test ROM inserted in its place. Since the size of the test program is no longer limited by the leftover space in the application ROM, more elaborate and sophisticated test programs can be devised.

For the two preceding cases, at least the kernel of the system under test must be operational. At first glance, this may seem a serious limitation. However, it is not as serious as one might expect. While it is true that the kernel must be operational for the tests to run, in reality, the kernel represents a very small, well-defined subportion of the system and can usually be brought up relatively easily using other means if it has failed. (Such methods are described in Chapters 6 and 7.) Once this is done, the diagnostics can be brought into play and troubleshooting resumed.

An example.   Signature analysis is one of the methods used to implement node-based circuit tracing (Chapter 7). However, it is inherently incapable of implementing functional testing. Thus it must be supplemented by some form of functional tests capability. Figure 4–18 illustrates one typical configuration. Here functional test routines reside in one corner of the application ROM. These routines may be designed into the product at the factory, or they may have to be devised by the user. In any case, the principles of this chapter apply. Note that since the routines reside in the memory of the unit under test, they must be written in the language of the processor. This is in contrast to the external tester case, where test software is often written in a high-level language in a universal form that is independent of the details of the actual system under test.

Run-Time RAM-Based Diagnostics

For systems with disks and operating systems (e.g., personal computers), diagnostic software is often provided by the vendor on disks. To test the system, these are called up by the user, loaded into RAM, and executed. Because of the space available on

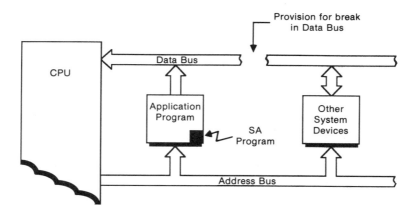

Figure 4-18:   Essence of a Signature Analysis configuration.

disks, diagnostics can be very elaborate. Memory diagnostics are a common example. Often memory diagnostics of the types described in this chapter (plus more) are included, providing the user with a battery of tests from which to choose. Again, a great deal of the system must be operational for these to run. Diagnostics may also include display tests, keypad tests, and others. Such tests are generally capable of identifying faulty system blocks and in some cases, actual suspect ICs.

4-13 SELF-TESTING

One of the areas where functional testing has found application is in the realm of self-testing. By "self-testing," we mean the ability of a product or system to assess its own functionality. Self-testing is useful in the production environment, in field testing, and for customer verification.

Power-Up Self-Test

Self-test capability proves especially useful in the field environment where a product falls into the hands of nontechnical customers. Typically, the self-test routines execute when power is switched on. Often the self-test does little more than assure the customer that the product is "working." It is a good way to build customer confidence.

Service-Oriented and Production-Oriented Self-Test

A more comprehensive set of self-tests may be provided for use by service personnel. These may be invoked, for example, by a special keystroke sequence or when a test jumper is installed. As above, such tests work only if the kernel of the system is functioning and able to execute the test software.

A specific example is illustrated in Figure 4-19. Here a service "test jumper" is interrogated, and if it is in the test position, testing proceeds. The example shown

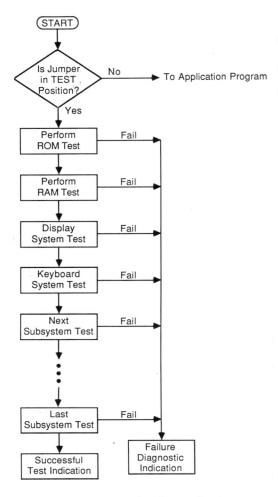

Figure 4-19: Diagnostic self-test logic.

performs pass/fail analysis of a small microprocessor-based system. All subtests shown are of the type discussed throughout this chapter. If all tests pass, the system is considered to be free from faults and able to perform its intended function. If any test fails, the operator is alerted.

For the display tests, the operator observes the patterns on the displays. If an error is detected, the operator stops the test. For the keyboard test, test software scans the keyboard, waiting for operator input. The operator must press each switch to verify its operation. When the specified "end of test" switch is operated, testing moves on to the next subtest. This process continues until the system is fully checked or until a fault is found.

4-14 SUMMARY

The functional tests described in this chapter may be used stand-alone or they may be used to implement level 1 of the general strategy of Chapter 3. Additionally, they may be built into commercial testers or the user may have to cast them into ROM (or EPROM) and install them into the UUT for testing. In Chapter 5 we consider a sophisticated μP socket tester that already has the basic tests built in; in Chapters 6 and 7 we consider other testers where the tests are not built in, but must be installed in the UUT by the user, either in a corner of the application ROM as in Figure 4–18 or in a separate debug ROM.[9]

REFERENCES

1. *Hands-On Troubleshooting Microprocessor Systems* (Course Notes), Integrated Computer Systems, Santa Monica, CA.

2. Donn, Edward S., and Michael D. Lippman, Efficient and Effective μC Testing Requires Careful Preplanning, *EDN*, February 20, 1979.

3. *Application Articles on Signature Analysis*, Application Note 222-2, Hewlett-Packard Co., Palo Alto, CA.

4. Application Note 00041, Micro Control Co., Minneapolis, MN.

5. Laurino, James A., A Quick March Test Checks Memory, *Electronics*, December 21, 1978.

6. Dupley, Bill, *Signature Analysis Application Examples* (Seminar), Hewlett-Packard Co., Palo Alto, CA.

7. *Guide to Testing Microprocessor Based Systems and Boards*, Millenium Systems, Inc.

8. Hardos, Barney, *Diagnostic Programming for Microprocessor-Based Systems*, Millenium Systems, Inc.

9. *9010A Micro-System Troubleshooter Operator Manual*, John Fluke Manufacturing Co., Inc., Everett, WA.

10. Hayes, John P., Testability Considerations in Microprocessor Based Designs, *Computer*, March 1980.

11. Lesea, Austin, and Rodnay Zaks, *Microprocessor Interfacing Techniques*, Sybex, Inc., Berkeley, CA, 1980.

12. Cannon, Don L., *Understanding Digital Troubleshooting*, Texas Learning Center, Dallas, TX.

13. Coffron, James W., Using and Troubleshooting the MC68000, Reston Publishing Company Inc., Reston, VA.

REVIEW QUESTIONS

4–1 Figure 4–4 shows one variation of a checkerboard RAM test. An alternate version works as follows. Memory is filled with a checkerboard background 01010101, 10101010, 01010101, 10101010, etc, then read back and verified. If no errors are found, memory is next filled with the inverse pattern 10101010, 01010101, 10101010, 01010101 and the test repeated. If an error is detected in either test, a branch is made to an error exit. Prepare a flowchart showing the logic of this test.

[9]Unless implemented via an external tester, in which case the test routines probably will reside in the tester also.

4-2 Code the test of Figure 4-4 for the processor of your choice.

4-3 Repeat Question 4-2 for Figures 4-5 and 4-7.

4-4 If it takes 90 s to test a certain RAM subsystem using an N-squared test, how long will it take to test a memory subsystem that is three times as large?

4-5 Consider the X-Y (matrix) keypad of Figure 4-20. An output port drives rows and an input port reads columns. Develop a flowchart showing the logic to test this keypad using the strategy described below. Assume an indicator as in Figure 4-16 to display test results.

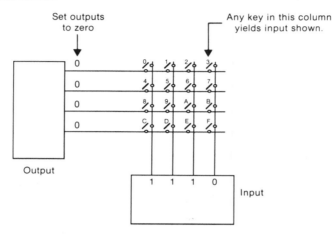

Figure 4-20

Test Procedure

1. Write all 0s to the output port to drive all rows low.

2. Read the input port to determine which key (if any) has been pressed. Display column information as indicated in Table 4-1.

Key	Indicator
3, 7, B, F	▨
2, 6, A, E	▨
1, 5, 9, D	▨
0, 4, 8, C	▨

▨ Indicator ON

3. Loop to step 2 and repeat continuously.

When no keys are pressed, all indicators should be blank. When a key is operated, the indicator for that column should come on. Table 4-1 summarizes test results for a properly functioning keypad. Note that key debouncing is not required. Why?

5

HARDWARE TROUBLESHOOTING USING μP SOCKET TESTERS

Tools based on μP principles are able to take advantage of the computer nature of the systems they are designed to test. In varying degrees, tools in this category perform analysis on the suspect system and assist in guiding the operator to the location of the fault. Figures 5-2 to 5-4 illustrate three commercial implementations of such testers. These instruments, although differing in detail and capabilities, have certain basic principles in common. Each employs functional testing using generic utility programs to localize problems to major functional blocks and a node verification and circuit-tracing strategy to trace failures to the faulty node level. They all thus implement troubleshooting in fundamentally the same fashion. In this chapter we highlight the basic test methodologies used by each, then focus on the Fluke 9010A MicroSystem Troubleshooter as an example of this class of troubleshooter.

PART A: μP SOCKET TESTERS (GENERAL)

Microprocessor socket testers interface to the system under test via a simple cabling arrangement as depicted in Figure 5-1. Working fundamentally the same as the processor that it has displaced, the tester takes over control of the system that it is testing, supplying to it all address, data, and control signals that the UUT processor normally would. For this reason, such testers are sometimes referred to as "in-circuit emulator" testers.

Several commercial implementations of μP socket testers are illustrated in Figures 5-2 to 5-4. Each includes a keyboard for operator selection of tests and entry of test parameters as well as a display for presentation of test results, operator prompts, and so on.

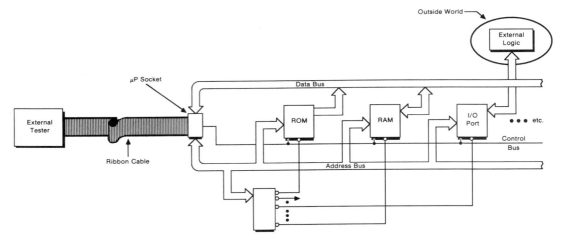

Figure 5-1: μP   Principle testers work in fundamentally the same fashion as computers and are thus able to take advantage of the computer nature of the systems they are designed to test.

Figure 5-2:   The Fluke 9010A MicroSystem Troubleshooter. Photo courtesy of John Fluke Mfg. Co. Inc.

Figure 5-3: The ET-2000 Micro
Trouble Shooter. Photo courtesy of
Applied Microsystems Corporation.

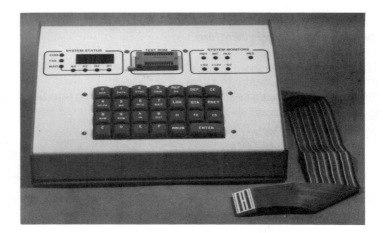

Figure 5-4: SST Tester. Photo courtesy of Creative Microprocessor Systems.

5-1 FUNCTIONAL TESTING

Functional test methods employed by these testers follow closely the strategies outlined in Chapter 4. Certain basic tests which are universal and independent of the unit under test are generally built in. Typical tests include a bus test, a set of read/write memory (RAM) tests, a read-only memory (ROM) test, plus a simple I/O port test. RAM test strategies minimally include a checkerboard or one of the other tests from Chapter 4. In some testers, more elaborate routines to test for pattern-sensitive failures and address decode problems are also included. ROM tests typically utilize a checksum, CRC algorithm, or direct comparison against a reference ROM.

Test requirements for system elements outside the basic kernel are generally unique and hence are not included as part of the built-in test set. Users must therefore develop their own custom tests for these subsystems. Depending on the tester in use, this may be a simple or modestly difficult task. Some testers, for example, provide built-in test functions that can be invoked by the user via pushbutton operation to test common off-kernel elements. (The Fluke 9010A features this capability.) Others require that test programs be developed in the code of the UUT processor and installed (via a debug EPROM) in the tester itself.

5-2 NODE VERIFICATION AND CIRCUIT TRACING

Several node verification strategies have also been devised. Basically, these work on the principle that since the tester is controlling the system under test, it knows when signals are valid on nodes, and hence it knows when to test them. There are, however, considerable differences in detail at the mechanization level.

Synchronized Probe Method

This scheme makes use of a logic probe whose operation is synchronized to the stimulus provided by the test box. Bus lines may be stimulated high, low, or continuously toggled and the probe caused to sample the stimulated line at its valid time, as illustrated in Figure 5–5. This not only verifies logic levels, it also verifies that the logic levels occur at the correct point in time.

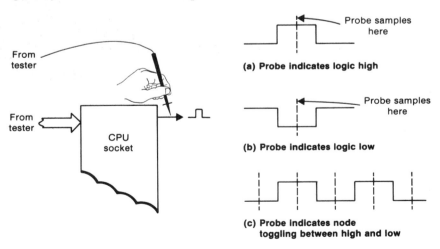

Figure 5–5: Synchronized probe sampling. Probe indicates logic level at instant of sampling.

The two general times of interest in this process are "address time" when addresses are valid on the buses and "data time" when data are valid on the buses, since all signals of interest coincide with one or the other of these times. The test instrument must therefore permit selection of which "time" to synchronize to. Generally, address-related signal measurements are made with the probe synchronized to address- and data-related signals with the probe synchronized to data. However, with some processors (such as the 6809), addresses are valid across the entire clock cycle and we can synchronize to either for address-related signals. For systems with multiplexed buses, greater care is needed. For example, consider the 8085. Low-order addresses are output on the multiplexed bus during address time (the early part of the cycle) and data during data time (the latter part of the cycle). If we want to see addresses, we must sample when they are valid (address time); if we want to see data, we must sample when they are valid (data time). Synchronization for this case is illustrated in Figure 5-12.

The Fluke 9010A uses this scheme. Its probe contains a set of indicator lamps to indicate the logic level observed at its tip. When a logic low is sampled, its "low" indicator lamp comes on; when a logic high is encountered, its "high" indicator lamp comes on; if a toggling node is probed, the indicator lamps come on simultaneously.

Using the synchronized probe technique, development of circuit tracing strategies is easy. To illustrate, consider Figure 5-6. Assume that we want to check address line A12 at devices U_5, U_{17}, and U_{19}. Proceed as follows. Synchronize the probe to address and set the tester to continuously toggle address A12. Now probe A12 at device U_5. Both indicator lamps will come on, indicating that the line is toggling correctly. Now probe at U_{17}. In this case, there is a break in the signal path and hence no activity is detected at U_{17}. To determine the location of the break, backtrack until the toggling reappears. Now test at U_{19}. In this case, A12 is shorted low after the buffer and does not toggle. The probe indicates that A12 is stuck at logic 0.

As a second example, consider Figure 5-7. In this case, suppose that we wish to verify the chip select input $\overline{CS}$. To stimulate $\overline{CS}$ for testing, read from (or write to) some location in the RAM to cause it to be selected. With the probe synchronized to address time, probe $\overline{CS}$. It should show low, as indicated in Figure 5-7(b). If $\overline{CS}$ is faulted as in part (c), the probe will indicate high.

With the ability to verify nodes or identify them as faulty as noted above, circuit tracing can be undertaken.

While Figures 5-5 to 5-7 illustrate the basic principle of synchronized node testing, there is much more to it than this. We will return to the topic in Part B when we examine the Fluke 9010A in detail.

Automatic Signal Identification

Since both the UUT stimulus and the probe sampling are controlled by the tester, it is possible to design a tester that not only samples nodes, but also automatically

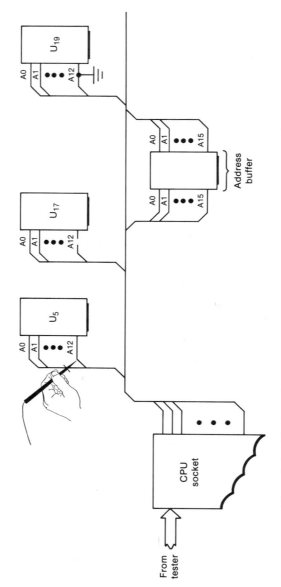

Figure 5–6: Circuit tracing. A12 has no faults at U₅; at U₁₇, there is a cold solder joint; at U₁₉, there is a solder bridge to ground.

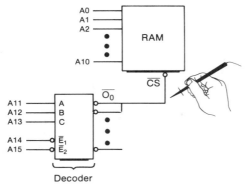

(a) Logic

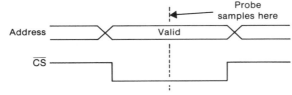

(b) Probe indicates node is low

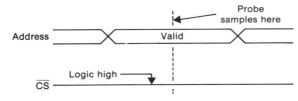

(c) Probe indicates node is high

Figure 5-7: Testing chip select $\overline{\text{CS}}$ using synchronized probe.

determines the identity of the node on which the probe is placed. This is the scheme used by the Applied Microsystems tester of Figure 5–3. The tester identifies unfaulted bus lines (address, data, and control) and displays their identity on the operator console using standard logic diagram terminology—for example, address line bit 5 is identified as ADDRESS LINE A–5. Automatic identification can simplify the node verification and circuit tracing process and help speed troubleshooting. Note, however, that faulted lines cannot be identified by this technique, and hence some alternative means of identification is necessary. In the case of the Applied Microsystems tester, signature analysis is used.

Circuit tracing using automatic signal identification follows the same basic strategy as that illustrated in Figure 5–6. For example, if A12 is probed at U_5, the console display will show ADDRESS LINE A–12. If A12 is probed at U_{19}, the tester will display the signature for a "stuck-at-zero node." At U_{17}, the tester will indicate a floating node (see Chapter 7).

Static Stimulus Method

Nodes can also be verified using static means. The tester of Figure 5–4 is based on this approach. Although it has some limitations, it is nonetheless useful for a wide variety of faults and is the least expensive of the techniques under discussion.[1]

Using the static stimulus approach, the tester outputs address, data, and control signals to the UUT like the previous testers. In its node verification and circuit tracing mode, however, it is stopped at this point. With the system stopped, logic levels throughout the UUT are static and hence can easily be verified. Synchronization is not even required—a simple hand-held logic probe or an oscilloscope will do. This permits verifying signal lines, decode and control logic, and so on. The principle is similar to that illustrated in Figures 5–6 and 5–7. (Troubleshooting using a manual SST tester is illustrated in Chapter 6.)

Signature Analysis Methods

Node verification and circuit tracing may also be effected by means of signature analysis.[2] As noted in Chapter 1, signature analysis uses a special data compression algorithm that uniquely identifies every node in a system (to a high degree of probability). This is exactly what we need for node verification and circuit tracing. However, the signature analysis approach suffers from the disadvantage that a data bank of known good signatures is needed, and this may not be available. Thus signature analysis, although suitable for production and service environments, is of little use in the design/development prototyping environment. (Troubleshooting using signature analysis techniques is discussed in Chapter 7.)

Another μP socket tester is the B2000 Microprocessor System Tester made by Polar Electronics (Guernsey) Ltd. It is a low cost unit intended for production or field service troubleshooting. Factory built-in tests are invoked by pre-programmed function keys. The unit features basic kernel tests and a fault tracing capability. Checks ROM using a checksum technique. Checks ability to read and write RAM. Tests ability to read from input ports and write to output ports. Checks for address and data bus shorts to Vcc and ground, other address lines or other data lines. A programmable loop program permits node level circuit tracing using an oscilloscope. A variety of personality pods support a number of popular processors.

PART B: μP SOCKET TESTERS (CASE STUDY: THE FLUKE 9010A)

We will now consider the Fluke 9010A as an example of this class of troubleshooter. However, the material, while specific to the 9010A, is presented in as general a man-

---

[1]It is estimated by the manufacturer that up to 90 percent of commonly occurring design prototype, production, and field-testing problems are static in nature.

[2]The first commerical μP socket tester, the μSA MicroSystem Analyzer for Millenium (introduced in 1977), implemented its circuit verification strategy using signature analysis.

ner as possible so that the reader can apply the underlying principles to similar testers made by other manufacturers.

The Fluke 9010A MicroSystem Troubleshooter is shown in Figure 5–2. It consists of a mainframe, an interface pod, and a troubleshooting probe. Featuring a set of built-in tests, it is able to exercise system buses, test ROM, RAM, I/O, and other bus devices as well as interrupt logic, status and control lines, and so on. The probe and mainframe are universal, while the interface pods tailor the mainframe to specific processors such as the 6809, 8085, Z80, 68000, and so on. A built-in cassette recorder provides for nonvolatile storage and transfer of test programs and data. The 9010A is intended for use in system design, prototype and production testing, and maintenance and field service. It is inherently capable of accommodating 8-, 16-, and 32-bit machines in either single-processor or multiple-processor configurations.[3]

The 9010A Console

The main instrument contains a keyboard and display to permit interactive troubleshooting. Figure 5–8 shows the layout of this keyboard and the troubleshooting

Figure 5–8:   9010A keyboard. Copyright © John Fluke Mfg. Co. Inc. Used with permission.

---

[3]Each portion of the system is tested separately with the particular processor removed and the 9010A installed in its place.

features available; most of these are invoked by single-keystroke operation. The 32-character display provides for presentation of test results, operator prompts, and other messages.

Testing Modes

Two modes of testing are provided—the immediate mode and the programmed mode.

Immediate mode.   In the immediate mode, testing is performed interactively from the console. The operator selects the desired test by pressing the applicable test key, enters test parameters as called for (memory boundaries, ROM signatures, etc.), performs the test, then analyzes its outcome before deciding what to do next. Here, successful testing relies directly on the operator's knowledge, skill, intuition, and experience. In practice, much troubleshooting is performed in this manner, possibly with the aid of some canned test software such as that discussed in Section 5-9.

Programmed mode.   In the programmed mode, troubleshooting steps are prestored in the 9010A's memory and executed much like a computer program. Programs may range from simple test routines used to assist the operator during immediate mode testing through customized functional test software to sophisticated "guided probe" fault routines that can guide the operator step by step through the troubleshooting process.[4]

Interactive Operation: Prompts and Error Messages

One of the features of the 9010A that makes it so easy to use is its interactive nature. During immediate mode testing, for example, it outputs prompts via its display console to guide the user step by step through the keyboard entry process, prompting for test parameters, address ranges, ROM signatures, and so on. Following the performance of tests, it displays results such as pass/fail status as well as details of actual faults found. User-written test programs can also take advantage of these capabilities.

5-3 CHARACTERIZING THE UNIT UNDER TEST: THE LEARN MODE

Testing with the 9010A requires that the user know where bus devices are located. If this information is not available, the 9010A's "learn" mode may be used to obtain it. In this mode the 9010A is able to learn the memory map of an unknown system and automatically classify devices as ROM, RAM, or I/O.

Example 5-1

To learn a system with an address map from 0000 to FFFF, select the learn mode by pressing the LEARN key (Figure 5-8), then key in the address range 0000 to FFFF. The

---

[4]Guided fault testing is beyond the scope of this book and will not be discussed.

9010A then works its way through the specified range, determining devices, their address boundaries, and in the case of ROM devices, their signatures as well. This information is stored as a set of "system descriptors."

Once a system has been learned, the user can interrogate the tester to determine its descriptors. To view a descriptor, press the appropriate view key (Figure 5–8). For example, if we press ROM view and the display shows ROM @ F800-FFFF SIG 0A39, this means that "LEARN" has found a block of ROM between address locations F800 and FFFF and that it has a signature of 0A39. Similarly, a RAM view message RAM @ 0000-07FF indicates a block of RAM between 0000 and 07FF. Using the information thus gained, the user can produce a map of the system as depicted symbolically in Figure 5–9. Once the descriptors for a given system have been learned, they should be documented for future reference. If you already know where devices are located, use LEARN only over ROM maps to determine their signatures. (These signatures must be learned from a known-good system.)

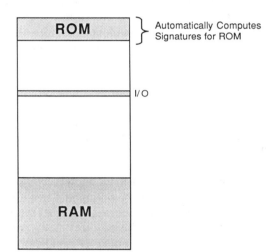

Figure 5–9:   Creating a memory map after learning a good system.

5–4 BASIC TESTS PROVIDED BY THE 9010A

Two basic sets of tests are built into the 9010A. A global set (designated BUS, ROM, RAM SHORT, RAM LONG, and I/O) provide large-scale testing of major functional subsystems. A local set (designated READ, WRITE, WALK, and RAMP) provides selective testing of individual memory and I/O locations as well as stimulus of individual bus lines for synchronized probe testing. Each test is invoked by operation of its like-named key (Figure 5–8). Following completion of a test, the 9010A halts and displays test results [1].

Large-Scale Tests

These tests automatically check the electrical integrity of system buses, the read/write capability of RAM, the data in ROM, as well as the correct functioning of I/O registers.

Bus system test.   BUS checks for bus faults. Undrivable control lines are identified, as well as address and data bus lines that are shorted high, shorted low, or tied together.

Example 5-2

Upon completion of a BUS test, the following message is displayed.

ADDR BIT 7 TIED HIGH

This error report indicates that address bit 7 is shorted high.

RAM module tests.   Two RAM memory tests (RAM SHORT and RAM LONG) are provided. RAM SHORT is a simple go/no-go test that identifies hard errors and gross RAM failures. RAM LONG is a more elaborate test that checks for harder-to-find errors, including pattern-sensitive failures. Both tests pinpoint many faults to the failed address and bit level.

Example 5-3

RAM DCD ERROR @ 10F6 BIT 1

This error message indicates that a decode error at address 10F6 (hex) has been detected. Specifically, it tells us that bit 1 is not being decoded properly to distinguish between addresses 10F6 and 10F7 [1].

ROM module test.   ROM uses a CRC algorithm. However, a signature from a known good ROM is needed for this test (usually obtained when LEARN is run on a known-good system). If no signature is available, a dummy ROM with a known signature may be substituted in its place.[5] If no dummy ROM is available, we can get by without the ROM test (although not as conveniently as when it is available).

I/O port register test.   A built-in I/O test checks for stuck register bits. It identifies address and bit positions where faults are found.

Local Level Tests

Now consider the local tests (designated Troubleshooting Functions by Fluke). These permit the operator to selectively test specific memory or I/O locations.

> *READ:* reads data from an operator-specified location and
> displays them on the console readout

[5]Use of a dummy ROM permits this test to verify ROM subsystem circuitry. However, it does not verify the application ROM.

WRITE: writes data keyed in by the operator to the location specified

RAMP: writes a binary incrementing pattern to the location specified

WALK: rotates a bit pattern at the location specified by the operator

Example 5-4: Troubleshooting Function READ

READ permits the troubleshooter to choose any location in the memory map of the system and read from it. This may be used to verify the operation of read-only devices, such as ROM and EPROM, input ports, keypads, and so on, or in conjunction with WRITE, to verify the correct operation of individual read/write locations, as in RAM.

To illustrate, assume that we want to verify correct operation of an input port. (This is illustrated in Figure 5-10 for a port with address 8000.) To verify the port, set logic levels on its input pins and read using the read command READ @ 8000. For the example shown, this will result in 51 hex appearing on the display. Ensure that each bit can input both a logic 0 and a logic 1. To avoid having to reenter the READ command for each new setting of input data, use the loop mode. Thus

READ @ 8000

LOOP

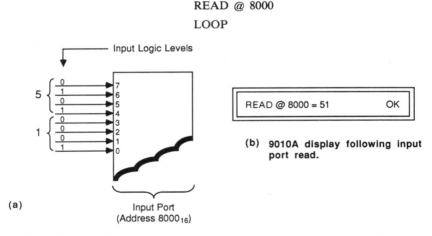

(b) **9010A display following input port read.**

(a)

Input Port
(Address 8000_{16})

Figure 5-10:   Verifying the correct functional operation of an input port using READ.

As each new data byte is set on the input pins, the display is immediately updated with the new value. In effect, this procedure implements a functional test of the input port subsystem.

Example 5-5: Troubleshooting Function WRITE

Similarly, WRITE may be used to verify writable locations, such as output ports, display subsystems, D/A converters, and so on, or when used in conjunction with READ, to verify the correct operation of individual read/write locations as in RAM.

To illustrate, consider an output port with address 8002 (Figure 5-11). To verify its operation, write selected patterns to the port and check logic levels at its output pins. The example illustrates writing 73 (hex) to the port. Verify that each bit can output both a logic 1 and a logic 0.

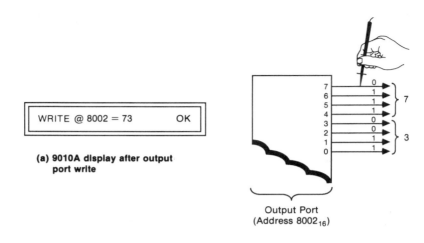

WRITE @ 8002 = 73   OK

(a) 9010A display after output port write

Output Port
(Address 8002_{16})

(b) Output logic levels following output port write

Figure 5–11: Verifying the correct functional operation of an output port using WRITE.

The built-in tests described above implement functional testing of basic kernel elements only. For logic subsystems outside the kernel, additional functional tests are needed. These are described in Section 5–8.

5–5 The 9010A TROUBLESHOOTING PROBE

To implement node verification and circuit-level fault tracing, the 9010A provides a troubleshooting probe (Figure 5–2). This probe is both a stimulus device and a monitoring device and may be operated either synchronously (synchronized to AD-DRESS or to DATA), or asynchronously (as a free-running, nonsynchronized logic probe). Consider first the synchronized mode.

Measurement mode. In the measurement mode, the probe reads in synchronism with the event to be viewed, causing the data at its tip to appear static. As noted earlier, this permits the tester not only to check for the presence of logic levels but also to check that they occur at the correct time.

Stimulus mode. In the stimulus mode, the probe can be made to force nodes high or low in synchronism with UUT events such as reads, writes, and so on. This permits the user to re-create missing UUT control signals if necessary.

Now consider the FREE RUN mode. In this mode, operation of the probe is not synchronized. In its measurement mode, it displays whatever logic levels occur at its tip; in its stimulus mode, it can be used to clock nodes high and low asynchronous to system operation.

For displaying logic levels, the probe contains a pair of red and green indicator lamps. Red indicates high and green indicates low. When a floating node is encountered, neither lamp lights. A node that is continuously toggling between 0 and 1 turns both lights on.

Stimulating UUT Circuitry for Test with the Probe

To stimulate circuitry for node verification and fault tracing, the 9010A provides a set of three toggling functions.

> *TOGGLE ADDR.* Toggle address toggles an operator-specified address bit from one binary state to the other.
>
> *TOGGLE DATA.* Toggle data toggles an operator-specified data bit from one binary state to the other.
>
> *TOGGLE DATA CTL.* Toggle data control toggles an operator-specified control line from one binary state to the other.

Either a single toggle action (0 → 1 or 1 → 0) or continuous toggling may be specified. To specify continuous toggling, use the loop mode. (Continuous toggling is normally used for fault tracing, as it facilitates probe observation.) Synchronize the probe to the toggling operation specified—normally, ADDRESS for ADDRESS TOGGLE and DATA for DATA TOGGLE. However, for some systems, we have considerable flexibility. For example, for the 6809, addresses are valid over the entire clock cycle and we can synchronize to either ADDRESS or DATA when tracing address lines. When testing data lines, however, we must synchronize to DATA, as the data valid time occurs only over the latter portion of the cycle. For systems with multiplexed buses, greater care must be exercised since the time of signal validity is affected by the presence of demultiplexing latches. To illustrate, consider the 8085 timing diagram of Figure 5-12. High-order addresses are valid throughout the entire cycle, but low-order addresses are not. Because of the latch and the timing of the demultiplexing strobe ALE (address latch enable), low-order addresses after the latch are not valid until the latter portion of the clock cycle (i.e., data time). On the other hand, low-order addresses prior to the latch are valid only during the address portion of the cycle. Thus, use Sync settings for the probe as indicated.

Example 5-6: Data Toggle

Data toggle is useful for tracing and troubleshooting data lines up to and beyond peripherals. Data lines may be toggled and the probe used to follow the toggling line. All bits but the one being toggled remain constant. A typical data toggle specification is illustrated below.

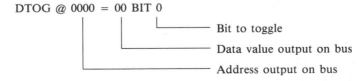

DTOG @ 0000 = 00 BIT 0

- Bit to toggle
- Data value output on bus
- Address output on bus

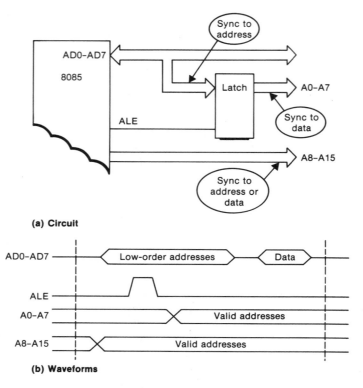

(a) Circuit

(b) Waveforms

Figure 5-12:   Probe synchronization for multiplexed buses. An 8085 shown for illustration.

Data toggle works by writing the specified data value to the address selected then it toggles the specified bit and writes it again. For the example indicated, the instrument will first write $0000\ 0000_2$ to address 0000_{16}, followed by $0000\ 0001_2$. The result is that bit 0 is toggled from 0 to 1. Because of the procedure used, we cannot toggle data bits at read-only locations (such as in ROM).

The address specification in the DATA TOGGLE command is needed to permit testing of address-specific logic, such as transceivers in buffered systems.

UUT circuitry can also be stimulated using the other troubleshooting functions: READ, WRITE, RAMP, and WALK. In the examples to follow, we will use whichever stimulus is most appropriate to the problem at hand.

5-6 A NODE VALIDATION STRATEGY

We now have the tools and techniques needed to evolve a node verification strategy. Using the circuit stimulation functions described above, the node of interest can be stimulated and the troubleshooting probe, synchronized to the event to be viewed, used to monitor its behavior. The basic procedure can be summarized as follows:

1. Examine the node of interest to see what signals (address, data, clock, etc.) affect it.

2. Select a test function to stimulate the node.

3. Determine when the node is active and synchronize the probe accordingly.[6]

4. Probe the node and compare the monitored result against that expected.

Nodes generally have two states (either an active state and an inactive state or alternatively, two active states). This means that two sets of tests are required. Illustrative examples are described below.

Example 5-7: Verifying a Chip Select

To illustrate, consider again the chip select input $\overline{CS}$ for the memory circuit of Figure 5-7. This node has one active state (low) and one inactive state (high).

Active-state test. Since only addresses are involved in creating $\overline{CS}$, we can synchronize to ADDRESS. To stimulate the node, read from or write to any location in the address range of the RAM. The RAM in this example is mapped from 0000 to 07FF. Thus we can stimulate it using

READ @ 0000

LOOP

We have used the LOOP mode to create a repetitive signal to facilitate probe observation. On each READ, the 9010A outputs address 0000 on the address bus. When decoded, this drives $\overline{CS}$ low, as illustrated in Figure 5-7(b). Now probe $\overline{CS}$. The green light should be on.

Inactive-state test. To verify the inactive state (RAM not selected), we can read from or write to some location not in the address space of the RAM. Set the probe to FREE RUN and probe $\overline{CS}$. The red light should come on, indicating that the node is high. (This test is needed to verify that the node is not stuck low.)

Example 5-8: Verifying a Write Control Clock $\overline{WR}$

As a second example, consider the write control signal $\overline{WR}$ of the Intel 8085. An examination of the 8085 data sheet shows that $\overline{WR}$ should go to its active (low) state at write time but remain in its inactive (high) state at all other times.

Active-state test. Since $\overline{WR}$ is active at data time, synchronize to DATA. Write to any arbitrary writable location in the address space of the system. Probe $\overline{WR}$. It should indicate low (its active state).

Inactive-state test. Set the probe to FREE RUN and repeat. Both lights should come on, indicating that $\overline{WR}$ is toggling between low (its active state) and high (its inactive state). (Use loop mode.)

Example 5-9: Verifying Read/Write (R/$\overline{W}$)

The read/write (R/$\overline{W}$) of the 6809 has two active states. On reads, it goes high; on writes, it goes low. It is active over the entire clock cycle. Thus we can synchronize to either ADDRESS or DATA. Test in loop mode.

---

[6]If the node is driven entirely from signals that are valid at address time, the probe can be synchronized to address. If it is driven by at least one signal that is active only during data time, synchronize to data. If signals are asynchronous, set the probe to FREE RUN.

Read-active-state test. Read from any location using READ. Probe R/$\overline{\text{W}}$. It should indicate red (high).

Write-active-state test. Write to any location using WRITE. Probe R/$\overline{\text{W}}$. It should indicate green (low).

The principles described and illustrated above can be used to devise tests for any circuit node of interest. If the test passes, the node has been validated; if it fails, troubleshooting as described next is in order.

5-7 A PRACTICAL HARDWARE TROUBLESHOOTING STRATEGY

We now have the tools and techniques needed to put together a practical hardware troubleshooting strategy. Specifically, we follow the general procedure outlined in Chapter 3. The testing order that we will use is almost always the same. We generally begin with BUS, since if the bus system is faulty, little else can be expected to function correctly either. RAM SHORT is usually next because it is fast and catches some faults missed by BUS. Thus the recommended order is

1. BUS
2. RAM SHORT
3. ROM
4. I/O

In the examples to follow, faults are specified in advance and the 9010A is used to find them. Although this is not the usual case, it is a good way to start the learning process. In later examples (the case studies of Section 5–10), faults are not specified in advance. This is, of course, the more realistic and interesting case.

The examples that follow are basically processor independent (although we reference specific processors such as the 6809, Z80 or 8085 to make them more realistic). You should therefore have no trouble following the solutions even if you are not familiar with the processor around which the example is based. In addition, although the examples use the Fluke 9010A Troubleshooter, the basic principles are quite general and hence, the methodology illustrated is transportable to similar testers made by other manufacturers.

Preliminary Check: Run UUT before Testing

Before beginning troubleshooting, it is wise to verify that there really is a problem by attempting to run the system using RUN UUT (run unit under test, Figure 5–8). The reason for this is as follows. First, it checks the CPU by substitution—if the system works with the 9010A installed but not with the CPU, the CPU is probably defective. Second, there are several practical problems associated with CPU sockets that can make the system appear to malfunction, such as improper seating of the CPU, bent or broken pins, dirty contacts, and so on. Sometimes the mere removal of the CPU and the substitution of the tester clears up such problems.

Example 5-10

The unit under test in this example is the single-board 8085 system of Figure B-7. Logic for the portion of the system of interest is reproduced as Figure 5-13. The fault here is a defective plate-through hole at the point marked X, resulting in an open circuit on address line A13.

Troubleshooting Log

Step 1. Try RUN UUT. It fails.

Step 2. Try BUS TEST. No faults are found. (BUS cannot find faults on the downstream side of the buffer.)

Step 3. Try RAM SHORT. For this system, RAM is mapped from 0800 to 0FFF. Thus key in the following sequence:

RAM SHORT @ 0800 − 0FFF

Following the test, an error message appears on the console indicating that none of the bits at address 0800 are read/writable.

Step 4. Since the RAM test uncovered a problem, let us concentrate on the RAM (Figure 5-14). Let us see what tentative conclusions can be drawn.

1. The RAM is not being accessed properly.
   (a) Could be a bad address.
   (b) Could be a bad read/write input $\overline{WE}$.
   (c) Could be a bad $\overline{OE}$ input.
   (d) Could be a bad chip select input $\overline{CS}$.
2. Could be a fault with the data bus.
3. Could be a defective RAM chip.

Let us test each of these in turn using the node verification strategies discussed above.

1. *Address interface.* Use ADDRESS TOGGLE to verify each pin in turn. No faults are found.
2. *Input* $\overline{WE}$. Since $\overline{WE}$ is driven directly by $\overline{WR}$, it may be tested as described in Example 5-8. No faults are found.
3. *Input* $\overline{OE}$. Note that $\overline{OE}$ is driven directly from $\overline{RD}$, which is active (low) during the data movement portion of the read cycle and inactive (high) at all other times. The test here is thus almost identical to that used to test $\overline{WR}$. Use loop mode.
   (a) *Active-state test.* Synchronize to DATA. Read from any arbitrary location in the address space of the system. Probe $\overline{OE}$. The probe should indicate low. It does.
   (b) *Inactive-state test.* Set the probe to FREE RUN and check $\overline{OE}$. Both lights come on, indicating that $\overline{OE}$ is toggling correctly—i.e., it is not stuck low.
   The $\overline{OE}$ test is now complete and no faults have been found.
4. *Chip select input* $\overline{CS}$. $\overline{CS}$ is driven from an address decoder conditioned by $\overline{RD}$ and $\overline{WR}$—thus its outputs are active only during data movement times. Thus:
   (a) *Active-state test.* Synchronize to DATA. Select any location to read or write and key in the applicable sequence for example, READ @ 0800. Set to the LOOP mode. Now probe $\overline{CS}$. It should be low. It is not. This means that a problem exists.

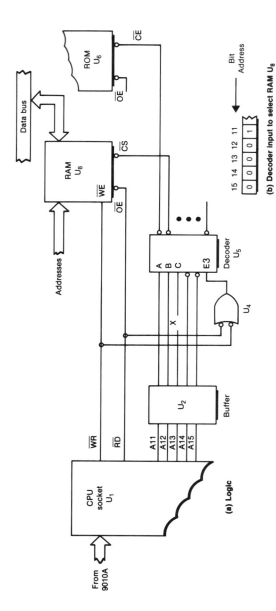

Figure 5-13: Fault is an open on address line A13 at the point marked X.

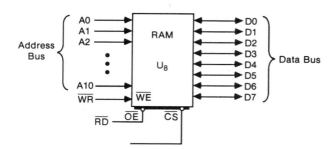

Figure 5-14:   Signals to be investigated.

Step 5. Backtrace to the decoder with the tester still in the LOOP mode (Figure 5-15). Note that the output of the decoder is faulty. Now check its inputs (still using the looping READ @ 0800 test). As noted in Figure 5-13(b), to select the RAM, address bit A11 should be high and address bits A12 and A13 should be low. Probing indicates that A11 and A12 are correct but that A13 is floating. Backtracing, we find that A13 is good (i.e., low) at the output of the address buffer U_2—thus we conclude that

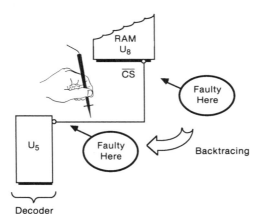

Figure 5-15:   Testing reveals a faulty chip select. Backtracking, we trace the fault to the decoder output.

there is a break somewhere between the output of U_2 and the input to U_5 (Figure 5-16). With the probe, follow the trace until the break is found. In this case, the signal checks okay from U_2 pin 13 to the plate-through hole; on the other side of the hole, it vanishes. Thus we have found the problem.

Note that the problem is not RAM related at all—we found it with the RAM test because this happened to be the first test that we ran that was affected by the fault. If we had started with the ROM test instead, we would have found the fault with about the same degree of effort—recall Example 3-11.

Example 5-11

The unit under test is again the 8085 system of Appendix B (Figure B-7). The fault here is a defective RAM chip (U_8).

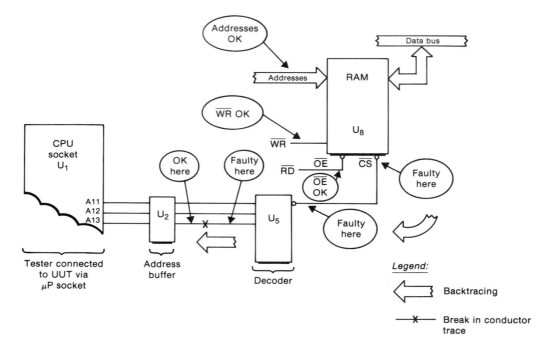

Figure 5-16: Further testing reveals a faulty input to U$_5$. Backtracing takes us to U$_2$, the address buffer. Its output tests okay . . . thus, the fault has been bracketed to the tace betwen U$_2$ and U$_5$.

Troubleshooting Log

> *Step 1.* Try RUN UUT. It fails.
> *Step 2.* Try BUS TEST. No faults are found.
> *Step 3.* Try RAM Short, as in Example 5-10. Again, an error message appears, indicating that none of the bits at address 0800 are read/writable.
> *Step 4.* Again, let us focus on the RAM. Possible faults here are the same as in Example 5-10. Thus test as follows:

1. *Address interface.* Use TOGGLE ADDRESS. No faults are found.
2. *Write enable* $\overline{WE}$. Test as in Example 5-10. No faults are found.
3. *Output enable* $\overline{OE}$. Test as in Example 5-10. No faults are found.
4. *Chip Select* $\overline{CS}$. Test as in Example 5-10. No faults are found.[7]
5. *Data bus interface.* Use TOGGLE DATA. No faults are found.

We have now completely bracketed the RAM with tested-good circuitry. The only conclusion left is that the RAM is defective and should be replaced.

[7]Note that we had gotten only as far as the active-state test in Example 5-10; thus you will have to devise the inactive-state test for this case. (Problem 5-1.)

5-8 FUNCTIONAL TESTING OUTSIDE THE BASIC SYSTEM KERNEL

While the examples above illustrate correct usage of the 9010A, we are at the moment constrained by the available (built-in) functional tests, since these are limited to kernel elements only. For subsystems outside the basic kernel, tests specific to the module of interest must be devised. We will consider a few, concentrating on those subsystems most commonly encountered. Initially, we will consider immediate mode testing. However, it will quickly become apparent that much testing can be more conveniently and effectively implemented via test programs. These will be considered also.

When studying the examples in this section, remember that the purpose of a functional test is to verify correct operation of the device or subsystem under test (or designate it as faulty). No fault tracing is inherent in this process.

Example 5-12: Functional Testing of Parallel Ports

Simple parallel ports may be verified functionally using READ and WRITE, as illustrated earlier (Example 5-4 and 5-5). More complex ports can be tested in a similar fashion. However, LSI devices such as the Intel PPI, the Motorola PIA, the Zilog PIO, etc. must be software configured prior to testing.

Functionally Testing a Motorola PIA

To illustrate, consider the PIA (peripheral interface adapter) from Motorola. (This device is described in Appendix A.) Here we will illustrate its basic mode as a dual 8-bit I/O port. Specifically, we will define port A for input and port B for output. Address assignments for this example are 8000 to 8003, as indicated in Figure 5-23(b).

As discussed in Appendix A, to define port A as input and B as output, set data direction register A to 00 and data direction register B to FF. In addition, we must configure both control registers. As indicated in Appendix A, a suitable control byte for this case is 04. Thus the configuration sequence is as indicated in Figure 5-17.

When initialization is completed, input and output sections can be tested as described earlier. For example, to test the input, apply known logic levels and verify using the read instruction: thus

READ @ 8000   (read port A)

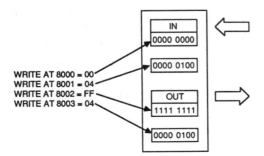

Figure 5-17: Configuring the PIA as a simple port with input on A and output on B.

Ensure that each bit can correctly input both a logic 0 and a logic 1. Similarly, to verify the output, use WRITE @ 8002.

Example 5-13: Functional Testing of a CRT Terminal Interface

Input and output sections of CRT terminal interfaces may be tested separately or together. In this example we illustrate the former. (The latter case is illustrated in Section 5-9.) Assume a 6809 processor interfaced to a CRT terminal via an ACIA (asynchronous communications interface adapter) with addresses 6000/6001 as depicted in Figure 5-18. (The ACIA is described in Appendix A.) Assume for this example, that the CRT is formated for 8 bits plus 1 STOP bit, and that the ACIA transmit and receive clock rates are 16 times the baud rate. The applicable control word in this case is 0001 0101 (i.e., 15 in hex; see Appendix A).

Port initialization. The first step is to reset the ACIA, then software configure it with the above control word. As indicated in Appendix A, to reset the ACIA, write the master reset code 03 (hex) to the control register. Thus

$$\text{WRITE @ 6000} = 03 \qquad \text{(reset the ACIA)}$$

$$\text{WRITE @ 6000} = 15 \qquad \text{(configure the ACIA)}$$

Transmit test. Once initialized, transmit logic can be tested. To test, write ASCII characters to the transmit data register (address 6001), then observe the CRT screen. For example, since the ASCII equivalent of A is 41 (hex), the command WRITE @ 6001 = 41 should output A to the screen. Similarly,

$$\text{WRITE @ 6001} = 42 \qquad \text{(should write B to the screen)}$$

$$\text{WRITE @ 6001} = 43 \qquad \text{(should write C to the screen)}$$

Continuing in this manner, all printable characters (and many control codes) can be verified.

Receive test. To test receive logic, read input characters (using READ @ 6001 in the LOOP mode) as keys are operated on the terminal keyboard. The ASCII equivalent of the key pressed should appear on the 9010A console display. Repeat for all keys of interest (printable or nonprintable).

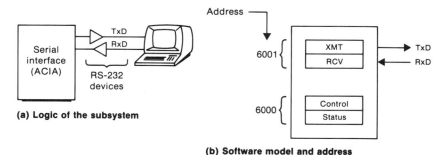

(a) Logic of the subsystem

(b) Software model and address assignments

Figure 5-18: Serial I/O subsystem under test.

Note that the tests described above do not check flag logic. This is considered in Section 5–9.

Example 5–14: Monotonicity Test of a D/A Converter

Troubleshooting function RAMP may be used to test D/A converters for monotonicity. RAMP writes a binary incrementing pattern to the selected port register, causing its contents to increment successively from 00 to its maximum value. The output of the converter is the analog equivalent of this input. By looping the operation, a repetitive signal is generated that can be viewed on an oscilloscope. Figure 5–19(b) shows the output for a good converter, while part (c) shows the output for a converter with stuck bits.

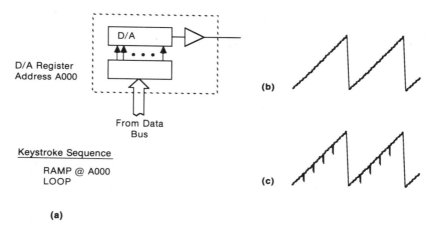

(a)

Figure 5–19:   Using RAMP to test D/A for monotonicity.

Example 5–15: Functional Testing of a Numeric Display System

To test seven-segment displays, use the 9010A to implement the "walking segment" test of Chapter 4. For the example indicated (Figure 4–14), a logic 1 turns on a segment— thus successively write a 1 to the display port register to test each bit position. Test steps are summarized below (assuming a display port with address 8004).

WRITE @ 8004 = 01   (turn on segment a only)

WRITE @ 8004 = 02   (turn on segment b only)

WRITE @ 8004 = 04   (turn on segment c only)

WRITE @ 8004 = 08   (turn on segment d only)

WRITE @ 8004 = 10   (turn on segment e only)

WRITE @ 8004 = 20   (turn on segment f only)

WRITE @ 8004 = 40   (turn on segment g only)

WRITE @ 8004 = 80   (turn on decimal point only)

Each digit in a multidigit cluster may be tested in this fashion (see Example 5–20).

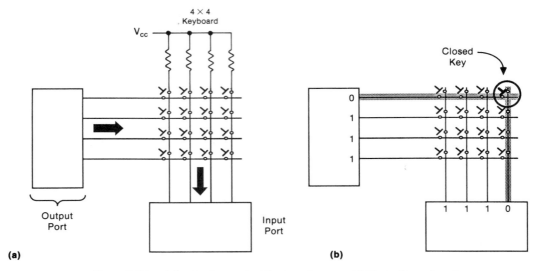

Figure 5-20: a) Logic of a scanned keyboard system. b) Illustrating a key closure.

Example 5-16: Functional Testing of a Scanned Keypad

Multiplexed keypads are frequently encountered in microcomputer systems. Figure 5-20 illustrates one approach. (A 16-key matrix is shown for illustration.)

The μP scans the keypad in a cyclic fashion, checking for key closures. To illustrate, assume a key closure as in Figure 5-20(b). The software scanning program successively writes a low to each output line and after each write, reads the input port. When a low is detected on read-in, scanning program logic determines which key was operated. For the example indicated, by noting the pattern 1110 on the output and 1110 on the input, program logic is able to deduce that key 3 was operated.

Testing using the 9010A Troubleshooter may be implemented similarly, or a simplified procedure as described below may be used instead. Assume an address of 8004 for the output port and an address of 8006 for the input port.

Procedure:

1. Write 00 to the output port using WRITE @ 8004 = 00. This sets all output lines low (Figure 5-21).
2. Now consider the input port. With no keys operated, all inputs are pulled high by the pull-up resistors. A read of the input port thus yields 1111 (i.e., F hex) on these four low-order input lines. (Note that since the high-order 4 bits are not used here, they are "don't cares." For simplicity, let us assume that the don't cares are zero. Thus, in this case, a read of the input port will show 0F hex.)
3. Now consider operation of a key. When a key is pressed, it shorts the intersecting row and column lines together and consequently pulls the corresponding input bit low. Now when the input port is read, the corresponding bit reads as a 0. Table 5-1 summarizes input patterns. If the test passes, we have verified the keypad and its associated interface electronics. If it fails, troubleshooting is in order (see Example 5-24).

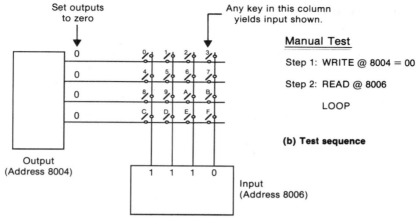

Set outputs to zero

Any key in this column yields input shown.

Manual Test

Step 1: WRITE @ 8004 = 00

Step 2: READ @ 8006

LOOP

(b) Test sequence

Output (Address 8004)

Input (Address 8006)

(a) Keypad

Figure 5-21:   With the 9010A in the LOOP mode, successively press keys and note console display.

TABLE 5-1   KEY COLUMN DATA[a]

Key	Input (binary)	Console display
3, 7, B, F	0000 1110	0E
2, 6, A, E	0000 1101	0D
1, 5, 9, D	0000 1011	0B
0, 4, 8, C	0000 0111	07

[a]The information of interest is contained in the four least-significant bits.

Table 5-1:   Unfaulted Key Test Data

Additional functional tests are considered in the programming section (Section 5-9) and in the problem set at the end of the chapter.

5-9 AUTOMATING TEST PROCEDURES: PROGRAMMING THE 9010A

Many of the functional tests of Section 5-8 and some of the circuit-tracing procedures of Section 5-5 can be simplified through the use of programs.[8]

[8]This section applies only to programmable members of the Fluke Micro System Troubleshooter family.

Programmer's View of the 9010A

The 9010A Troubleshooter contains an internal memory of 10K bytes for program storage plus a group of sixteen 32-bit registers for data storage and manipulation [2]. Programs are written in a high-level format using the same tests, functions, and operations as used for immediate mode testing (i.e., READ, WRITE, RAMP, etc.). Test sequence keys (IF, GOTO, =, as shown in Figure 5–8) help direct program logic. Labels are used to identify key points in programs for program loops, decision points, and so on. Messages can be included to advise the operator of results as well as to provide prompts for operator action.

Once a program has been created, it is entered via the console keyboard (Figure 5–8) into the 9010A's memory using the procedure detailed in the 9010A's Programming Manual [2]. It can then be executed. Programs may be stored on cassette for future use.

Programming the 9010A

We will illustrate programming by means of examples. Let us begin with the functional tests considered in Section 5–8.

Example 5–17: An I/O Port Functional Test

I/O ports may be tested in several ways. In this example, we will simply read the input port and write its data to the output port for verification. Let us use the Intel parallel peripheral interface (PPI) here. (It is described in Appendix B.) We will consider a test here for mode 0 only.

Let the PPI be I/O mapped with address assignments 40 to 43 as indicated in Figure 5–22. Let us select ports A and C for output and port B for input. To configure the PPI as indicated requires a control byte of 82 hex (Appendix B). Write this byte to the control register using WRITE @ 10043.[9]

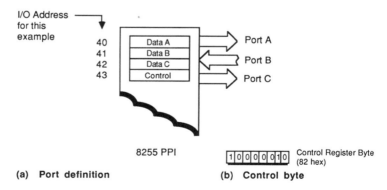

(a) Port definition   **(b) Control byte**

Figure 5–22: Port configuration. Writing the configuration byte 82 configures A and C for output and B for input.

[9]Note the 1 required in front of the port address. It tells the 9010A that the device is I/O mapped.

A program listing follows. The third step (READ @ 10041) copies data from the input port to the 9010A,[10] while the fourth and fifth steps write it back to the output ports. The last instruction loops the program back to "LABEL 1" to repeat the process.

WRITE @ 10043 = 82	(configure B = input, A and C = output)
1: LABEL 1	
READ @ 10041	(read from port B, address 41)
WRITE @ 10040 = REGE	(write to port A, address 40)
WRITE @ 10042 = REGE	(write to port C, address 42)
GOTO 1	

When execution has been started, set logic levels on input pins port B and verify logic levels at output ports A and C.

Loop-Back Tests

I/O devices can also be tested using a loop-back technique. (The output is externally jumpered back to the input.) This permits easy and rapid testing of both input and output ports simultaneously and is applicable to any port, parallel or serial.

With this scheme, patterns are written to the output port, read back through the input port, and compared by program logic. If the two values agree, the test passes and the next pattern is selected and tested. If any mismatch occurs, the program stops and displays both the data out and the data in. An examination of the two patterns permits the operator to determine which bits failed and whether they failed high or low. Various sequences of patterns may be used, including rotating bits, counting sequences, and so on. Rotating bits provide a fast test; counting sequences test all possible combinations but take longer.

Example 5-18: Parallel Loop-Back Test

A "rotating bit" test for the Motorola PIA is shown in Figure 5-23. General program logic is indicated in the flowchart, while details are contained in the comment section of the listing. Register 1 is used to output the current bit pattern, while Register E receives the value read in. Program logic compares the two values using an IF statement. If the two numbers agree, execution proceeds to Label 2 and a new value is output. However, if an error is detected, (i.e., the value read in does not match the value written out), execution drops through to the display command DPY. This command writes to the console display the value written and the corresponding value read in (i.e., the contents of Registers 1 and E respectively). From these, the operator can determine which bit or bits failed the test. Tests for other ports are similar—only the initialization steps and the register addresses need be changed.

---

[10]Register E is the intermediate register for READ and WRITE operations. A READ command copies data into E, while a WRITE command outputs the contents of E to the device or location specified in the WRITE command [2].

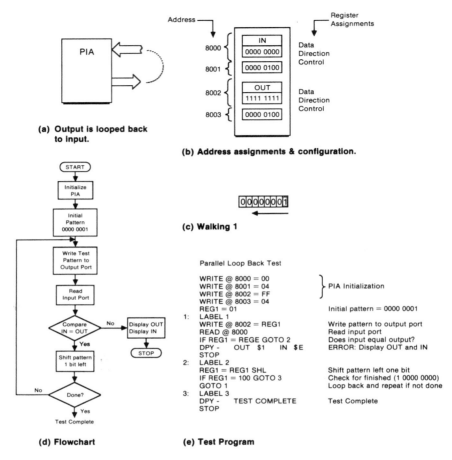

(a) Output is looped back to input.

(b) Address assignments & configuration.

(c) Walking 1

(d) Flowchart

(e) Test Program

Figure 5-23: Parallel Loop back test of PIA.

Example 5-19: Serial Loop-Back Test

Figure 5-24 shows logic for a serial I/O test (the Motorola 6850 ACIA). This test checks flag logic in addition to transmit and receive logic. The procedure is general and with changes in detail can be used to test any serial I/O port.

Example 5-20: Functional Testing of Numeric Displays

This is an automated "walking segment" test for multidigit clusters. (Six digits are illustrated in Figure 5-25.) Two ports are used in this design, one to select digits and the other to select segments. To test, select a digit, then walk its segments as described in Example 5-15. Repeat for each digit. Steps are summarized below. (Logic for the example shown requires a 1 to select a digit and a 1 to turn on a segment. Other designs may require the opposite. In this case, complement the corresponding test patterns.)

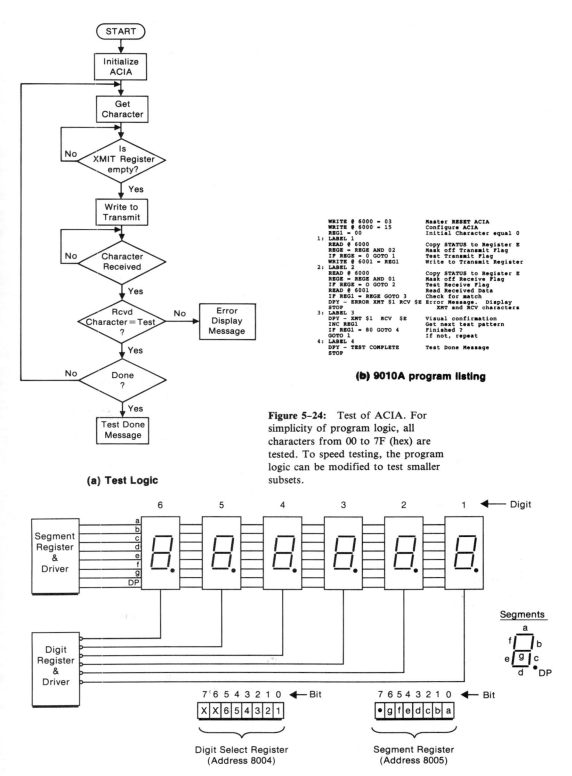

```
WRITE @ 6000 = 03        Master RESET ACIA
WRITE @ 6000 = 15        Configure ACIA
REG1 = 00                Initial Character equal 0
1: LABEL 1
   READ @ 6000           Copy STATUS to Register E
   REGE = REGE AND 02    Mask off Transmit Flag
   IF REGE = 0 GOTO 1    Test Transmit Flag
   WRITE @ 6001 = REG1   Write to Transmit Register
2: LABEL 2
   READ @ 6000           Copy STATUS to Register E
   REGE = REGE AND 01    Mask off Receive Flag
   IF REGE = O GOTO 2    Test Receive Flag
   READ @ 6001           Read Received Data
   IF REG1 = REGE GOTO 3 Check for match
   DPY - ERROR XMT $1 RCV $E  Error Message.  Display
   STOP                      XMT and RCV characters
3: LABEL 3
   DPY - XMT $1  RCV  $E Visual confirmation
   INC REG1             Get next test pattern
   IF REG1 = 80 GOTO 4  Finished ?
   GOTO 1               If not, repeat
4: LABEL 4
   DPY - TEST COMPLETE  Test Done Message
   STOP
```

(b) 9010A program listing

Figure 5-24: Test of ACIA. For simplicity of program logic, all characters from 00 to 7F (hex) are tested. To speed testing, the program logic can be modified to test smaller subsets.

(a) Test Logic

Figure 5-25: Conceptual representation of display system.

Test Strategy:

1. Select the least significant digit by writing 01 to the digit select register.
2. Turn on segment a by writing the pattern 01 to the segment select register.
3. Turn on segment b by writing the pattern 02 to the segment select register.
4. Continue in this manner until all segments and the decimal point of digit 1 have been verified.
5. Select the second digit by writing the pattern 02 to the digit select register. Test all segments of this digit in the manner described above in steps 2 to 4.
6. Repeat for all remaining digits.

Figure 5–26 shows a flowchart and a program listing for this test. Note the delay. It holds the patterns long enough for viewing. Note also that Registers 3 and 4 are used to store the port addresses. This makes it easy to change the program to test display systems with different port addresses. The principle described here is general and the procedure may be adapted to other display systems.

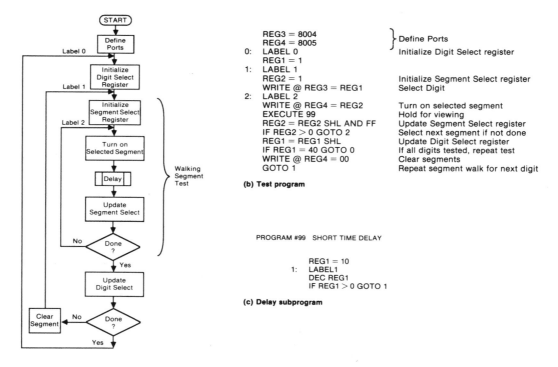

Figure 5–26: Walking Segment Test for 7-Segment display. Test continuously repeats.

Interactive Testing: Operator Prompts and Messages

Programming also permits us to incorporate interactive operation into our test procedures. For example, messages can be output to the console at run time to advise the operator of test results, to prompt for input of data or test parameters, or to advise the operator of the next action to be undertaken. Such interactive testing can be used, for example, to lead unskilled operators back through a fault sequence to the initial fault cause.

Example 5-21

To illustrate, consider the automatic address identification program of Appendix E. This program automatically identifies address bus lines and displays their identity on the operator console using standard logic diagram terminology. For example, if the probe is placed on address bus line 12, the display will show ADDRESS 12. On the other hand, if the node probed is not an address line, the message NOT AN ADDRESS will be output instead.

The program also includes some operator prompts. For example, after checking a node and displaying its identity, it prompts the user to move the probe to the next point of interest via the message POSITION PROBE-PRESS CONT. This tells the operator to move the probe to the next node and press the CONTINUE key on the operator console (Figure 5-8).

A similar program for automatic data bus identification is also included in Appendix E. These two programs can be used instead of the ADDRESS TOGGLE and DATA TOGGLE functions. Their use can greatly speed the troubleshooting process.

5-10 TROUBLESHOOTING CASE STUDIES

We now have the tools and techniques required to extend the basic troubleshooting procedures described in Section 5-7. The following case studies illustrate typical hardware troubleshooting sessions and the thought processes that go into finding unknown faults.

In the following examples, we describe principal steps but do not include detailed operational procedures. For such procedures, the reader is referred to the appropriate operator's manual [1 and 2].

Example 5-22

The system here is a 6809-based machine control system that uses limit switches to monitor machine operations and solenoids to position final control elements. The position of the solenoids (extended or retracted) is determined by the application program acting on information gathered from these switches. The system has been in operation for a long time. Now, however, a problem has developed that manifests itself as incorrect operation of solenoid 3 (Figure 5-27). In the application environment solenoid 3 is controlled by bit 3 of the output port indicated, acting on status gathered by switches connected to PIA inputs PB0 and PB1.

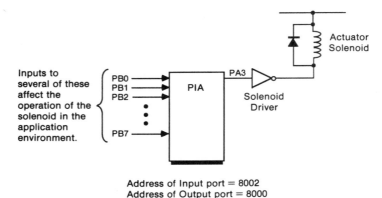

Address of Input port = 8002
Address of Output port = 8000

Figure 5-27: Solenoid fails to function properly in the application environment.

Problem Analysis and Troubleshooting Log

The problem could be caused by a number of things, including the following:

1. Output bit PA3 of the PIA may be faulty.
2. The solenoid or its driver may be faulty.
3. Input bits PB0 or PB1 of the PIA may be faulty.
4. There may be a failure in one of the external circuits feeding PB0 or PB1.

There are also other possible causes since many circuits affect system operation in the application environment. However, because of symptoms observed, it is reasonable to start investigation at the PIA.

  Step 1: PIA initialization. The first step is to configure the PIA. The procedure is similar to that of Example 5-12. (Note that Port A is now output and Port B is now input.)

  Step 2: Output port and solenoid test. To check output bit 3 and the solenoid circuit, drive it to its extended and retracted positions.

Procedure

1. To activate solenoid 3, set bit PA3 high using the command WRITE @ 8000 = 08. This outputs the binary pattern 0000 1000. (All other bits have been left at 0 to avoid actuating solenoids not under test.) In response to this, solenoid 3 correctly moved to its extended position.
2. To retract solenoid 3, set PA3 low by writing 0 to it using WRITE @ 8000 = 00. In response to this, the solenoid retracted correctly.

Since both tests passed, the problem is not in the output port, the solenoid or its driver circuitry.

  Step 3: Input port. We need to test PB0 and PB1, as they both affect solenoid operation in the application environment. Limit switch L1 feeds directly into PB0, but limit switch L2 input passes through a gate which is conditioned by an enabling signal (Figure 5-28). Test as follows.

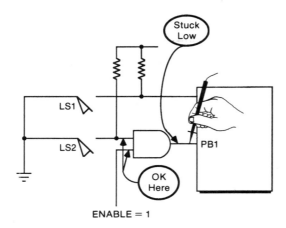

Figure 5-28: Input PB1 is found to be faulty.

Procedure

1. Set both limit switches to their logic 1 (open) state. Set the gate enabling signal high using external means.
2. Read the input port using READ @ 8002. In this case, PB0 indicates logic 1 (as it should). However, PB1 indicates a fault (it reads as logic 0).
3. Check logic levels at the AND gate using the probe in the FREE RUN mode. Results are indicated in Figure 5-28.

As indicated, the AND gate is properly conditioned by the enabling signal and the logic level from limit switch 2 is correct. However, its output is stuck low. This suggests one of the following problems:

1. The AND gate is defective.
2. The input PB1 of the PIA is defective (internally shorted to ground).
3. There is a problem with the printed circuit trace between the output of the AND gate and the input of the PIA. (However, this is not likely, as the system functioned correctly up to the time of the fault.)

Using the methods of Chapter 10, check for the specific failure. (In this case, it was a bad AND gate.)

Example 5-23

The system for this example is Z80 based (Figure C-5).

Troubleshooting Log

> *Step 1: Try RUN UUT.* The following error message appears:
>
> ACTIVE FORCE LINE @ 0000 - LOOP ?

The second line of the error message is

STS BTS 0001 0000 - LOOP ?

Reviewing the 9010A Operator's Manual, we find that a 1 in the binary string above means that the corresponding status bit is stuck in its active state. Checking the decal for the Z80 (Figure 5-29 part a), we see that bit 4 corresponds to the RESET input. From our knowledge of the Z80, we know that it should always be high except during reset. The message above indicates a fault. Therefore, we conclude it must be stuck low.

Step 2. To determine the cause of the stuck RESET line, investigate using the probe (Figure 5-29 part c). Since this circuitry is asynchronous, set the probe to the FREE RUN mode. Backtracking, we find that the output of $U_{9(b)}$ is faulty (stuck low). Check-

	Signal		Control lines
7	PWR FAIL		$\overline{MREQ}$
6	—		$\overline{M1}$
5	—		$\overline{WR}$
4	$\overline{RESET}$[a]		$\overline{RD}$
3	$\overline{INT}$		IORQ
2	$\overline{NMI}$		$\overline{RFSH}$
1	$\overline{BUSRQ}$[a]		$\overline{HALT}$[b]
0	$\overline{WAIT}$[a]		$\overline{BUSAK}$[b]
[a]Forcing lines. [b]User writable.			

(a) Status and control assignments for the Z80.
Copyright © John Fluke Mfg. Co. Inc. Used with permission.

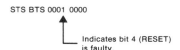

STS BTS 0001 0000

Indicates bit 4 (RESET)
is faulty.

(b) Meaning of the error message

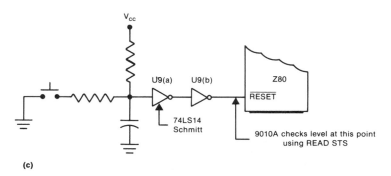

(c)

Figure 5-29:   Troubleshooting a problem in the Reset circuit.

ing its corresponding input, we find that it is also faulty. Now check $U_{9(a)}$. Its input follows the switch as expected, but its output is frozen. This suggests a faulty inverter. When we replaced the inverter, the problem disappeared.

Example 5-24: Troubleshooting a Multiple-Fault Problem

The system for this example has three faults. Most of the principles and practices described throughout this chapter and Chapter 3 are used here.

The unit under test. The unit under test is 8085 based, as illustrated in Figure B-7. In this example, assume that the unit has just come off the production line and thus can have a variety of faults, such as bad plate-through holes, improperly etched traces, poor solder joints, solder bridges, faulty components, and so on.

Fault symptoms. The unit contains a small ROM-based monitor that outputs an operator prompt to the hex display on power-up. However, when this particular unit was pulled off the production line, the prompt message was not displayed properly and the system failed to function as expected.

Troubleshooting Log

There are a number of possible reasons why the display is incorrect. Many circuits affect system operation in the application environment, and a fault in any one (bus, ROM, RAM, etc.) could be the cause. Let us therefore proceed through the BUS, RAM, and ROM tests, as they take little time. All pass. Let us now turn our attention to the display subsystem itself.

Step 1. Use the "walking segments" test described in Example 5-20 to test the display subsystem. It fails. All segments of digits 1 to 4 check okay except segment g. However, digits 5 and 6 remain completely blank. This test clearly indicates a problem with the display subsystem. Let us therefore concentrate on it (Figure 5-30).

Step 2. Investigate the segment g circuitry of digits 1 to 4 as follows:

1. Attempt to turn on segment g by writing 1 to bit position 6 of the segment port register using the WRITE command. No success.
2. Now check the segment g circuitry between the segment port U_{12} and the display itself. Use the probe in the FREE RUN mode, since the logic level we want to check is static (i.e., latched in the segment port). As indicated in Figure 5-31, it is faulty.
3. Since the output of U_{12} is faulty, let us test its input. However, since we are no longer on the latched side of the port, we cannot simply test using the FREE RUN mode. However, the inputs to U_{12} are data bus lines. Thus synchronize to DATA and use TOGGLE DATA. The bit of interest is D6. It is found to be faulty at the input of U_{12} but is good at the output of U_{10} (Figure 5-31).
4. Since the signal is good at U_{10} but bad at U_{12}, the fault must be an open somewhere between these two points. Using the probe, trace until it is found, then repair it.
5. Run the "walking segment" test again to verify the repair. This time, digits 1 to 4 pass, but digits 5 and 6 remain blank.

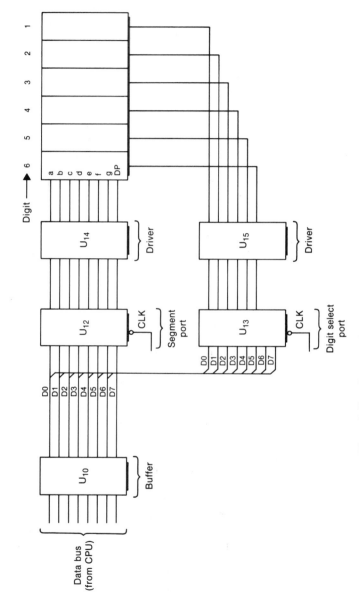

Figure 5-30: Conceptual representation of the display subsystem.

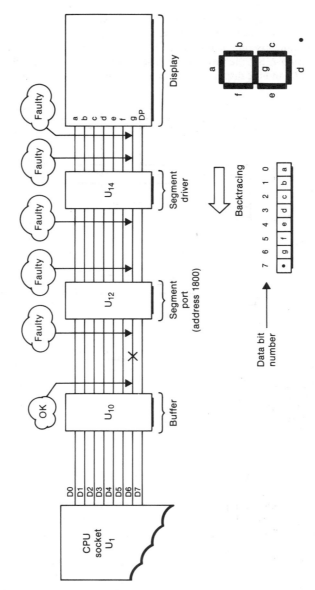

Figure 5-31: Result of investigating "Segment g" circuitry.

Since digits 1 to 4 function correctly, we know that the segment driver portion of the display system is working. The most logical place to look for problems is therefore in the digit select and driver circuitry for digits 5 and 6. Let us begin with digit 5.

Step 3. To set up the test for digit 5, write 0001 0000 (10 hex) to the digit select register U_{13} to select digit 5 (Figure 5-32), then write FF to the segment port U_{12} to turn all its segments on. In response to this, digit 5 remains blank.

Step 4. Set the probe to the FREE RUN mode and check the digit select line between U_{13} and the display. As indicated in Figure 5-32, it is faulty. Synchronize to DATA

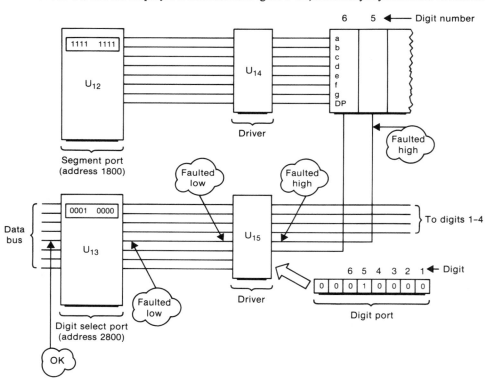

Figure 5-32: Investigation of Digit 5 Select Circuitry.

and using TOGGLE DATA, check data bit 4 on the bus side of port U_{13}. As indicated, it tests okay. We have now isolated the fault to a small section of circuitry consisting of U_{13}, U_{15}, and the trace between them. Visual examination reveals a solder splash. The short is removed. When the "walking segment" test is run again, all digits pass.

Step 5. Try RUN UUT. The system works partially, but seems unable to read from key 7. This suggests a problem in the keypad subsystem.

Step 6. The keypad subsystem logic is shown in Figure 5-33. To test this circuit, use the method described in Example 5-16. Key 7 fails the test.

Step 7. Since key 7 failed, let us investigate its circuitry. Write 00 to the scan port (U_{13}) to drive all its output bits low. Now consider Figure 5-34. Using the probe in FREE RUN, probe point x. It is high, as it should be. Now press key 7. Point x should go

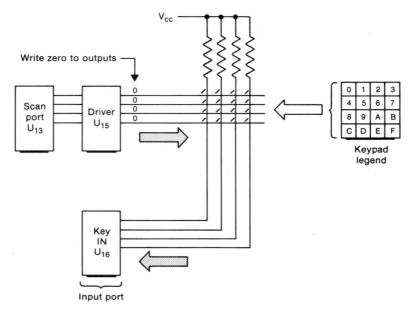

Figure 5–33:   Keypad circuit details.

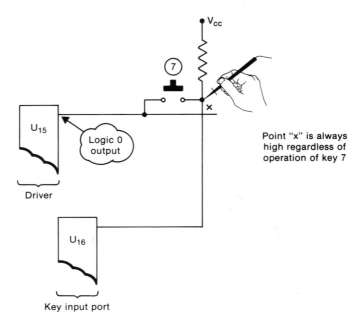

Figure 5–34:   Detecting faulty pushbutton. Use probe in the FREE RUN mode.

low as key 7 is operated (shorting it to the low output from U_{15}). However, it does not. This suggests a faulty key. Replacing the key clears up the problem.

Step 8. Try RUN UUT. The subsystem now functions correctly with no further problems.

5-11 TESTING INTERRUPT SYSTEMS

Interrupt systems commonly employ an LSI I/O port or an interrupt controller to interface interrupt-based peripherals to the CPU. In its simplest form, the interfacing device contains interrupt status (flag) bits and interrupt enable bits. When an interrupt request is received by the controller, internal logic sets the corresponding interrupt request flag bit. If this bit's companion enable bit is active, the request is passed to the CPU. If the request is not reaching the processor, it may be because the flag bit logic is malfunctioning or because enable bits are set wrong. Both of these conditions can be checked using READ. For example, to check a flag, force an interrupt request, then read the contents of the flag register. If the flag did not set, check the interrupt request signal to ensure that it meets specifications (rise and fall times, logic level, etc.). An oscilloscope may be used for this purpose. If all of these check out, the controller is probably faulty and should be replaced.[11]

If the flag sets correctly but the request is still blocked from reaching the processor, use READ to check the register bits that enable/disable the controller from passing the request to the processor. If any control register configuration bits are found to be incorrect, use WRITE to correct them, then repeat the test.

To determine whether interrupt requests are actually reaching the processor, use the "read status" feature of the 9010A (Interrupt request inputs are CPU status inputs and thus can be read directly.) The READ STS capability reads the status of these lines right at the CPU socket. To illustrate, assume a Z80 system with the following result:

$$\text{READ @ STS} = 0001\ 0111$$
$$\text{↑}$$
$$\text{L} \overline{INT} = 0$$

Figure 5–29(a) shows bit assignments for the Z80 status inputs. The result above clearly shows that the interrupt request line $\overline{INT}$ is stuck in its active (low) state at the CPU input.

It should be noted that there are many different interrupt controllers on the market and testing will have to be tailored to the controller and the system under consideration. The comments above illustrate only the general principle.

---

[11]The procedure described here amounts to a functional check of the controller. If you are unable to read from or write to the controller's registers, there may be faults in the external circuit. This should be checked according to the methods of Section 5-10.

5-12 TROUBLESHOOTING 16-BIT SYSTEMS

Let us now consider a 16-bit example. It should be noted, however, that, in principle, there is no fundamental difference between troubleshooting a 16-bit system and an 8-bit system—the difference is largely one of detail. This is illustrated in the following example.

Example 5-25: Troubleshooting a 68000 with a Dynamic RAM Problem

The system here is 68000 based. Its block diagram is illustrated in Figure D-1.

Troubleshooting Log

Step 1. Try RUN UUT. The system does not function.

Step 2. Try BUS test. It passes.

Step 3. Try RAM test. It fails. An error message appears indicating that none of the bits at the first RAM location are read/writable. This suggests a problem that affects the whole RAM subsystem.

Step 4. As indicated in Figure D-1, the RAM in this system consists of a group of 16 dynamic RAM chips. Let us begin investigating the RAM subsystem by testing its address interface using TOGGLE ADDRESS or the address identification program. All test faulty (Figure 5-35).

Step 5. As indicated in Figure D-1, dynamic RAM addresses are multiplexed to the RAM subsystem using 74LS153 multiplexers. Details for this circuit are broken out in Figure 5-35. Testing addresses at the outputs of the multiplexers as above indicates that they are also faulty.

Step 6. On the input side of the multiplexers, addresses connect directly to the address bus. Testing here indicates that they are all okay.

To understand the operation of the multiplexer circuit, note that pairs of addresses connect to each section of the 74LS153s. Under direction of its control circuit, the multiplexer steers one or the other of these two addresses to the RAM. Selection of the required address is governed by control inputs A and B. For example, to pass address A8 (multiplexer chip 1), control input A must be low at address valid time. Let us devise a test to check it.

Step 7. Since control input A must go low at address valid time to pass A8, synchronize the probe to ADDRESS, then toggle A8 (using ADDRESS TOGGLE). Now probe input A. It is stuck high (Figure 5-35).

Step 8. Now backtrack to the device driving input A (U_{39}, pin 11). It is also stuck high (Figure 5-36).

Step 9. U_{39} is a quad D flip-flop whose function is to help steer row, column, or refresh addresses through the multiplexer. Investigation as indicated in Figure 5-36 (using FREE RUN) reveals that its CLR input is stuck in its active (low) state, constantly holding the device reset.

Step 10. Backtracking to the device driving CLR takes us to U_{23}, pin 8. It, too, is stuck low. Testing its inputs, we find input pin 10 stuck low (Figure 5-36). Pin 9, however, has activity on it and is thus likely okay.

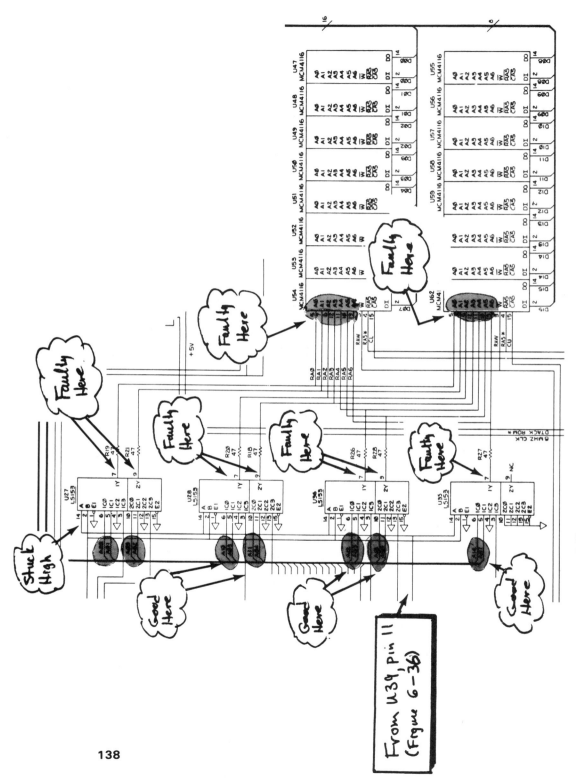

Figure 5-35: All addresses test faulty at the RAM chips and at the outputs of the multiplexers. Address inputs to the multiplexers are good. Multiplexer control input A is stuck high.

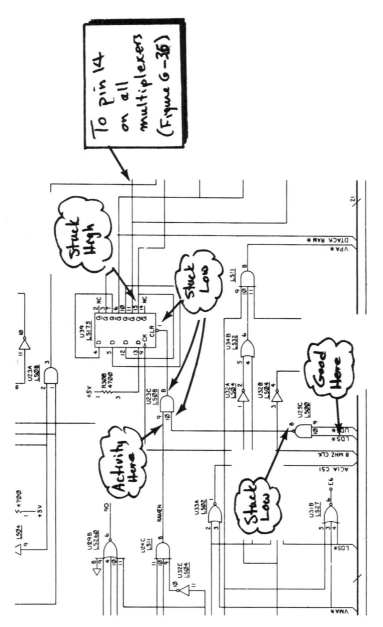

Figure 5-36. Backtracking from the multiplexer (Figure 5-35) brings us to the 74LS175 quad flip-flop. Further, backtracking narrows the problem to U25 or U23. Courtesy of Motorola, Inc.

139

Step 11. Backtracking takes us to U_{25}, pin 8, which is also stuck low. Testing the inputs, they test okay. We have now narrowed the fault to the node level and conclude that either U_{25} or U_{23} is at fault. (Since the system worked prior to the fault, it is unlikely that the trace between them is at fault.)

Step 12. Determine the failed circuit element using the methods of Chapter 10. (In this case, it was U_{25}.)

After the faulty device was replaced, the system returned to normal operation.

The examples considered above provide a good cross section of what can be done using the 9010A. However, the topic will not be pursued further here. Anyone with a clear understanding of the principles and methodologies of this chapter and that of Chapter 4 should have little trouble extending the basic idea to cover the many practical troubleshooting situations that are likely to be encountered in practice.

5-13 SUMMARY

The examples in this chapter clearly illustrate the power of the computer principle control and stimulus method as implemented by the 9010A. Even for the most complex problems, we were never faced with more than a small piece of the system to deal with at any given time. We did this by partitioning the system and separating the major steps. Initially, for example, we focused on the big picture and ignored all low-level circuit detail. As testing progressed, we shifted our attention more and more from the general to the specific, progressively ignoring the big picture as we narrowed the search to the node level. Ultimately, we were left with a relatively small portion of circuitry to examine in detail. In this manner, we reduced the solution of a large complex problem to a series of smaller, more manageable ones.

REFERENCES

1. *9010A Micro-System Troubleshooter Operator Manual,* John Fluke Manufacturing Co., Inc., Everett, WA.
2. *9010A Micro-System Troubleshooter Programming Manual,* John Fluke Manufacturing Co., Inc., Everett, WA.
3. Cassas, Don, Portable Tester Learns Boards to Simplify Service, *Electronics,* June 16, 1981.
4. *Guide to Testing Microprocessor Based Systems and Boards,* Millenium Systems, Inc.

REVIEW QUESTIONS

5-1. Consider the RAM chip select $\overline{CS}$ of Example 5-11. Devise a test to verify its inactive state.

5-2. Consider the circuit of Figure B-7. Assume that ALE (address latch enable) is open circuited. In the manner of Example 5–10, outline a set of troubleshooting steps that would lead to finding this fault.

5-3. Consider the circuit of Figure A–6. Assume a faulty PIA. In the manner of Example 5–10, outline a set of troubleshooting steps that would lead to finding this fault.

5-4. Consider the circuit of Figure C–5. Assume that gate U_8 fails. In the manner of Example 5–10, outline a set of troubleshooting steps that would lead to finding this fault.

5-5. Consult the timing waveforms for the Z80 (Appendix C). Devise a set of tests to verify $\overline{\text{MREQ}}$.

5-6. Consider the circuit of Figure A–6. The operator can no longer interact with the system via the CRT terminal connected to the ACIA via the RS–232 link.

(a) There are many possible reasons why this is so. List at least six possible reasons.

(b) Assume that the fault is a bad baud-rate generator. In the manner of Example 5–10, outline a set of troubleshooting steps that would lead to finding this fault.

5-7. The D/A converter of Figure C–5 fails a monotonicity test.

(a) List all possible reasons why the test may have failed.

(b) Assume that the fault is a bad 74LS374 latch. Outline a set of steps that would lead to finding this fault.

(c) Repeat part (b) if inverter $U_9(c)$ fails.

5-8. Consider the ACIA test of Example 5–19. While the test functions correctly for the type of errors that it is designed to detect (namely, bad bits in data words), it does not detect errors in parity nor errors in framing. Extend the test to cover these errors as well. (You will need an ACIA data sheet for this.)

6

HARDWARE TROUBLESHOOTING USING THE STATIC STIMULUS APPROACH

Static Stimulus Testers[1] provide a relatively powerful, easy-to-use approach to hardware troubleshooting at a very low cost. As hardware troubleshooting tools, they are well suited to the needs of many small firms and individuals who do not need the capabilities,the speed, or the convenience of the more powerful dynamic units.

The static stimulus testing concept was pioneered by James Coffron. Several commercial implementations are available, including a μP-controlled version (Figure 5–4) and a manual version that uses switches and LEDs. Alternatively, users can put together their own version from a few hundred dollars worth of parts using the information contained in this chapter and Appendix F. In this chapter we describe the manual concept and illustrate its use in troubleshooting.

6-1 OVERVIEW OF STATIC STIMULUS TESTING

Essentially, a manually controlled processor emulator, the SST described in this chapter, permits the user to directly access system elements (ROM, RAM, I/O ports, etc.) and test them for functionality, as well as stimulate and monitor system buses and their attendant decode and control logic to implement node verification and circuit-level fault tracing. Since the basic strategy is hardware based, the target system does not even have to be able to run software—thus SST testers are just as able to test and debug prototype hardware as they are finished products.

[1]Static Stimulus Tester and SST are registered trademarks of Creative Microprocessor Systems, Inc., of Los Gatos, California. Both manual and μP-based versions are available from them.

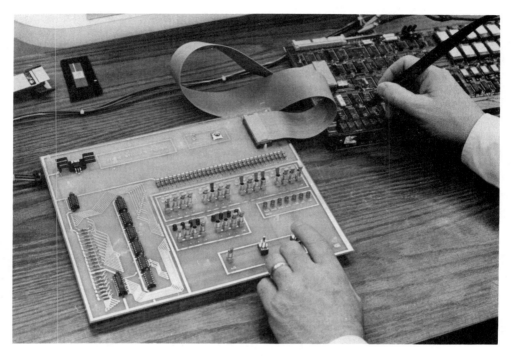

Figure 6-1: A typical manual tester.

A typical manual tester is depicted in Figure 6-1. Testing using this device is illustrated in Figure 6-2. During troubleshooting, the μP from the suspect system is removed from its socket, and the test box, substituted in its place, supplies to the unit under test all signals that the actual processor normally would. To emulate the behavior of the processor, the user operates switches in the appropriate sequence to duplicate, at manual speeds, the normal bus operation of the processor, while using the LEDs to view system responses. Except for its speed of operation the SST looks to devices on the bus, much as the processor that it has displaced.

Principles of Static Stimulus Testing

To appreciate how a static tester can substitute for a dynamic processor, it is necessary to understand clearly how a microprocessor system works. From the point of view of circuitry surrounding the CPU, the processor performs two basic operations—it reads data from the data bus and writes data to it. In addition, it generates addresses and a small number of control signals [1]. As long as these signals are present and correct, it does not matter where they come from. With the SST approach, these signals originate from a test box.

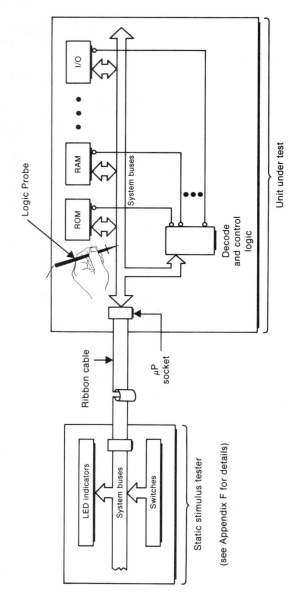

Figure 6-2: Conceptual representation of static stimulus tester in use.

To illustrate, consider a read operation. Traditionally, we view this transaction as a single dynamic event; a closer examination reveals, however, that it is not a single event at all but rather a series of separately identifiable, although related operations [2]. For purposes of illustration, we have selected a 6809 processor. Figure 6–3 shows system waveforms as they appear in vendor catalogs. The major steps in a 6809 read transaction can be summarized as follows:

1. The processor places the address of the desired location on the address bus.
2. The processor sets the R/$\overline{\text{W}}$ line high.
3. The processor asserts the E line high.

At this point, all signals needed are present and the selected device responds by outputting its data onto the data bus. The system is now essentially still and will remain so until changed by the processor as it moves on to the next cycle. Note, however, that with the SST substituted for the system processor, the unit under test is no longer under the control of a CPU—it is under the direct manual control of the operator. The operator is able to stop the process at this or any point in the cycle and hold it as long as necessary. When stopped, the operator can, by observing the indicator lamps, determine the status of bus lines, read memory and I/O locations, and so on, as well as, via its switches, "reach" into writable locations and manipulate or change their contents. In addition, it can stimulate and monitor system buses, combinational logic, and other internal system workings to permit node-level circuit tracing using simple test tools such as a hand-held logic probe or an oscilloscope. This permits the troubleshooter to trace circuit paths throughout the stopped system and check for correct behavior of all circuits. Since the system is stopped, the user can take as long as necessary. This is the method of static stimulus testing.[2]

The static approach does have some limitations, however. For one, it can only be used to trace circuits in the stopped (static) mode. This makes it most useful for debugging "hard" failures since such faults exist whether the system is operating at

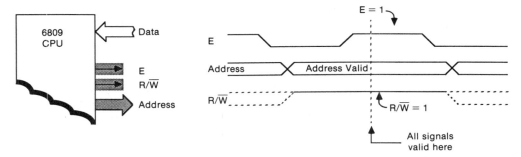

Figure 6–3:   Bus signals output by the processor during a Read Cycle. 6809 system shown for illustration.

[2]A little thought will show that these comments are quite general and applicable to other processors (Z80, 8085, etc.).

normal speeds or at "static" speeds.[3] Errors caused by timing, pattern sensitivity, and so on, will not be picked up. Another potential concern is its inability to test dynamic RAM. However, a close examination of dynamic RAM circuitry shows that the only nonstatic element that it cannot test is the RAM cell itself. All peripheral support circuitry is composed of nondynamic logic and can therefore be tested. In addition (Section 6-5), the basic strategy can be augmented to permit testing of dynamic RAMs using functional tests of the type described in Chapter 4.

An Example Static Tester

Figure 6-4 shows typical circuitry for the tester we are considering here. Shown are circuits to generate address, data, and control signals as well as circuits to display system status. Debounced switches are needed for some control signals (particularly

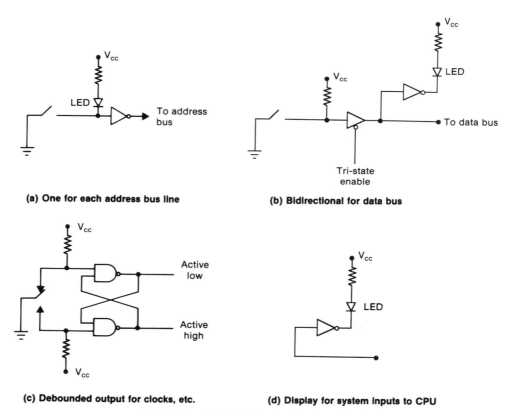

(a) One for each address bus line   (b) Bidirectional for data bus

(c) Debounded output for clocks, etc.   (d) Display for system inputs to CPU

Figure 6-4:   Typical static stimulus tester circuits.

[3]Note that correct operation in the static environment does not necessarily guarantee correct operation in the dynamic (running) environment. However, if it does not operate correctly in the static environment, it definitely will not work in the dynamic environment.

clocks and latch strobes); others, such as address and data signals, may use nondebounced switches. Tri-state devices are needed for bidirectional bus circuits.

The circuits of Figure 6-4 may be used to put together a tester for any processor. Appendix F summarizes logic requirements for several popular processors. Since the test box logic requires considerable current, it should be fitted with its own power supply. As a refinement, you may wish to add hexadecimal displays to show address and data information in a more convenient format.

6-2 SST READ AND WRITE OPERATIONS

To read and write memory and I/O locations, the user must output to the bus the same sequence of signal events that are normally supplied to it by the processor.

The Basic Write Procedure

To illustrate, consider a 6809 write. (Circuitry for the 6809 tester is shown in Figure F-1). Proceed as follows:

1. Set the address of the location of interest on the 16 address switches A0 to A15.
2. Set the data to be written on the eight data switches D0 to D7.
3. Assert the read/write line to its active-low (write) state via the R/$\overline{\text{W}}$ switch.

As this point, the location should be accessed and data from the tester should be present at its input (Figure 6-5).

4. To complete the transaction, strobe bus clock E via its pushbutton. Return R/$\overline{\text{W}}$ high. This writes the data to the selected location.

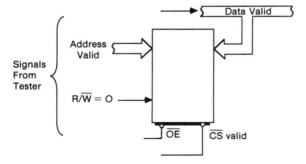

Figure 6-5: Illustrating an SST write operation.

The Basic Read Procedure

The basic read procedure is similar. For the 6809:

1. Set the address of the location to be accessed on the 16 address switches A0 to A15.

2. Assert the read/write line to its active-high (read) state via the R/$\overline{\text{W}}$ switch.
3. Assert bus clock signal E high via its pushbutton.

At this point, all signals necessary to access the specified location are present and its data should appear on the data bus, where they can be observed on the SST indicators.

For other processors such as the 8085, Z80, and so on, similar procedures are used. The Z80 procedure, for example, is virtually identical to the above, although it must include an $\overline{\text{MREQ}}$ (memory request) for memory transactions and an $\overline{\text{IORQ}}$ (I/O request) for I/O transactions. The 8085 sequence is somewhat more involved because of its multiplexed bus. In this case, the sequence must include an ALE (address latch enable) strobe for demultiplexing the bus plus an IO/$\overline{\text{M}}$ select to differentiate between memory and I/O transactions. (Operational steps for the 8085 are detailed in Appendix F.)

6–3 FUNCTIONAL TESTING

Functional testing can be implemented using the read and write capability just described.

ROM Test

To verify ROM, read successive locations and compare against system documentation. If they agree, the test passes. If they do not, there is a fault.

The problem with this approach is that it is tedious and error prone, and thus it is practical to check only a relatively few locations. This obviously does not result in very comprehensive testing. However, if the test passes, the ROM is probably okay. At the very least, we can be reasonably sure that its bus interface and control logic are free from faults. If the test fails, however, something is definitely wrong. A failed test indicates either a bad ROM or a fault in some related circuit. In any event, the problem has been narrowed to the point where circuit-level fault tracing can take over.

RAM Test

The RAM test is implemented as described in Chapter 4. Use the test box to write data to memory and read it back for verification. A simple approach is to test using alternating 1s and 0s to implement the checkerboard test described in Section 4–4. Again, it is practical to check only a relatively few locations, and thus the RAM confidence level is quite low. However, a successful test verifies basic RAM subsystem logic, including all interface and control logic. A failed test indicates either a bad RAM or a fault in some related circuit.

I/O Test

Input ports and output ports (including parallel ports, serial ports, display systems, keypads, A/D converters, D/A converters, etc.) can be tested functionally using this read/write capability. The procedure is exactly as outlined in Chapter 4, except that the tests are performed at manual operating speeds. For example, to verify output ports, write known test patterns using the write procedure described above, then with a probe, verify logic levels at the port's external pins. Similarly, to verify input ports, apply known logic levels at input pins, then use the read capability of the test box to verify the data. Software-configurable I/O ports will, of course, have to be initialized. This is readily done using the write capability of the test box. In a similar manner, keypad logic and display systems can be verified. Continuing in this manner, many hardware elements can be checked statically.

Example 6-1: Functionally Testing a Parallel I/O Port

To illustrate, consider an Intel PPI. As described earlier, the PPI is a typical general-purpose LSI parallel I/O device with several software-configurable modes. In this example, let the PPI be I/O mapped with address assignments 40 to 43 as indicated in Figure 6-6. To configure the device in mode 0 as shown requires a control byte of 82

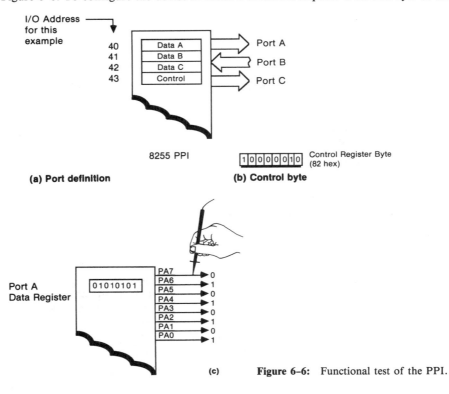

Figure 6-6: Functional test of the PPI.

hex (see Appendix B). To configure the port, we must duplicate the 8085 signal sequences (Figure B–2). Proceed as follows:

1. Set the address of the control register (43 hex) on the low-order address switches.
2. Latch this address into the demultiplexing latch by strobing ALE via its pushbutton.
3. Set switch IO/$\overline{\text{M}}$ to the logical high state to define the operation as I/O.
4. Set the control register configuration byte 82 (hex) on the data bus switches.
5. Strobe $\overline{\text{WR}}$ via its pushbutton to latch these data into the control register.

For this example, the port is I/O mapped, and address lines A8 to A15 take no part in the selection process. They are thus "don't cares."

Verifying output ports. To verify an output port, use the procedure of Chapter 4. With the test box, write patterns to its output pins and verify with a probe. Verify that each bit can output both a logic 0 and a logic 1. A particularly convenient pattern to use is the alternating 1/0 pattern 01010101 (55 hex) used previously. Repeat with the complementary binary pattern 10101010 (AA hex).

Verifying input ports. Input ports are handled similarly. Apply a known set of logic levels to the inputs of the port, then use the read capability of the test box to verify. Ensure that each bit can correctly input both a logic high and a logic low.

If the port passes all tests, it can be designated operational.

Example 6–2: Functionally Testing Numeric Display Systems

As a second example, consider the numeric display system of Figure 5–25. Testing follows exactly the procedure outlined in Section 4–8. First, select a digit for testing by writing the appropriate select pattern to the "digit select" register. Next, write the pattern to turn on segment a to the segment register. Test all segments in this fashion. Repeat for each digit in the cluster.

6–4 NODE-LEVEL CIRCUIT TRACING

Now consider circuit tracing. Since all bus signals (address, data, and control) originate at the tester and are controlled via switches, any line can be stimulated (set high, set low, or toggled) by the operator (using the corresponding switch) and the stimulated line traced using common test equipment such as a logic probe or an oscilloscope.

Circuit tracing is easily implemented using the toggling approach. To illustrate, consider the circuit of Figure 6–7. Suppose that we wish to follow address line A12 throughout the system. To do this, probe A12 at the first point of interest and toggle switch A12. The probe indicator should flicker between high and low. Now move to the next point of interest and again toggle switch A12. In this manner, the integrity of signal lines, combinational logic, and so on, can be verified or faults detected if they exist.

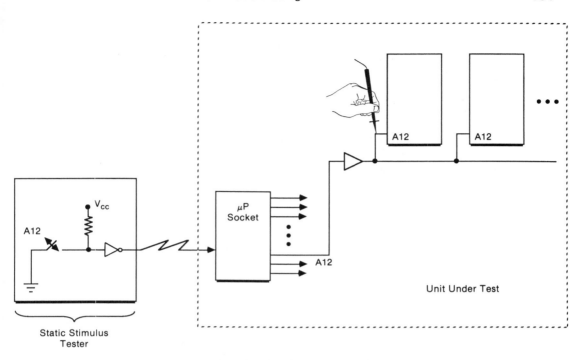

Figure 6-7: Circuit tracing using the SST system. Toggle A12 and observe the response on the probe.

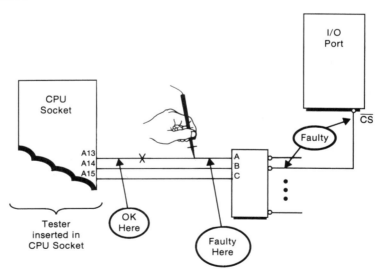

Figure 6-8: Circuit testing using the SST method. Place probe on line of interest and toggle the corresponding switch. Here, probe indicates toggling on A13 at CPU but not at input to decoder.

Example 6–3: Verifying Chip Select Logic

To illustrate, consider the circuit of Figure 6–8. Suppose that the I/O port shown is not accessed properly. To investigate, set address lines A13, A14, and A15 to select the port. (Since the port is connected to output $\overline{O_1}$ of the decoder, set A13 = 1 and A14 and A15 both to zero using the address switches on the test box.) Now probe $\overline{CS}$ of the port. It should be asserted low. If it is not, backtrack to the output of the decoder and probe there. If decoder output $\overline{O_1}$ is not asserted, check address inputs A13, A14, and A15 by placing the probe on the address input of interest, then toggle its corresponding switch. Verify each input in turn. If a fault is found, backtrack to the CPU socket and check there. Continue tracing along the suspect line until the fault is found. For the example shown, A13 does not toggle at the decoder but does at the CPU socket. This means that a fault exists somewhere between the CPU socket and the decoder. Further investigation reveals a break at the point marked X.

6–5 AUGMENTING THE SST FUNCTIONAL TESTS

As noted, manual RAM and ROM tests have low confidence levels. In addition, the static approach does not permit functional testing of dynamic RAM. To overcome these shortcomings, we can augment the SST approach with full-speed dynamic testing implemented using programs contained in a debug ROM. A suitable set of programs (devised as per Chapter 4) are coded in the language of the UUT processor, cast into ROM (or EPROM), then installed in the system ROM socket.[4] The SST is then disconnected and the UUT processor replaced. On power-up (assuming that the kernel is working),[5] operation vectors to the set of test routines in the debug ROM and testing ensues.

6–6 TROUBLESHOOTING CASE STUDIES

We now have the tools needed to implement the basic strategy of Chapter 3. The methodology will be illustrated by means of examples. In the first example, we start with a known fault and show how static stimulus testing leads us directly to it. In the next example, we do not specify the fault in advance (the usual troubleshooting problem), but via systematic testing, deduce the fault. Note that in each case, the steps in the solution sequence are governed by common sense.

Example 6–4

The unit under test is the single-board, 8085-based system of Figure B–7. The fault here is a defective input buffer (U_{16}) in the keypad circuit. The system had been used regularly until it failed. Now there is no response from the keypad. The system has a very limited

---

[4]Alternatively, instead of using a separate debug ROM, it is sometimes possible to include test programs in an unused section of the application ROM.

[5]If the kernel is inoperational, use the test box to troubleshoot it and restore it to service.

built-in self-test routine that checks ROM and RAM on power-up. The power-up message indicates no faults with either.

Problem Analysis and Troubleshooting Log

Since ROM and RAM test correctly and the correct message appears, we can assume that the kernel of the system and the display are working. It seems logical therefore to focus immediately on the keypad circuitry itself. The portion of the circuit of interest is reproduced in Figure 6-9. In the application environment, the system does not respond to the keypad. Let us therefore investigate this logic.

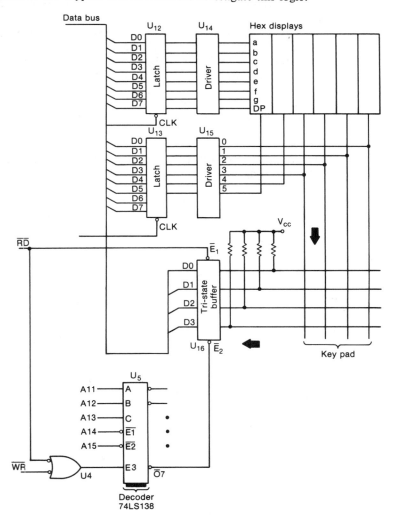

Figure 6-9: Portion of keypad logic under investigation.

Step 1: Keypad logic setup. Set up the keypad logic to read keys as follows:

1. Using the "write" procedure, write 00 (hex) to latch U_{13} (address 2800_{16}). This sets all outputs low.[6]
2. Now set the tester to read the keypad input buffer U_{16} (address 3800_{16}). Set $\overline{RD}$ to it slow state. Leave $\overline{WR}$ high.

At this point, U_{16} should be selected and keypad data should be enabled onto the data bus and appear on the SST data bus indicators. Now press keys. As each key is pressed, its equivalent (as summarized in Table 5-1, Section 5.8) should be displayed. Nothing happens.

Step 2: Verifying keypad input. Now operate keys and probe the corresponding inputs to U_{16}. (Inputs should go low when keys in that row are operated.) All inputs test correctly.

Step 3: Enable inputs. Probe $\overline{E1}$ of U_{16}. It indicates low, as it should. Toggle $\overline{RD}$. $\overline{E1}$ follows, as it should. Repeat for $\overline{E2}$. (It is also driven from $\overline{RD}$ through the decoder.) It also tests okay.

Step 4: Data bus interface. Probe the data bus connections D0 to D3 at U_{16} and toggle the corresponding SST data bus switch. All test okay.

At this point, we have bracketed U_{16} with independently verified circuitry (Figure 6-10). The only conclusion left is that U_{16} is faulty. When U_{16} was replaced, the system returned to normal operation.

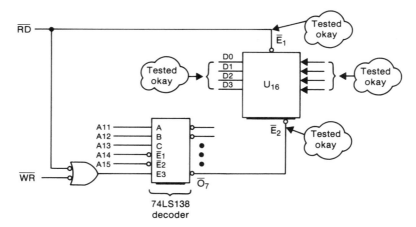

Figure 6-10: Checking keypad logic. Test indicates that U_{16} is faulty.

Example 6-5

The system here is a 6809-based machine control system that uses limit switches to monitor machine operations and solenoids to position final control elements. The position of the solenoids (extended or retracted) is determined by the application program acting on information gathered from these switches. The system has been in operation suc-

[6]The read and write procedures for the 8085 are detailed in Appendix F.

cessfully for a long time. Now, however, a problem has developed that manifests itself as incorrect operation of solenoid 3 (Figure 6-11). In the application environment, solenoid 3 is controlled by bit 3 of the output port indicated, acting on status gathered by limit switches feeding PIA inputs PB0 and PB1 respectively.

Problem Analysis and Troubleshooting Log

The problem could be caused by a number of things, including the following:

1. Output bit PA3 of the PIA could be faulty.
2. The solenoid driver could be faulty.
3. Either PB0 or PB1 inputs of the PIA could be faulty.
4. There may be a failure in one of the external circuits feeding PB0 and PB1.

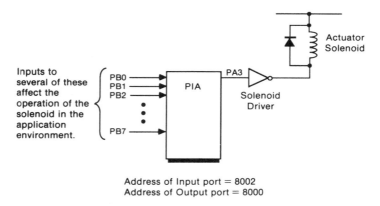

Address of Input port = 8002
Address of Output port = 8000

Figure 6-11:   Solenoid fails to function properly in the application environment.

There are other possible causes, such as a failure in the portion of the ROM chip containing the solenoid actuation routine, a problem in RAM memory where intermediate data for the solenoid routine is accumulated, and so on. However, because of the symptoms observed, it is reasonable to start troubleshooting at the PIA.

Step 1: PIA initialization. The first step is PIA initialization. Here we must configure all B-side lines for input and all A-side lines for output. As noted in Appendix A, this is done by setting the contents of Data Direction Register A to FF and the contents of Data Direction Register B to 00. Set their respective control registers to 04 (hex) as indicated in Appendix A.

Procedure

1. Press RESET on the UUT to clear all PIA registers. (This automatically configures Data Direction Register B for input.)[7]

---

[7]Using the UUT reset works here. However, some systems (the 8085, for example) use a Reset Out (generated by the CPU) to reset peripheral devices. In this case, the Reset Out must be part of the SST design (see Figure F-2).

2. Write the configuration byte FF to Data Direction Register A using the write procedure.
3. Write the configuration byte 04 to control registers A and B.

With the PIA thus configured, we can now turn our attention to input and output operations. Let us begin with the output port.

Step 2: Output port. Test output bit PA3 to determine whether it can output both a 1 and a 0 correctly.

Procedure

1. To activate solenoid 3, set output bit 3 high by writing the pattern 0000 1000 (08 hex) to port A. (All other bits have been left at 0 to avoid actuating solenoids not under test.) In response to this, solenoid 3 correctly moved to its extended position.
2. To retract solenoid 3, output logic 0 to bit position 3 by writing the binary pattern 0000 0000 (00 hex) to port A. In response to this, solenoid 3 retracted correctly.

Since both tests passed, the problem is not in the output side of the PIA or in the solenoid or its driver.

Step 3: Input port. Test both input bits PB0 and PB1, as they both affect solenoid actuation in the application environment. Input bits PB0 and PB1 originate from limit switches. As indicated in Figure 6–12, L1 feeds directly to PB0, but L2 is conditioned by an enabling signal. Test as follows:

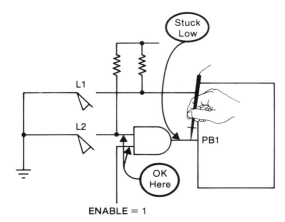

ENABLE = 1

Figure 6–12: Input PB1 is found to be faulty.

Procedure

1. Set both limit switches L1 and L2 to their logic 1 (open) state. Set the gate enabling input high using external means.
2. Read the input port using the READ procedure. In this case, PB0 = 1, as it should. However, PB1 shows 0. Thus PB1 is faulty.

Step 4: With the probe, check logic levels at the AND gate. Results are summarized in Figure 6–12. As indicated, the gate is properly conditioned by the enabling signal and the logic level from limit switch 2 is correct. However, its output is faulty. This suggests one of the following problems:

1. The AND gate is defective.
2. Input PB1 of the PIA is defective.
3. There is a problem with the printed circuit trace between the output of the AND and the input to the PIA. (However, this is not likely, as the system functioned correctly up to the time of the fault.)

Using the methods of Chapter 10, it was determined that the fault was a bad AND gate.

6-7 SUMMARY

The examples considered above have barely scratched the surface of what can be done using static stimulus techniques. Interrupt systems, analog subsystems, display controllers, and so on, can all be tested using the SST. However, the topic will not be pursued further here. Anyone with a clear understanding of the principles and methodologies of this chapter and that of Chapter 4 should have little trouble extending the basic idea to cover the many practical troubleshooting situations that are likely to be encountered in practice and for which the SST approach is suitable.

REFERENCES

1. Zumchak, Eugene M., *Microcomputer Design and Troubleshooting,* The Blacksburg Group, Inc., Blacksburg, VA, 1982.
2. Coffron, James W., *Proven Techniques for Troubleshooting the Microprocessor and Home Computer Systems,* Prentice-Hall, Inc., Englewood Cliffs, NJ, 1984.
3. Coffron, James W., *Z80 Applications,* Sybex, Inc., Berkeley, CA, 1983.
4. Coffron, James W., Serially Testing a Board's States Takes the Trickiness Out of Debugging It, *Electronics,* January 27, 1982.

REVIEW QUESTIONS

6-1. Consider the circuit of Figure B–7. Assume that ALE (address latch enable) is open circuited. Outline a set of troubleshooting steps that would lead to finding this fault.

6-2. Consider the circuit of Figure A–6. Assume a faulty PIA. Outline a set of troubleshooting steps that would lead to finding this fault.

6-3. Consider the circuit of Figure C–5. Assume that gate U_8 fails. Outline a set of troubleshooting steps that would lead to finding this fault.

6-4. Consider the CRT terminal and serial interface of Figure 4–12(a).
   (a) Detail the steps that can be used to write printable characters to the screen in order to test output logic.
   (b) Detail the steps that can be used to read characters from the keyboard in order to test input logic.

6-5. Consider the numeric display system of Figure 5–25. Detail the set of steps that can be used to test each display in this cluster.

6-6. Consider the circuit of Figure A–6. Assume a faulty baud rate generator. Outline a set of troubleshooting steps that would lead to finding this fault.

6-7. The D/A converter subsystem of Figure C–5 is faulty.
   (a) Assume that the fault is a bad 74LS374 latch. Outline a set of troubleshooting steps that would lead to finding this fault.
   (b) Repeat part (a) if inverter $U_{9(c)}$ fails.

7
SIGNATURE ANALYSIS

Signature analysis is an offshoot of the old analog troubleshooting technique of injecting a signal into a circuit and comparing the waveforms produced within the circuit against the expected waveforms. The major difference is that in the digital environment, we are no longer concerned with the actual shape of the waveforms on the various nodes. Rather, we are concerned only with whether they are right or wrong. The signature analyzer provides this go/no-go test by reducing the complex data streams to an easily verifiable four-digit signature. If the signature obtained matches the expected signature, the node is functioning correctly. Otherwise, there is a problem. There is no such thing as an almost-right signature.

Figure 7–1 shows a typical signature analyzer, the Hewlett-Packard 5004A. The instrument is relatively simple. There are two sets of probes: a data probe for sampling the individual nodes and a control pod for controlling the data capture process. These topics will be discussed in greater detail shortly. The front panel has a few buttons for control of the operating parameters and a four-digit seven-segment readout for displaying the signature.

Actual troubleshooting with signature analysis is a simple procedure which in its most basic form requires little understanding on the operator's part of the circuit being tested. The operator simply compares the signature obtained against the expected one and, upon finding a discrepancy, backtraces through the circuit until the source of the fault is identified. This simplicity makes signature analysis well suited to a service depot or production environment, where relatively unskilled personnel can test and troubleshoot a large number of systems fairly quickly.

In this chapter we look at how system problems can be effectively diagnosed using a combination of functional testing and traditional signature analysis in a manner similar to the general troubleshooting methodology developed in Chapter 3. In

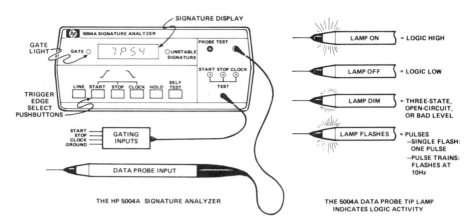

Figure 7–1: The HP 5004A signature analyzer. Courtesy of Hewlett-Packard Company.

addition, a considerable portion of the chapter is devoted to the general theory of signature analysis operation, and how signature analysis can be implemented within a microprocessor-based system. This information is intended to provide the troubleshooter with a basic understanding of the process being used. It is not intended to be a comprehensive guide to signature analysis design.

The final section of this chapter examines some enhancements introduced into the signature analysis field in recent years, and how these enhancements have countered many of the traditional arguments against signature analysis.

7–1 UNDERSTANDING THE SIGNATURE ANALYSIS CONCEPT

There are three main aspects to the signature analysis process: stimulus, data capture, and data compression. *Stimulus* is used to create state change activity on the system nodes. This activity is essential for the signature analysis process. *Data capture* is responsible for sampling the activity on the node in a manner that yields usable bit-stream information. Finally, *data compression* reduces this bit stream into the four-digit number known as the signature. Figure 7–2 illustrates the interrelationship of these three aspects.

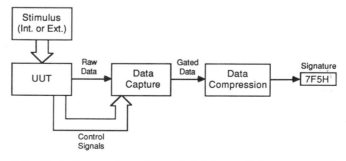

Figure 7–2 Block diagram of signature analysis being applied to a system under test.

The necessary stimulus is provided by the UUT if signature analysis capabilities were included in the system design or by an external stimulus instrument. In later sections we look at the theory of UUT-implemented stimulus. External stimulus is discussed in the section on enhancements.

Data capture and compression are implemented within the signature analyzer. We now examine these two aspects in detail.

Data Compression

Although the mathematics behind the data compression algorithm are quite complex, the general concept is fairly easy to grasp. As shown in Figure 7-3, data

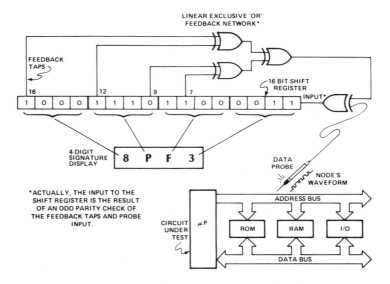

Figure 7-3: Data compression circuitry in a signature analyzer. Courtesy of Hewlett-Packard Company.

compression is implemented in hardware using a 16-bit shift register with linear feedback. Thus the actual data input to the shift register is a function of both the incoming data stream and the data that currently exist within the register—that is, its past history.

The incoming bit stream is not limited to 16 bits. Captured data, modified by the feedback network, will simply pass through the register until the capture control logic ends the data sampling process. At this point, the residue of the bit stream remaining in the shift register forms the signature which is displayed to the operator. It should be noted that the display character set differs from normal hexadecimal characters as shown in Table 7-1. This was done to avoid confusion between similar characters, such as the number 6 and a lowercase b.

The data compression algorithm was developed by Hewlett-Packard and is used by most manufacturers of signature analyzers. The algorithm is both data and time dependent and is capable of 100 percent detection of single-bit errors. That is, a single-

TABLE 7-1 SIGNATURE DISPLAY
CHARACTER SET

Digit	Display	Digit	Display
0000	0	1000	8
0001	1	1001	9
0010	2	1010	A
0011	3	1011	C
0100	4	1100	F
0101	5	1101	H
0110	6	1110	P
0111	7	1111	U

bit difference between two bit streams is guaranteed to result in different signatures. The algorithm also has a 99.998 percent success rate at detecting multiple-bit errors in the captured data. Readers interested in the mathematics behind the algorithm can refer to an article by Robert Frohwerk [1].

Data Capture Process

During data capture, the signature analyzer reads in the bit-stream information being generated by the stimulus. The period when the analyzer is reading data is known as the *measurement window,* or *gate.* Since the gate must be synchronous with the testing stimulus, all control and sampling signals are derived from the unit under test. There are three main signals used for control of the data capture process: start, stop, and clock.

The *start* signal tells the analyzer to open the measurement window so that data can be read in. The *stop* signal closes the window, signifying that data capture is complete, and the resultant signature is then displayed. The *clock* signal synchronizes the analyzer's sampling circuitry to the unit being tested. This process is illustrated in Figure 7-4. This illustration points out some important features about the capture process. One should note that the gate is actually controlled by the clock and not by the start and stop signals themselves. The start and stop inputs are sampled on the active clock edge just as the data probe input is. When the sampling circuitry detects a state change on these inputs corresponding to the selected active edge, the gate is opened or closed on the clock edge following the start or stop edge, respectively. Because of this, the designer must ensure that the chosen setup provides a clock edge both before and after the start and stop edges. Problems often result from an oversight of this fundamental detail.

Each of the three signals can be set independently for rising or falling active edges. The choice will vary, of course, depending on the type of system, the signals chosen, and the type of stimulus being run. Some analyzers also have a *clock qualifier* input which can be set to HIGH, LOW, or DON'T CARE active levels. A clock edge will be valid only if the level at the qualifier input agrees with the preset active level.

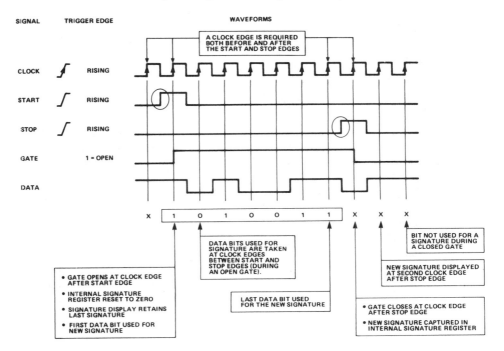

Figure 7-4: Basic gate operation. Courtesy of Hewlett-Packard Company.

In the example above, we have shown a relatively short gate for illustrative simplicity. In actual troubleshooting, gates are typically much longer. The analyzer imposes no upper limit on the length of time the gate can be open. However, the new signature will not be displayed until after the gate is closed. Thus very long gates can make for extremely tedious debugging. Generally, it is advisable to keep gate periods to under half a second.

This invites the question: How long does the gate have to be open? The gate must be open only as long as it takes to stimulate the node through all its functional states. For example, suppose that we wished to test the data within a particular ROM. We would set the window to open when the stimulus accessed the first ROM location and close when the last ROM location had been reached. This will be discussed further in the next section when we look at signature analysis tests for various devices. Of course, we must also choose a clock that will sample all the functional states. The reliability of the error-detection algorithm is of little consequence if the bit in error does not get clocked into the analyzer.

Sources for the start, stop, and clock signals will also vary according to the application. Generally, these signals can be obtained from hardware which is intrinsic to basic system operation. Examples of these would be address lines, chip selects, and read and write strobes. However, some tests may require the addition of analysis-specific hardware to generate an appropriate control signal. An example of this would be a flip-flop which is triggered by the stimulus program to produce a start or stop edge. It is desirable to minimize such hardware overhead for a couple of reasons:

1. It adds to the size and cost of the system.
2. It increases the complexity of the control circuitry.

Control and clock circuitry should be as simple as possible. An error in this circuitry could mislead the operator into thinking the fault lies in the circuitry being tested. Later, we look at examples of control signal sources which are appropriate for the various tests.

Before leaving this topic, we should look at how the operation the gate is affected by two things common to most microprocessor-based systems: noise and three-state nodes.

Signature analysis is generally unaffected by noise on the start, stop, and data signals. This is because most of the noise occurs away from clock edges and is therefore not detected by the analyzer. Figure 7–5 illustrates some typical noise occurrences in relation to the clock signal. The only type of noise that can cause problems

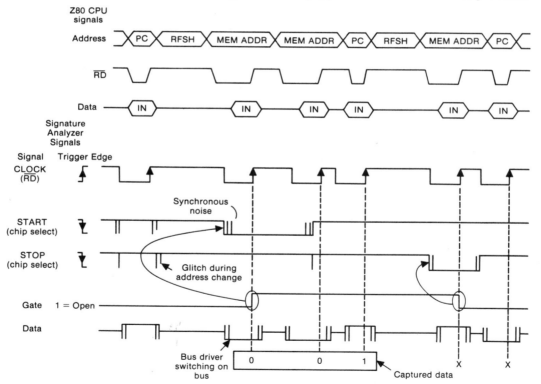

Figure 7–5: Noise rejection in a Z80 based system.

is random asynchronous noise which occurs right at a clock edge. In that case, the noise can affect the start or stop times of the gate or the level of the data being sampled.

Noise on the clock signal is far more serious since a noise spike will appear to the analyzer as a valid clock edge. This can result in variations in gate length or, as shown in Figure 7-6, in extra data being clocked in. Either case will result in incorrect signatures.

Ground noise induced in long ground leads can also be a problem when measuring high-frequency data (greater than 5 MHz). In such instances, the extra ground lead on the data probe can be connected to a ground near the nodes being probed.

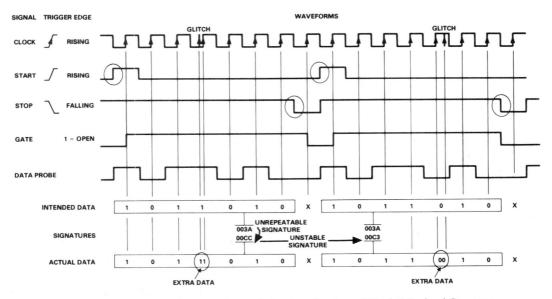

Figure 7-6:   Incorrect signatures due to clock noise. Courtesy of Hewlett-Packard Company.

Three-state devices are a common occurrence in the bus-oriented systems that this book deals with. On the surface, they would appear to pose a problem since the undefined state should cause problems in achieving signature predictability. However, this is not the case.

First, it is usually easy to select a clock that samples the nodes only while valid data are available. In this case, we avoid the third state entirely. If, however, our test requires us to sample during the third state, the front-end circuitry of the analyzer will define an undefined data sample as being the last valid level on the node before going into the third state. This is illustrated in Figure 7-7.

Finally, we must remember that the signature analyzer contains "real" circuitry, with all its inherent limitations. It is therefore necessary that we be aware of two important timing constraints.

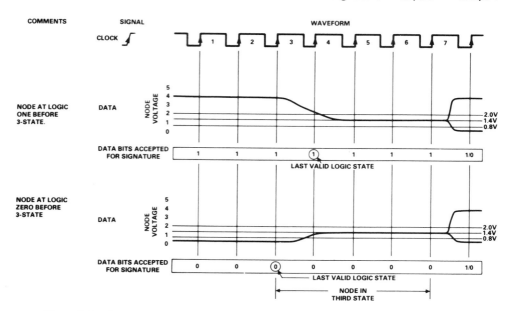

Figure 7-7: Data sampling on a three-state node. Courtesy of Hewlett-Packard Company.

The first is the *clock input rate.* All signature analyzers have a maximum rate at which data can be sampled. In the case of the HP 5005A, this is 25 MHz.

Second, the design must not violate the setup time requirements of the analyzer. *Setup time* is defined as the minimum length of time that the data or start/stop signals must be present and stable before the clock edge occurrence. This is illustrated in Figure 7-8.

The troubleshooter must ensure that the timing specifications of the chosen analyzer are not exceeded by any of the signature analysis tests to be performed. Timing requirements are always specified in the operation manual for the signature analyzer.

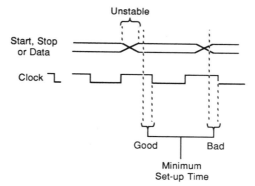

Figure 7-8: Signature analyzer set-up time.

7-2 SIGNATURE ANALYSIS STIMULUS CONCEPTS

As mentioned earlier, a fundamental concept in signature analysis is that of the "wiggling line," where the node changes between one logic state and the other. To produce this activity, it is necessary to stimulate the nodes in a manner that exercises all the functional states of a particular node. The method by which this is accomplished varies depending on the type of device being tested. However, no matter how the stimulus is produced, the resultant signatures must be both repeatable and stable. Let us now look at what we mean by these terms [2].

Signatures are considered *repeatable* if the same signature is obtained every time a measurement is made, assuming that the measurement is made on identical nodes in identical good products using identical stimulus and measurement parameters. Unrepeatable signatures are usually a result of some device not being properly initialized before beginning stimulus. As mentioned earlier, noise on the clock can also result in unrepeatable signatures. When gathering good signatures, one can test for repeatability by turning the system off, then on again and repeating the measurements. This will ensure that all devices being tested have been properly initialized. Signatures should also be gathered from as many known good systems as is feasible. This, too, will ensure that all devices are properly initialized and will help detect borderline operating conditions that could cause setup time violations in some systems.

Signatures are considered *stable* when two consecutive measurements produce the same signature for all measurements. If two adjacent measurement cycles produce different signatures, the signatures are unstable. Grossly unstable signatures will result in a changing or unreadable display. However, a single unstable signature occurrence can be indicated only by the unstable signature light on the front panel of the signature analyzer. This light will come on for a short period whenever two adjacent signatures differ. Unstable signatures usually occur due to the gate length changing from cycle to cycle, or varying circuit response to the stimulus. To prevent instability, the designer must provide a clean clock signal and ensure that the stimulus always produces the same data pattern while the gate is open.

Circuit Stimulus

There are two basic types of stimulus which can be employed in signature analysis testing. Each type is inherently suited for testing of only a portion of a total system, so both types must be included to provide complete testing stimulus capability.

The first type of stimulus is called *free-running*. It is a hardware-based stimulus which allows the microprocessor to cycle through its entire addressing range, thereby allowing the operator to test and troubleshoot the bus system, address decode logic, and ROM(s): the "kernel" of the system. Free-running is very important since it requires only the microprocessor IC to be functional in order for it to run. With it, we can debug enough of the system for it to be able to run more sophisticated circuit stimulus.

This leads us into the second type of stimulus, the *signature analysis stimulus program*. This is a series of ROM-based software routines which provide for the sometimes complex stimulus techniques required by the system's outlying circuitry. This type of stimulus is effective for testing RAMs, I/O devices such as keyboards and displays, sequential logic, interrupts, and programmable devices. It is, of course, dependent on the kernel being up and running so that the system can execute these routines.

In the following sections, we take a detailed look at how these two stimulus techniques can be implemented in typical microprocessor-based systems.

7–3 FREE-RUNNING

Free-running is defined as the sequential cycling through all possible addresses by the microprocessor. This provides activity on all address lines, thereby allowing the operator to test the address bus and the decoding circuitry, which is a function of the address. As explained in an earlier chapter, the address put out by the microprocessor is a function of the data received on the data bus. The data bus therefore serves as a feedback loop which is essential for the operation of a healthy system, but which proves to be a major obstacle when trying to debug the system kernel.

The key to making a system free-run, then, is to break this feedback loop and provide the microprocessor with data that will allow it to cycle through its addressing range. An example of how this can be done is shown in Figure 7–9. In this example, we are showing a 6800-based system which allows for the simplest implementation due to its separate bus structure. The data bus is broken mechanically by means of

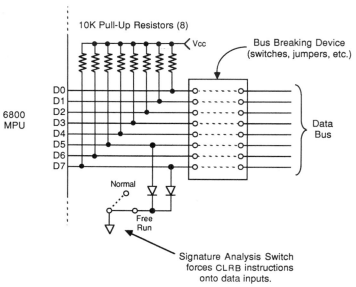

Figure 7–9: Breaking a non-multiplexed data bus.

a jumper plug and socket, or through DIP switches. The break must be placed between the microprocessor and the first (physically) device on the data bus. The instruction to be read in is implemented using pull-up resistors (for a logic 1) and grounded diodes (logic 0). A switch removes the ground so that normal operation is not affected by the diodes. In this case, the CLRB (clear accumulator B) instruction is chosen since it requires a minimum number of diodes.

On power-up or reset, the microprocessor will read this instruction and execute it. Since the instruction is internal, requiring no further reads or writes, the microprocessor will increment its address by one and read in the next instruction to be executed, which, of course, is the CLRB. Thus the process of reading and executing will force the address bus through its entire range continuously until the operator manually halts the test.

In the case of a system that uses a multiplexed bus scheme, the implementation is slightly more difficult. Here we cannot just ground the diodes since this would affect the address put out on the bus. One solution is shown in Figure 7–10. In this example, which uses an 8085 microprocessor, the read strobe from the 8085, labeled as $\overline{RD}$, is used to ground the diode. Since the strobe is low only during the data portion of the cycle, the address part of the cycle is not affected.

Now that we have our microprocessor free-running, we must devise some means for the signature analyzer to make use of this stimulus by defining appropriate start, stop, and clock signals. Since the highest address line (A15 in a 64K addressing range)

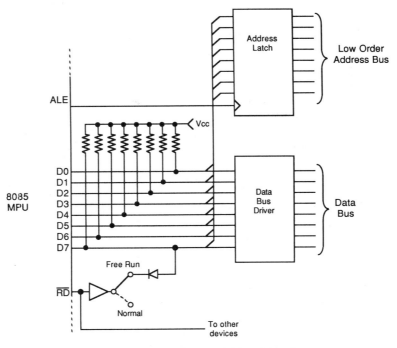

Figure 7–10: Breaking a multiplexed data bus.

has only one positive (or negative) edge per address cycle, it is a logical choice for both the start and stop signal. This is shown in Figure 7–11. Both start and stop are set to trigger on the positive edge. In this way, the analyzer gate is open for the entire address range of the microprocessor.

The signal chosen for the clock will depend on the microprocessor being used. The choice should be a simple signal which will provide one clock edge per address state at a time when the address is valid. In an 8085 or Z80 system, the rising edge of the read strobe is a good choice. For a 6809 system, we could use the falling edge of the E clock signal.

Note that although this scheme will test the address bus and memory-mapped decode logic, it cannot be used for testing the data bus. This is because free-running causes the system to address RAM in some part of the address map, where undefined random data exist. Since these data will always be different, repeatable signa-

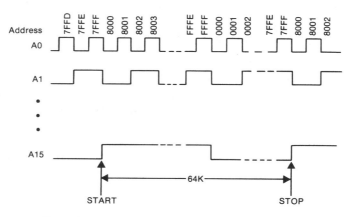

Figure 7–11: Controlling the gate for free-run stimulus.

tures cannot be obtained for the data bus with this test setup. It will also not test the system's write logic (since only reads are being performed) or any I/O addressing circuitry.

We can, however, use a subset of the free-run stimulus to test both the data bus and the system ROM. Let us assume that we have an 8085-based system with ROM in the address range 0000–07FF. In this example, we open the measurement window only during the time when the ROM is being addressed. To do this, we connect the start and stop lines to the chip select for the ROM. The start is set to trigger on the falling edge (indicating the system access of the first ROM location) and the stop is set to the rising edge (which occurs after the last ROM access). This is illustrated in Figure 7–12.

As before, the read strobe is used for the clock signal. Since the gate is open only when the ROM is accessed, the data that appear on the data bus will be a function of the contents of the ROM only. Since these data are constant, repeatable signatures can be obtained for the data bus. If the system contains more than one ROM, the test can be repeated for each one using the appropriate chip select to control the

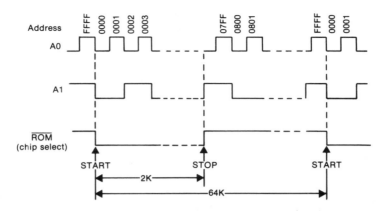

Figure 7-12: Controlling the gate for ROM free-run stimulus.

gate. If the faulty system passes this test, the operator will have a high level of confidence in both the data bus and in the ROM and its associated circuitry.

It should be noted here that while a free-run test, or any signature analysis stimulus, is being run, unexpected events are generally unwelcome. For this reason, provisions should be made for disabling any interrupts normally used by the system for the duration of the testing. We will look at how we can test interrupts a little later.

With the free-run stimulus, the kernel can be debugged to a high level of confidence, thereby allowing the troubleshooter to proceed to debugging the rest of the system circuitry.

Let us now look at an example that should help to clarify the theoretical discussion so far. In this example, we proceed step by step through a typical debugging session, where we will use signature analysis under free-run stimulus to isolate a fault in the system kernel. The example chosen is the same one used in previous chapters, where we have a broken connection between the address buffer and the decoder chip. In this way, we see not only how to employ signature analysis to locate a fault, but also the similarities between using this particular method and those discussed previously. For convenience, the section of the circuit we will be dealing with is reproduced in Figure 7-13.

Let us proceed. At this point, we have attempted to boot-up the UUT and found that it will not even execute the startup self-test routines. After a preliminary investigation into power levels and clocks, we decide to use signature analysis to test the operation of the boot ROM and its associated circuitry.

1. Our first step is to connect the signature analyzer to the UUT and set its control parameters according to the test specifications. In the signature analysis documentation, the following information is given.

$$\begin{array}{lll} \text{START} & \uparrow & \text{A15} \\ \text{STOP} & \uparrow & \text{A15} \\ \text{CLOCK} & \uparrow & \overline{\text{RD}} \end{array}$$

V_{cc} signature: 0001

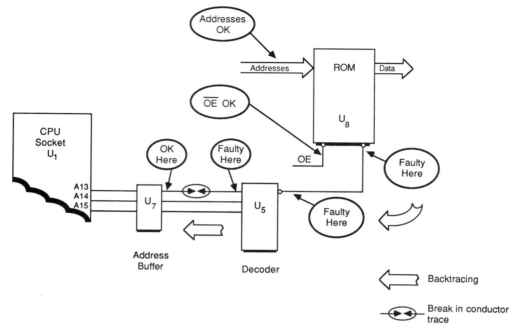

Figure 7-13:   Example system circuitry.

This tells us that both the start and stop inputs are connected to address line 15 and the clock input is connected to the $\overline{RD}$ output of the 8085. All signals are set for rising active edge. Many test documents will also include a characteristic V_{cc} *signature.* This is the signature produced when the data probe is placed on a constant HIGH level, using the given stimulus and test setup conditions for that application. Testing this before starting signature gathering gives the troubleshooter a high level of confidence that the analyzer has been correctly hooked up and the stimulus is operating as expected.

2. Next, we set up the UUT so that it will go into free-run when it is powered-up. This involves setting the bus break switches to their open positions and setting the free-run switch to connect the $\overline{RD}$ strobe to the diodes, thereby placing the selected single-byte instruction onto the 8085 data inputs during the data portion of the cycle.

3. With the signature analyzer on, the UUT is powered-up. The gate indicator on the front of the analyzer should be flashing, indicating that the measurement window is opening and closing as the microprocessor cycles through its address field. The V_{cc} signature should now be checked to ensure that the test setup is correct. Having done that, we can proceed with confidence into our investigation of the suspect circuitry.

4. The investigative procedure we follow from this point on does not differ significantly from that outlined in earlier chapters. A suitable starting point is to check

the functionality of the address bus. Since we suspect a problem with accessing the boot firmware, the address bus signatures should be checked at the appropriate ROM input pin. Moving our data probe from pin to pin, we find that the address bus signatures are all correct. When collecting signatures you will notice that the unstable signature light on the analyzer will flash briefly when the data probe is placed on a different node. This is normal and is caused by the signature changing from one node to the next.

It is interesting to note that the free-run signatures for the address bus are the same for all microprocessors with 16 address lines. (This assumes that the start and stop are connected to the most significant address line and that the clock is any signal which is active once per instruction cycle during a period when address information is valid.) This common set of signatures is shown in Table 7-2.

We should note that these signatures apply only to analyzers that use the HP data compression algorithm. The Fluke 9010A, for example, offers signature analysis capabilities but does not use the HP algorithm.

TABLE 7-2 FREE-RUN
ADDRESS SIGNATURES FOR
ALL MICROPROCESSORS WITH
16 ADDRESS LINES

A0	UUUU	A8	HC89
A1	5555	A9	2H70
A2	CCCC	A10	HPP0
A3	7F7F	A11	1293
A4	5H21	A12	HAP7
A5	0AFA	A13	3C96
A6	UPFH	A14	3827
A7	52F8	A15	755P

5. The next logical step (since we cannot test the data bus using free-run stimulus) is to test the ROM control lines. These include the output enable and the chip select. Here our probing reveals an incorrect signature on the chip select.

6. Backtracing, we find the same incorrect signature at the output of the decoder. We must now determine if this is indeed the bad node or if the problem is farther upstream. This is done by checking the signatures of all inputs to the decoder.

7. Testing the inputs, we find correct signatures on all pins except pin 3. Here the signature should have been 3C96 since it is connected to address line A13. However, the display shows either 0000 or 0001 (the signature will depend on the last valid state sampled since the pin is floating at an undefined level) and the LED on the data probe tip shows no activity.

8. Backtracing further, we see that the signature at the address buffer is correct. Thus we can conclude that there is a discontinuity between the buffer and the

decoder. Using the tools and methods described in Chapter 10, we identify the source of the problem: a bad plate-through hole.

Some general comments on this example can be made here. First, it again illustrates how the basic methodology can be utilized, regardless of the implementation details. (In a later section, we will see that signature analysis actually forces some minor variations on the approach developed in Chapter 3.) Where we might have looked for a toggling line with the Fluke 9010A, we now check the validity of a four-digit number. The overall approach, however, remains the same.

Second, the mechanics of testing used in the example are applicable to any signature analysis test. These can be summarized in three basic steps.

1. Connect the analyzer and set its operating parameters according to the test specifications.
2. Set the unit to produce the desired stimulus.
3. Probe the system nodes and compare the signatures obtained to the expected values.

These steps remain the same whether we are testing an address bus with free-run, or a display shift register using a complex stimulus program. We look at the latter approach in the next section.

7-4 PROGRAMMED STIMULUS

To move beyond the kernel of the system, we require more sophisticated stimulus than free-running can provide. Beyond the relative simplicity of the bus structure there can lie many varied and complex circuits for tasks such as memory control, data acquisition, input/output, and communication, to name but a few. It is beyond the scope of this chapter to provide the reader with a detailed study in specific application stimulus design. Rather, we look at programmed stimulus from a generalized viewpoint with the following questions in mind.

How can programmed stimulus be implemented within the framework of a typical bus-structured system?

What type of stimulus is suitable for a particular type of device?

Programmed Stimulus Implementation

There are a number of ways in which the programmed stimulus software can be implemented in the system hardware. The key in all these methods is providing the microprocessor with access to the stimulus software so that it can be executed.

One method is to replace the boot ROM (the ROM containing the code which is executed first upon startup or reset) with a test ROM containing the stimulus software. The testing software is then executed in place of the normal software when the system is turned on. Although this method requires no system ROM overhead, it has a few disadvantages. Namely, a separate ROM is required for troubleshooting, the ROM requires a socket that can lead to operating problems due to poor pin-socket contact, and there is the danger of damage to both system and test ROMs due to improper handling.

Another method is to include the stimulus software within an existing system ROM. Generally, the test software is only 5 to 10 percent of the total program length and so does not pose an excessive burden on the required ROM space. One can then use jumpers to readdress the portion of ROM containing the stimulus software so that it is executed in place of the normal system software. Or one can define the stimulus software to be executed when an interrupt line is activated by a switch or jumper.

The test software will usually contain a number of separate routines for testing different devices in the system. Some means to select these individual routines is therefore necessary. One way is to have switch settings that can be read onto the data bus. The software can then use these settings to determine which routine to execute. These switches can be existing ones which serve a different purpose under normal system operation or a dedicated switch bank which is used only for test selection. In either case, the read circuitry for the switches should be as simple as possible since the operator must be sure that it is working before attempting to run the stimulus routines.

Stimulus Software Routines (General)

The essential feature of any stimulus routine is that it exercises the circuitry under test through all functional states. The stimulus need not be meaningful in terms of normal circuit operation as long as each node receives activity for the signature analyzer to monitor.

The stimulus routine must provide initialization for any device requiring it. This could range from setting a control latch to outputting a programming sequence to a programmable device. Failure to do so could result in improper operation of the circuit or unrepeatable signatures to be generated.

No matter what type of device is being tested, the signature analyzer must be provided with suitable start, stop, and clock signals. If suitable control signals are not intrinsically available (such as the highest address line when performing free-run stimulus), they must be created by the stimulus routine. A common technique is to do a dummy read to an upper address location before beginning the stimulus. This causes the highest address line to toggle so that it can be used as a start/stop trigger. This method requires that the test software be located in the lower half of the address space. If this is not practical, one can use a latch or flip-flop dedicated to testing. The routine would set the latch at the start of the stimulus and reset it upon completion.

When choosing the clocking and control scheme, one must be careful that the signature analyzer timing requirements are met. One should also remember that it is the clock which actually controls the gate, so there must be a clock edge both before and after the selected start and stop edges. The following example illustrates this point. See reference [2].

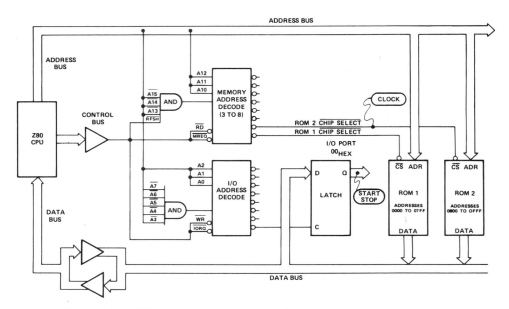

Figure 7–14: Z80 system with signature analysis control signals. Courtesy of Hewlett-Packard Company.

In this example, we have a Z80-based system in which a test program in ROM 1 is stimulating ROM 2. A simplified circuit schematic is shown in Figure 7–14. The test program in ROM 1 reads all locations in ROM 2 onto the data bus so that the ROM and its associated circuitry can be tested. In this scheme, the test routine sets a latch to go high before reading the first location in ROM 2, then resets the latch after the last location is read. The idea is to use this latch output to control the start and stop lines, while the chip select for ROM 2 is used to clock in the data. However, in its present form this test routine will not work because the gate is never opened. The reason for this is shown in Figure 7–15.

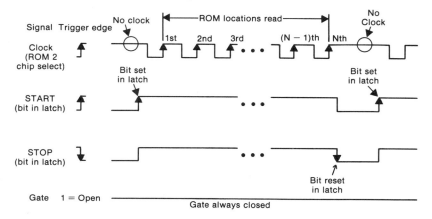

Figure 7–15: Original ROM stimulus program timing diagram.

Looking at the timing diagram, the reason for this failure becomes apparent. The test program accesses the ROM only after the start edge is produced and before the stop edge. As a result, there is no clock edge before the start edge or after the stop edge. Thus the edges are never detected and the gate remains closed.

The solution to this problem is quite simple. Modify the test routine to perform a dummy read of ROM 2 before setting the latch. The data from this read are not used for the signature but provide the necessary clock edge so that the start and stop edges can be detected. This is shown in Figure 7-16. In general, such problems are easily avoided if one takes the time to understand both the signature analyzer and the behavior of the system under test.

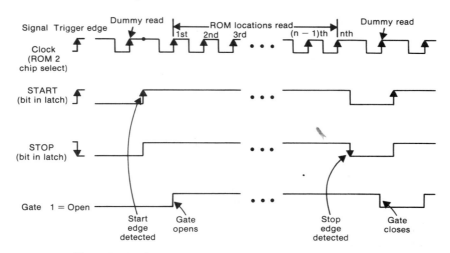

Figure 7-16:   Corrected ROM stimulus program timing diagram.

Device Testing Concepts

A typical microprocessor-based system will contain a variety of devices from memory components and control logic to digital and analog I/O for interfacing the system to the real world. Each device group has its own specific requirements for effective signature analysis application. Furthermore, some types of circuitry do not lend themselves to signature analysis very well, if at all. In the following paragraphs, we will look at the various device groups and how programmed stimulus relates to them [3].

ROMs

ROMs are one of the simplest types of devices to test. One merely has to check the outputs while applying all possible input possibilities. Because of this simplicity, ROMs can be effectively tested using free-run stimulus, as explained earlier. However, in a system containing many ROMs, performing a free-run test on each is both tedious and a waste of time. Once we have used free-run to verify the ROM containing the test routines, we can use programmed stimulus to test the other ROMs quickly and easily.

In the programmed approach, ROMs are tested using a combination of signature analysis and the functional testing techniques discussed in Chapter 4. As was explained earlier, ROMs can be verified by applying a checksum or CRC test to its contents and comparing the result to the expected value. Using this idea, we can develop a test routine that not only tests all the ROMs but which will tell us which ROM is bad. The flowchart for such a routine is shown in Figure 7-17.

In this routine, the measurement window is opened and the testing algorithm is performed on each ROM until a bad ROM is found or all ROMs have been tested.

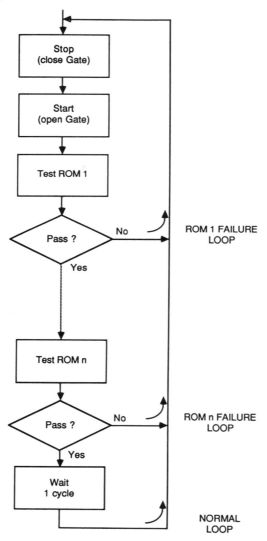

Figure 7-17: ROM test routine flowchart.

When this happens, the program will loop back and close the measurement window. What this does is create a measurement window whose length is dependent on which ROM (if any) is at fault.

The question now arises: Where do we place our data probe while running this test? The answer is: any convenient node that is at a constant logic 1. Since the data on such a node are constant, the signature produced will depend only on how long the measurement window is open for. Thus the signature will indicate whether the test completed successfully or how far it got before failing. A simple table of characteristic signatures can be provided to tell the operator which ROM was detected as "faulty." Again, it is worth emphasizing that a ROM test failure does not necessarily indicate a bad ROM chip. The problem could lie in supporting circuitry, such as bus buffers or enabling logic. Further node-by-node testing is still required to identify the source of the problem. However, the test serves to reduce the task to a manageable level by isolating the fault to a fairly small area. The corollary to this is that successful completion of the test verifies not only the ROMs but all support circuitry associated with them also. The only drawback to this scheme is that it finds only the first bad ROM. The fault must then be corrected before subsequent ROMs can be tested.

RAMs

As explained in Chapter 4, proper testing of RAM devices can be a complex and time-consuming process. In a system with a large amount of RAM, performing the various pattern sensitivity tests can take hours. Usually, such thoroughness is not necessary but even a series of basic tests, such as checkerboard and walking ones and zeros, can take several minutes. As such, it is not practical to perform node-by-node signature analysis on RAMs. However, we can combine functional testing with signature analysis using a loop-on-fail program structure as we did for ROMs.

If the system uses dynamic RAMs, the program must also test for proper operation of the refresh circuitry. A simple functional test would be to store data in the RAM, enter a wait loop to force the refresh circuitry to maintain the data, then check the stored data for any changes. Again, a loop-on-fail structure would yield a unique signature for refresh problems. For further testing, one could synchronize the signature analyzer to the refresh circuitry by connecting start/stop to the MSB of the refresh address and the clock line to the refresh clock. This is useful for identifying the faulty node in asynchronous refresh circuits implemented with discrete logic.

Decoding Circuits

It is generally not necessary to write specific test routines for decoding logic, as most can be adequately tested using free-running stimulus. In cases where decoding is not fully tested during free-run, as in an I/O-mapped decoding structure, the circuitry can be checked during the programmed stimulus for the devices they enable.

Interrupts

The interrupt structure of a system can range from a simple hard-wired connection between a device and a microprocessor interrupt input, to complex prioritized multiple-interrupt structures using programmable interrupt controllers. Whatever scheme is used, it is essential that any asynchronous circuits involved be synchronized or removed to allow proper control of the test situation. One possibility is to break the connection between the asynchronous circuitry and the microprocessor. The interrupt can then be triggered manually and the signature analysis interrupt service routine can synchronously test the circuitry associated with the interrupt.

Usually, signature analysis will require a different interrupt-handler routine than the one used in normal operation in order to provide meaningful stimulus to the circuitry. This can be accomplished in a couple of ways. One could replace the system ROM containing the interrupt handlers with a test ROM holding the signature analysis handlers. Or the normal handlers could check to see if the system was in normal or testing mode, then branch to the appropriate routine. The pros and cons for either implementation are basically the same as discussed earlier for overall programmed stimulus implementation.

In the case of multiple interrupt structures, the software should provide for selective disabling of interrupts so that one can be tested without the fear of interference from other interrupts. Signature analysis, unlike normal operation, does not allow for nesting interrupt handlers.

Keyboards

There are basically three types of keyboard circuits found in microprocessor-based systems: nonscanned, encoder scanned, and microprocessor scanned.

Nonscanned keyboards, often used in systems with only a few control keys, are relatively easy to test. A simple strategy is to use software to enable the keyboard input buffers and trace the signal with a logic probe. (Many signature analyzer data probes also function as logic probes.)

Encoder scanned keyboards are often untestable with signature analysis. This is because they generally operate asynchronously to the rest of the system, and the internal timing control signals are not available for use by the signature analyzer.

However, microprocessor scanned keyboards, like the one shown in Figure 7–18, can be tested using signature analysis. The test routine outputs patterns to the scanning latch and reads data from the input buffer. The signatures obtained will vary according to which key is closed. These can be documented in a table of good signatures for each key closure.

Displays

Displays come in many forms, from LEDs and seven-segment displays to CRT raster scan displays. Any type of display is intrinsically capable of providing clues to problems in its circuitry. A common practice is to exercise the display during power-up

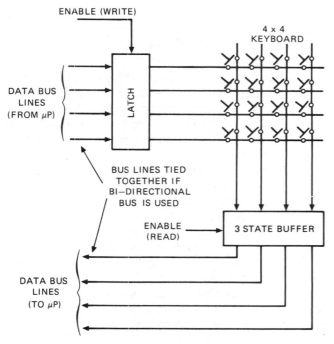

Figure 7-18: Microprocessor scanned keyboard. Courtesy of Hewlett-Packard Company.

self-tests, so that the operator can make a visual check of its operation.

If the display is totally under microprocessor control, it can be tested very easily by stimulating the various nodes and obtaining signatures. Many types of displays, though, are largely independent of the processor. Although this eases the burden on the processor during normal operation, it makes testing more difficult since such displays generally contain circuitry that is asynchronous to the kernel. In such cases, one may have to include hardware to force the display circuitry into sync with the processor, or else test it independently using timing signals from within the display logic to control the signature analyzer.

Input/Output Ports

I/O devices range from simple latches and buffers to programmable ports such as the Motorola 6821 or the Intel 8255. These devices are most easily tested if provision is made in the hardware for looping back outputs to inputs. The stimulus software can then write out, and read back, all possible bit patterns onto the data bus for signature gathering.

Multiprocessor Systems

A typical multiprocessor system will have a single processor for overall system control and one or more slave processors for performing specific tasks. Such systems will usually share the same bus structure to allow common access to the various devices. An example of this would be a system using an 8086 CPU for main control, an 8087 Numeric Data Processor for performing floating-point mathematical computations, and an 8089 I/O Processor for high-speed I/O transfers. Bus arbitration logic ensures that only one processor has control of the bus at a time.

Signature analysis cannot be used to provide an exhaustive functional test of the slave processors' internal instruction set any more than it can for the CPU. However, it can test the slave processor's ability to communicate over the common bus by utilizing the slave timing and control signals. For such testing, additional hardware may be required to prevent other processors from attempting to take control of the bus while the measurement window is open.

As an example, let us consider a typical direct memory access (DMA) device, a common feature in systems that require large amounts of data transfer between the system core and outlying peripherals such as disk drives. Figure 7–19 illustrates the handshaking process between the processor and the DMA controller.

Upon receiving a request for data transfer from a peripheral device (e.g., floppy disk controller), the DMA controller sends a *bus request* signal to the CPU. The DMA requires control of the bus so that it can transfer data directly between the disk controller and RAM. Upon receiving this signal, the processor will send setup information to the DMA controller and issue a *bus grant* signal, indicating release of bus control. The DMA signals acceptance of this by sending a *bus acknowledge* signal. During the time that the bus acknowledge is asserted, the DMA controller has control of the bus.

The bus acknowledge provides a convenient source for the analyzer start and stop signals. The system clock can be used for the analyzer clock since the DMA controller is a synchronous device. A typical test routine would provide for a known

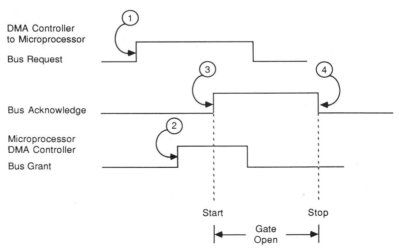

Figure 7–19: CPU-DMA Controller handshaking signals.

source of data and initiate the DMA process. The operation could then be tested by probing for signatures on the data bus [4].

Although much more could be said on the topic of programmed stimulus, we will stop here. The examples above are sufficient to give the production or service technician an insight into, and appreciation for, the varied and complex strategies that go into producing a troubleshooting approach which is both simple and effective.

7-5 APPLYING THE GENERIC APPROACH TO SIGNATURE ANALYSIS

In Chapter 3 we looked at a generic troubleshooting methodology that could be applied no matter what specific testing implementation was chosen. For review purposes, we can summarize this three-level approach as follows:

Level 1: Isolate the fault to a specific subsystem using functional tests.

Level 2: Isolate the fault to a particular node within that subsystem using any appropriate node-level troubleshooting equipment.

Level 3: Identify the source of the fault within the node as explained in Chapter 10.

In the case of traditional signature analysis, where the testing and stimulus are handled entirely within the UUT, we are forced to modify this approach somewhat. In such instances we require a certain amount of functional hardware to be able to execute the level 1 functional tests. If enough of the kernel is not working to permit these tests to be run, we must perform some level 2 and level 3 troubleshooting to get the kernel operational. Once the kernel is operating correctly, we can then return to our general methodology to expand the kernel in a systematic manner.

In the case where signature analysis is implemented using external stimulus, the original approach is still valid since we are providing a functional kernel outside the UUT. Thus the external tester can functionally test the UUT's own kernel as well as its other subsystems.

It should be noted that to this point we have assumed that the UUT is equipped to perform the functional tests required by the topmost level. If such capabilities have not been included, the task of implementing the three-level approach becomes more difficult. It then becomes the responsibility of the troubleshooter to write the necessary software, and implement it either by replacing the boot ROM or using an external tester. Unfortunately, this is not always possible because of lack of equipment or expertise. Without the ability to isolate faults within manageable blocks, then, the signature analysis process can become very tedious and slow. The top-down approach should therefore be an important precept not only for troubleshooters, but also for people involved in designing signature analysis into a product.

7-6 SIGNATURE ANALYSIS ENHANCEMENTS

In recent years, there have been three major developments in the signature analysis field: composite signatures, automatic signature comparison, and external stimulus systems. The first two allow for faster and more accurate troubleshooting, while the latter permits signature analysis to be used in systems that were not originally equipped for it. Let us now take a closer look at each of these developments.

Composite Signatures

Composite signature analysis was developed by Hewlett-Packard and is currently available in the HP 5006A signature analyzer. A *composite signature* is simply the sum of all individual signatures gathered to produce it. The aim of this development is to greatly reduce the number of signatures that the troubleshooter must reference in the debugging process. This, in turn, speeds up the analysis process and reduces the likelihood of human error.

A simple example will show how this works. Let us say that we wish to verify the address lines going to a particular IC. Using traditional signature analysis, the operator would place the probe on an address line, look at the display to see the signature, then look up what the expected signature is in a table of signatures or on an annotated schematic. If this line proved to be correct, the process would be repeated with the next address line, and so on.

Using the composite approach, the operator would place the probe on an address line, press the data probe switch to gather the signature for summation, and then move on to the next line. When all lines have been probed, the operator checks the displayed composite signature against the documented value. If the signature is correct, an entire chip's address bus has been verified using only one signature.

Suppose, however, that the composite signature obtained was incorrect? It is not necessary to reprobe all the lines individually to find the bad one. The HP 5006A stores the last 32 signatures gathered for individual inspection. The operator can simply scroll through the stack of signatures until the bad one is located. Hewlett-Packard estimates that between 5 and 35 minutes of debugging time can be saved per circuit board by using composite signature analysis.

Good composite signatures can be obtained from existing documentation simply by converting each individual signature to normal hexadecimal representation, summing the values, and converting the resultant sum back to standard signature representation. Carries beyond 16 bits are simply discarded. This process is illustrated in Figure 7–20.

We should note that composite signatures have a slightly higher chance of not detecting errors since there is a small probability that two bad signatures could cancel each other out in the sum. This probability increases with the number of individual signatures used to produce the composite. For this reason, it is recommended that composite signatures be limited to 20 signatures or less, where the probability of missing an error is negligible [5].

LINE	SIGNATURE	HEX
DØ	1 5 F 3	1 5 C 3
D1	2 7 H 9	2 7 D 9
D2	1 1 6 4	1 1 6 4
D3	C A P Ø	B A E Ø
D4	7 1 7 F	7 1 7 C
D5	4 H A 8	4 D A 8
D6	3 C 2 5	3 B 2 5
D7	8 1 A U	+ 8 1 A F

Total ... ②8 5 D 8

Discard

Composite Signature 8 5 H 8

Figure 7-20: Generating a composite signature.

Automatic Signature Comparison

Automatic signature comparison (ASC) refers to a test system's capability to verify whether a signature is good or bad without the need for the operator to check the value against documentation. This ability eliminates one of the biggest complaints about signature analysis: the extensive documentation required. Traditional signature analysis documentation is both cumbersome and costly to produce. There is also the risk of human error, both typographical and comparitive, which it introduces into the diagnostic process. By removing or lessening the human involvement in the verification process, ASC makes signature analysis faster, less expensive, and more accurate.

How this process is implemented varies between manufacturers. The following systems that use ASC illustrate this.

Data I/O Corporation calls their process *Signature Verification* and uses it in their 1310A Signature Verifier. This process differs slightly from the industry standard in that it uses a 24-bit signature consisting of the standard 16-bit signature and an additional 8-bit signature. Only the standard signature is displayed, but the internal comparison circuitry compares all 24 bits. Signature information is stored in removable EPROM modules that plug into the front of the unit.

Signature gathering from a good unit must be done manually. The operator places the probe on the desired node and presses the STORE button on the front panel twice. This stores the signature in the EPROM module. Up to 500 signatures can be stored in an EPROM module. The system will not store V_{cc} or ground signatures.

When troubleshooting, the unit can be set for manual or automatic operation. The *manual mode* is basically the same as a normal signature analyzer. In *automatic mode,* the unit will check the obtained signature against the signatures stored in the module. If a match is found, the FOUND LED on the data probe is lit and a short beep is sounded. In addition, if the signature has been obtained before (within the last 500 samples), the unit will beep twice. This alerts the operator to the possibility that the probe was inadvertently placed on the same pin twice. If the signature obtained is not found in the stored values, the NOT FOUND LED is lit and a long beep is sounded.

Hewlett-Packard offers a more sophisticated (and expensive) system in the 55005A Logic Troubleshooting System. It consists of an HP-85 personal computer and an HP 5005B Signature Multimeter connected over an HP-IB interface bus. The HP 5005B functions as a "front-end" unit for obtaining the signatures. The actual ASC is implemented within the HP-85 using specialized software.

In addition to storing signature information, the system also can hold data concerning the circuit topology: that is, whether a node is an input or an output, and which device pins are connected together on each node. This information is used for the guided testing mode of operation. Each data base can hold signature and circuit topology information for 576 nodes. Permanent storage is on cassette tape or floppy disk with each being able to store typically 20 to 30 data bases.

Control of the system is provided through softkeys and menu displays which guide the operator through the functions. The two major functional modes are LEARN and PROBE, with additional functions provided for listing data bases and managing data base files.

The LEARN mode allows the operator to collect and edit node information, and specify test setup conditions, for a particular test data base. Node information can be gathered from a good unit using the signature multimeter or typed in manually from existing documentation. Whether in the LEARN or PROBE mode, the operator is not allowed to proceed until the characteristic V_{cc} signature has been checked to ensure proper setup conditions. When collecting signatures for storage, duplicate measurements are flagged to alert to a possible misprobe. The operator can then append the pin to a previous node, identify it as a separate node with the same signature, or redo the measurement in case of a misprobe.

In the PROBE mode, the system assists the operator in troubleshooting in much the same manner as we have looked at in this book. When a faulty node is detected, the system identifies the device whose output is driving the node, and directs the operator to probe the inputs for that device. In this way, the operator can backtrace through the system to the source of the fault without having to refer to schematics. The system also provides a printed report of the trace history and the faulty node [6].

The reader should note that the troubleshooting approach outlined earlier in this chapter does not change when using these instruments. Rather, the speed and accuracy of that approach is enhanced, since the operator is freed from the mundane aspects of the analysis and so can concentrate more on intelligently isolating the fault source.

Signature Analysis through External Stimulus

Given the effectiveness of signature analysis in a production or service depot environment, it is unfortunate that most microprocessor-based products on the market today are not equipped for providing signature analysis stimulus. However, in most cases, signature analysis capabilities can be retrofitted into such products using some form of external stimulus.

The simplest external stimulus device is a free-run test fixture which can be built in the lab for only a few dollars. Although the specific design will vary depending on the microprocessor used, the general idea of the test fixture is to provide a means of breaking the data bus so that the processor can cycle through its address field.

Figure 7-21 shows how this can be implemented for a 6800-based system. In this design, the microprocessor from the UUT plugs into the test fixture, which, in turn, plugs into the processor socket.

The address and most of the control lines are simply fed straight back into the UUT. The data bus, though, is not fed through, and a NOP instruction is hardwired onto the data pins of the processor. Also, any asynchronous inputs, such as $\overline{\text{HALT}}$ and $\overline{\text{IRQ}}$, are tied off to their nonactive levels to prevent unwanted interruptions. Essentially, we are doing the same thing as when we enable the built-in stimulus for free-running.

Of course, the effectiveness of this test fixture is limited to those portions of the kernel which can be diagnosed using free-run stimulus. The majority of the UUT is still out of reach of signature analysis. However, if the UUT already contains some functional testing capabilities for outlying circuitry, the test fixture can be a cheap solution to getting enough of the system working to run these tests. Readers interested in building test fixtures for a variety of 8-bit processors should consult an article by Andrew Stefanski [7].

For full stimulus capabilities, a much more elaborate tester is needed. The tester must be equipped to provide custom-programmed stimulus in addition to free-run,

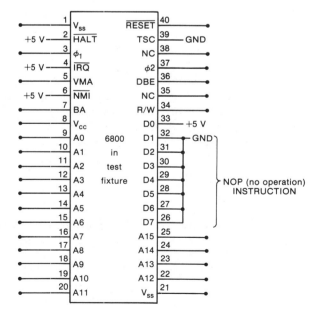

— To corresponding pin in UUT socket

Figure 7-21: 6800 free-run test fixture. Courtesy of Hewlett-Packard Company.

and should provide some built-in functional tests for ROM and RAM. Up until the early 1980s, Hewlett-Packard, Data I/O Corporation, and Millenium Systems all marketed some type of external stimulus system for signature analysis. Unfortunately, these products are no longer supplied by these companies.

However, the void left by the demise of these testers appears to have been filled by the introduction of a new product from Applied Microsystems Corporation. The ET–2000 Micro Trouble Shooter can best be described as a hybrid test system, combining features such as those found in the Fluke 9000 series, with signature analysis and even some node-level analysis, as discussed in Chapter 10. Some of the features offered by this system include:

1. Built-in bus, ROM, and RAM tests
2. Signature analysis, including external stimulus
3. Real-time execution of UUT or custom test code
4. A short-circuit locator that tracks down the physical cause of the short
5. A process dubbed Signal Identification, which identifies all address, data, and control signals, or combination of, when probed by the operator

Retrofitting signature analysis to a product offers the same advantages as built-in analysis capabilities. Once implemented, it is a quick and effective tool for semiskilled personnel to debug microprocessor-based systems. However, it, too, requires time and expertise to implement properly and one must decide if the volume of testing warrants the cost of this development.

7-7 SUMMARY

Signature analysis applies the old waveform comparison techniques of the analog world to modern microprocessor systems. Although complex in design, its simplicity at the debugging level makes it a cost-effective means for troubleshooting microprocessor-based systems in a high-volume environment. Recently introduced enhancements have served to improve the speed and accuracy of this approach.

REFERENCES

1. Frohwerk, Robert, *Signature Analysis: A New Digital Field Service Method,* Application Note 222-2, Application Articles on Signature Analysis, Hewlett-Packard Co., Palo Alto, CA.

2. *Guidelines for Signature Analysis,* Application Note 222-4, Hewlett-Packard Co., Palo Alto, CA.

3. *A Designer's Guide to Signature Analysis,* Application Note 222, Hewlett-Packard Co., Palo Alto, CA.

4. Robinson, J. B., *Modern Digital Troubleshooting,* Data I/O Corporation, Redmond, WA.

5. *Troubleshooting with Composite Signatures,* Application Note 222–6, Hewlett-Packard Co., Palo Alto, CA.

6. *Increasing Productivity in Manufacturing and Service with a Logic Troubleshooting System,* Application Note 222–5, Hewlett-Packard Co., Palo Alto, CA.

7. Stefanski, Andrew, *Free Running Signature Analysis Simplifies Troubleshooting,* Application Note 222–2, Application Articles on Signature Analysis, Hewlett-Packard Co., Palo Alto, CA.

8

INTRODUCTION TO LOGIC ANALYZERS

Logic analyzers are oscilloscope-like instruments that provide a visual representation of the signal flow activity in a system. They permit the user to troubleshoot either hardware faults or software faults. In the state mode, the user can track program flow and view software execution directly on the screen. This permits checking for flaws in program logic as well as for the correct execution of instructions, memory and I/O reads and writes, and so on. In the timing mode, the user can view logic signal activity on system buses and search for hardware-related problems such as noise glitches, skewed signals, intermittent timing failures, and other extraneous conditions that may foul system operation. It is this ability to debug and integrate both facets of system operation that is the real strength of logic analyzers, and which makes them an almost indispensable tool in the product development environment. Efficient use of a logic analyzer requires considerable system knowledge and skill on the part of the user.

Logic analyzers are most useful if the kernel of the system under test is functional and able to execute software. However, they can be used to debug a faulty kernel even though not ideally suited to such a task. In Chapter 9 we look at some techniques for doing this.

8-1 THE BASIC LOGIC ANALYZER

Figure 8-1 shows typical logic analyzer architecture. The unit consists of a data acquisition subsystem, one or more memories, trigger logic, a formatter, and a display subsection plus operator controls.

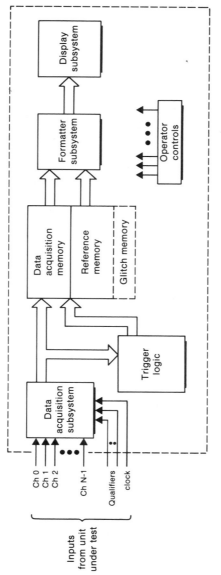

Figure 8–1: Logic Analyzer architecture.

In use, the analyzer is connected to the system under test by mechanical probes as depicted in Figure 8-2(a). The UUT is then started and data are gathered in real time during normal system operation as depicted symbolically in part (c). Signals of interest include address, data, and control. To better appreciate the use and limitations of the analyzer, let us consider each of the blocks of Figure 8-1 in more detail.

Data Acquisition Subsystem

The data acquisition subsystem captures and conditions data for storage. It takes one sample on each channel for every cycle of the sampling clock (which may come from the UUT or be internally generated) as depicted in Figure 8-2(c). The sample is digitized and stored in the data acquisition memory as a corresponding set of 1s and 0s. In most analyzers, the digitization consists of a comparison of the input signal against a predefined threshold. Signals higher than the threshold are stored as logic 1; signals lower than the threshold are stored as logic 0. Some analyzers permit the user to specify standard logic family thresholds such as TTL or to specify the threshold quantitatively as a voltage level.

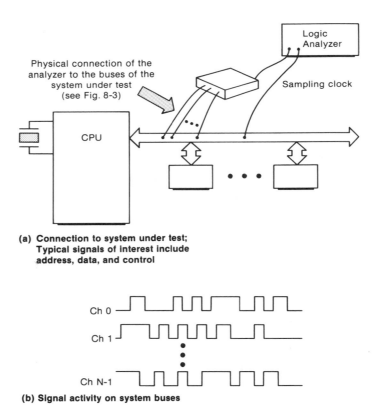

(a) **Connection to system under test; Typical signals of interest include address, data, and control**

(b) **Signal activity on system buses**

Figure 8-2: Data is clocked into the analyzer memory for analysis.

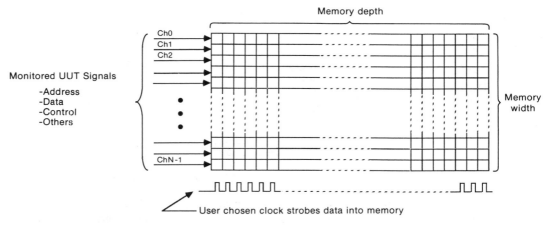

(c) Symbolic representation of analyzer memory

Figure 8-2   (Contd.)

Several schemes for interconnecting logic analyzers to the unit under test are illustrated in Figure 8-3. Whereas early analyzers provided only the simple clip set depicted in part (a), modern analyzers generally provide mass connection alternatives such as depicted in parts (b) and (c). Although the clip set scheme provides generality (the user has to individually connect clips to signal points and thus the function of

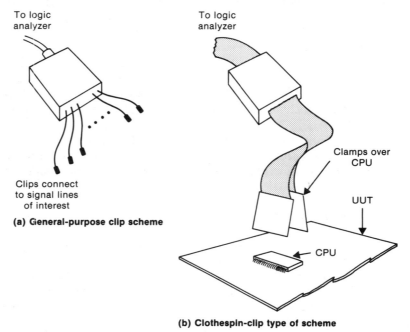

Figure 8-3:   Various schemes for connecting the analyzer to the UUT.

To logic
analyzer

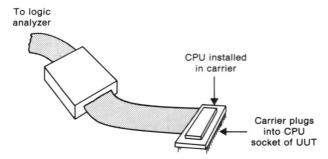

CPU installed
in carrier

Carrier plugs
into CPU
socket of UUT

(c) Carrier socket scheme   **Figure 8-3**   (Contd.)

each line is defined by the user), it is generally impractical for the wide-word-size analyzers now in use. The newer schemes of parts (b) and (c) speed and ease the interconnection task by tailoring the connection to the pin-outs of the target processor, automatically assigning inputs as address, data, and control. Although they lack generality, they provide great convenience for accessing signals at the CPU. For capturing signals not available at the CPU socket however, clip sets are still necessary.

Analyzer Memories

The primary memory is the data acquisition memory. It is used to store test data samples. The reference memory (if provided) permits saving of historical data (i.e., a previous sample) for future comparisons. This feature permits investigation of intermittent phenomena such as noise glitches[1] by permitting comparisons of successive captures of the same data stream.

Memory size is quantitatively described in terms of its width (number of channels of data that can be stored) and its depth (number of samples per channel that can be saved). Memory widths range from eight channels by 256 words on low-end products to 64 channels (or more) by several thousand words for top-of-the-line models.

Sometimes a third memory is provided for storing glitch data.[2] Data from this memory are merged with data from the acquisition memory during display to permit observation of short-duration glitches for use in investigating hardware-related problems.

The User Interface

User interaction with the analyzer is by console keys. Most modern analyzers use a menu-based scheme where operational choices (test parameters, trigger conditions, sampling intervals, etc.) are displayed on the screen and the operator selects options according to the needs of the test by pressing the appropriate keys. Some higher-price models use a disk operating system where the menu of operating choices is kept.

[1]A glitch is a short anomaly on an input which may be faster than the sample period of the analyzer.

[2]An alternative method of dealing with glitches is through the use of glitch latch circuitry. Both methods are discussed in Chapter 9.

The Format and Display Subsystem

Modern analyzers provide an integral CRT for display of captured data. Although there are several possible modes of display available, we consider here only the basic timing and state display modes. Higher-priced models may include an optional printer as well.

Timing display mode.   In this mode, the user visualizes system activity as a set of logic signals on system buses and uses the analyzer much like a multichannel oscilloscope. This is depicted in Figure 8-4. Note that since only 1s and 0s are stored during data capture, electrical characteristics (such as signal rise and fall times) are lost. Thus the waveforms look like idealized textbook waveforms. Note the easy identification of the noise glitch.[3] The time display format is most useful for investigating hardware-related problems.

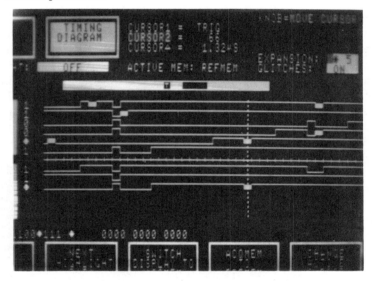

Figure 8-4:   Timing mode display is useful for signal investigation.

State display format.   In this mode, the user visualizes system activity as a sequence of binary states representing the programmed operation of the processor. The basic concept is illustrated in Figure 8-5(a). Here captured data are shown as a series of binary words with each bit position corresponding to an input line (channel) with the bit value being the logic level of the corresponding line when it is sampled. The state diagram can be thought of as a timing diagram rotated by 90 degrees as in part (b).

The binary representation of Figure 8-5(a) is inconvenient and is now seldom used—instead, modern analyzers convert and display captured data in hexadecimal

[3]Using the analyzer shown, the glitch is easily identified. However, not all analyzers are this good at highlighting glitch problems. This is considered in more detail in Chapter 9.

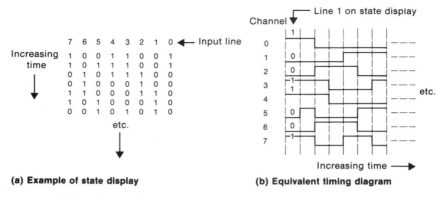

(a) Example of state display

(b) Equivalent timing diagram

Figure 8–5: Relationship between state and timing representations.

or octal format. However, such representations are still inconvenient, as the operator must mentally convert codes to processor mnemonics to understand the logic of the program. For this reason, most analyzers also incorporate disassemblers to automatically translate binary codes to mnemonic codes. The resulting display is much more meaningful, as illustrated in Figure 8–6. Note that signal line inputs have been grouped according to function (address and data). Note also that hex numbers are used where appropriate, as for example to represent addresses. Regardless of the display mode, a scrolling feature provides for rolling the display to permit examination of portions of the captured data not currently on the screen.

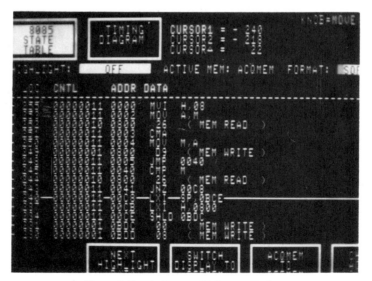

Figure 8–6: A disassembled state display.

8-2 TRIGGERING

The constant flow of signals over system buses presents the user with far more information than can be handled. With present analyzers capable of processing many megabytes per second, capturing and reviewing any more than a small portion of this data stream becomes impractical. For this reason, logic analyzers permit the user to select from the data stream only that portion of signal flow activity that is of interest to the problem at hand. The "trigger" facility of the analyzer implements this capability. Triggering is used to define when the analyzer should start the capture process (or stop it).

To understand the concept of triggering, consider Figure 8-7. Shown symbolically is system bus activity from start of execution to end of execution. Somewhere in here lies the data that we want to examine. To capture this data, we define a "trigger event"—a condition or set of conditions that must exist on the system buses to start or stop the capture process. During setup, the user arms the analyzer by keying in the trigger conditions via the operator's console; during test, the analyzer monitors the system buses watching for the defined trigger event to occur. When the trigger event is detected, data capture is effected. Thus, in its simplest form, a trigger is a comparison of acquired data against a reference value set by the user during setup.

There are two basic trigger modes, referred to as pretrigger and posttrigger, respectively. These are illustrated in Figure 8-7. Note that in both cases, the amount of data retained by the analyzer is equal to the depth of its memory.

1. *Pretrigger.* This is the dominant mode by far and is illustrated in Figure 8-7(b). In this mode, the analyzer begins to capture data as soon as the system is started and continues to capture data until the trigger event is encountered. At this point, capture ceases. Data is retained equal to the depth of memory. This provides the user with a record of UUT execution history leading up to the trigger event. If a fault point is selected for the trigger, the prefault data capture may provide some clue as to why the fault actually occurred.

2. *Posttrigger.* In this mode, data capture starts when the trigger event is encountered.[4] In this case, the record shows the system's execution history following the trigger point. If a fault point is selected for the trigger, the record will show postfault system behavior (i.e., what effect the fault had on subsequent system operation).

Center Triggering

Most modern analyzers combine the two modes so that the trigger point can be centered and execution history preceding and following the trigger point displayed. Again, by choosing a faulty system operation as the trigger event, the user can observe operational symptoms leading up to the fault as well as the system's response to the

[4]This trigger mode is much like that provided on oscilloscopes.

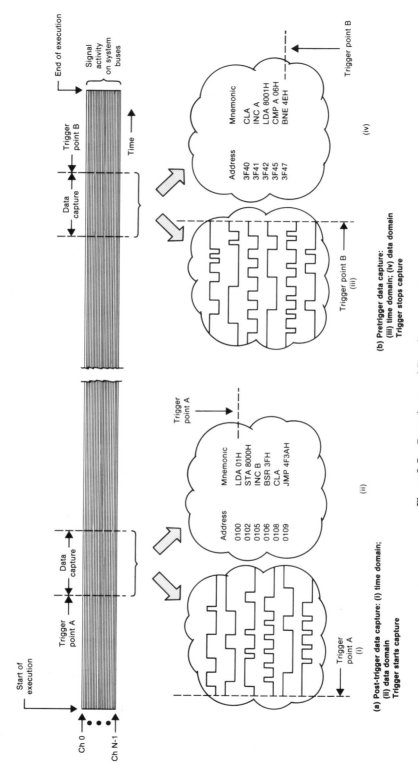

Figure 8-7: Post-trigger and Pre-trigger concept.

**(a) Post-trigger data capture: (i) time domain;
(ii) data domain
Trigger starts capture**

**(b) Pretrigger data capture:
(iii) time domain; (iv) data domain
Trigger stops capture**

198

conditions created by the fault. Hopefully, from this information, the nature of the fault can be deduced. This is the method of logic analysis.

One of the simplest trigger conditions of practical interest is the occurrence of some specific bit pattern on some set of bus lines such as a particular address or data word (bit pattern recognition). For example, analyzers are often used to track program execution from startup to some particular address in the program. To achieve such a capture, the operator selects the desired address as the trigger and uses the pretrigger mode. The system is then started and data capture commences. When the address is reached, capture ceases and the results appear on the screen.[5]

Don't-Care Conditions

When defining a trigger condition, we sometimes are interested only in matching specific bits or groups of bits. Others may not be important. To handle this situation, most analyzers permit "don't-care" specifications. These permit the user to tell the trigger hardware that any value (high or low) will satisfy the trigger condition. Usually, don't-care conditions are represented by the letter X.

Modern logic analyzers provide a host of triggering capabilities, ranging from the relatively simple offerings of low-cost analyzers to ultrasophisticated capabilities of top-of-the-line models. Features include simple combinational triggering (bit pattern recognition as described above), the ability to trigger on the Nth occurrence of an address (for investigating software loops), to delay capture until N clock cycles after the trigger event (delay by clock), to trigger on some complex Boolean combination of logic patterns on buses, to trigger only when certain sequences of events occur, and so on. Such capabilities permit great selectivity in data capture (to help unravel the complexities of modern software) and are discussed and illustrated in Chapter 9.

8-3 DATA SAMPLING

As noted in Figure 8-2(c), data are clocked into the system via a sample clock. The source of this clock will be internal or external, depending on whether data are being gathered synchronously or asynchronously.

Asynchronous Clocking

This mode is used for time-domain analysis. Sampling is via a free-running clock internal to the analyzer, and hence it is not synchronized to the UUT clock. Sampling intervals are user selectable and usually range from nanoseconds to hundreds of milliseconds, depending on the needs of the application. This is detailed in Chapter 9. The display here is presented as a timing diagram.

[5]Data retained will, of course, only equal the memory size of the analyzer.

Synchronous Clocking

This mode is used for data-domain analysis. Here we are interested in monitoring sequential machine states—that is, the analyzer must be able to emulate the read cycle of the processor. Since data are read by the analyzer much as they are read by the UUT processor during normal operation, the sample clock must be perfectly synchronized to the UUT clock. For this reason, it is derived from the unit under test using the clock input depicted in Figures 8-1 and 8-2. During setup, the user connects the analyzer clock input to the desired UUT clock source (such as E for the 6809 or $\overline{WR}$ or $\overline{RD}$ for the 8085 and so on), then arms the analyzer to sample on the appropriate clock transition (low to high or high to low). This is illustrated in Example 8-1.

Example 8-1: A Simple Synchronous Clock Example

To illustrate, assume that we want to track program execution but only want to gather and display data for read cycles. To do this, connect the analyzer clock input to the read clock of the UUT. To illustrate, consider the Z80 system of Figure 8-8. Here we have connected the analyzer clock input to the system READ signal $\overline{RD}$. Via operator controls, specify the rising edge for the clock. Now, since data are gathered only on the rising edge of $\overline{RD}$, only read-cycle data will be captured—signal activity for all other cycles is simply ignored.

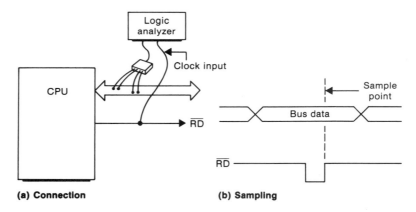

Figure 8-8: Capturing Read cycles.

Multiple clocks.   Depending on the sophistication of the analyzer, additional clock inputs may be provided (some analyzers provide up to a dozen or so). With multiple clock capability, the user is able to define more precisely the data to be captured. Typically, the user can specify some Boolean (or other) combination of the various clock inputs as the equivalent clocking condition. This is illustrated in Example 8-2 for a two-clock example.

Example 8-2: Boolean Combination of Clocks

To illustrate, assume an Intel-type clock scheme (clocks $\overline{RD}$ and $\overline{WR}$). Further assume that we want to capture data for both reads and writes. To effect this, connect one clock to the read clock ($\overline{\text{RD}}$) of the unit under test, and the second to its write clock ($\overline{\text{WR}}$). Set the active edge for each, and specify the logical OR of the two clocks. Since data are gathered when $\overline{\text{RD}}$ goes high or when $\overline{\text{WR}}$ goes high, capture is effected for both read cycles and write cycles.

Clock qualifications.   Many data that appear on system buses during test may not be relevant to the problem under consideration and if gathered, forces the user to sift through quantities of extraneous material to find what is really wanted. In addition, the unwanted data take up valuable memory space. To circumvent these problems, the user is able to "qualify" the clock with other system events so that only those phenomena of interest are actually recorded. To implement this capability, clock qualifier inputs (as depicted in Figure 8–1) are provided. During setup, the user connects these qualifiers to the appropriate signal points in the UUT and via the setup menu, defines which clocks are to be qualified as well as how they are to be qualified.

Example 8–3: Clock Qualification

For example, suppose that we want to capture input data from a specific I/O port during read cycles. To illustrate, assume a Z80 system with a PIO. Connect the clock to the UUT's $\overline{\text{RD}}$ clock, select rising edge clocking, then qualify it by the select signal of the port as depicted in Figure 8–9. Specify active low for the qualification signal via the setup menu. For the example illustrated, data are gathered only when the port is selected AND a read cycle occurs.

The difference in philosophy between the two sampling approaches (synchronous and asynchronous) described above can be traced to the difference in philosophy between the needs of the hardware user and the needs of the software user. The hardware user is interested in observing timing waveforms exactly as they occur, complete with noise glitches, timing skew, and other spurious phenomena that may be present. Thus the measurement must faithfully capture, store, and reproduce these data. The software user, on the other hand, only wants the analyzer to see what the CPU sees—thus the analyzer need only sample data from the bus at the instant of clock transitions just as does the normal CPU. Anything that occurs on the buses between clock transitions is of no interest in this mode.

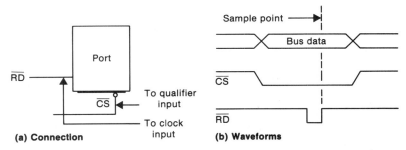

(a) Connection   **(b) Waveforms**

Figure 8–9:   Illustrating clock qualification. Here, $\overline{\text{RD}}$ is qualified by $\overline{\text{CS}}$. Data will only be stored when $\overline{\text{CS}}$ is low.

8-4 TROUBLESHOOTING WITH A LOGIC ANALYZER

When faced with a malfunctioning system, it may not be apparent at the outset whether the problem is software based or hardware based. Regardless of the source of the problem, however, faulty operation generally manifests itself as a bad set of data on system buses. We will therefore begin by considering the use of the analyzer in the state-domain mode, which offers the operator the better overall picture of this activity.

Troubleshooting Using the State-Domain Mode

In principle, troubleshooting using the state-domain mode is straightforward—with the analyzer connected to the system under test, execution is started and a sample of data is captured. By comparing the actual system behavior (as displayed on the analyzer screen) against that expected, the point at which the problem appears can be found. This is illustrated in Figure 8-10. Part (a) shows the actual program as

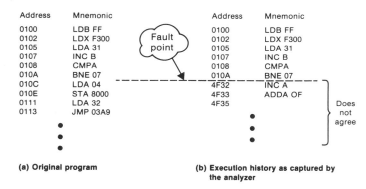

(a) Original program

(b) Execution history as captured by the analyzer

Figure 8-10:   Illustrating a fault capture in the execution history.

it is written. If no faults (in software or hardware) exist, execution will proceed exactly as indicated. If, however, a fault occurs, execution may depart from the expected sequence. In this example, the fault causes execution to get lost as in part (b).[6] The problem may be due to software or hardware. At this point, we do not know. In any event, the record clearly indicates a fault.

Although the concept above is simple in principle, there are many practical difficulties that must not be underestimated. First, as discussed in Chapter 1, microprocessors contain many feedback paths that cause errors to spread throughout the system, propagating through good and bad circuits alike, corrupting data on circuit nodes in an unpredictable fashion as depicted symbolically in Figure 8-11. Second, most programs contain software loops, subroutines, and so on, and the point

[6]Following the fault indicated in Figure 8-10(b), we are more likely to encounter an unintelligible jumble rather than a neat, recognizable program sequence as indicated.

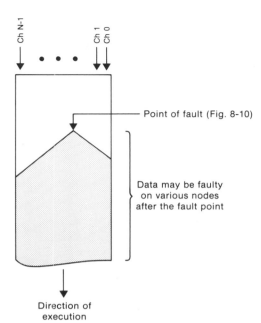

Point of fault (Fig. 8-10)

Data may be faulty
on various nodes
after the fault point

Direction of
execution

Figure 8-11: Characteristic bus failure pattern. Node data becomes corrupted as effect of the fault spreads.

at which a fault is actually detected in the program may be far removed in time from the failure (hardware or software) that created the error in the first place. Third, we may not know at the outset whether the problem observed is due to a hardware fault or a software fault and one of the things we must do is try to establish which it is.

To capture the fault point and surrounding data for analysis, we must set a trigger point. If we have some idea where to begin (as we often do), we can select the trigger point accordingly. If we do not, we may have to record many iterations of data capture before a successful capture is effected. In some cases, it is simply a matter of progressively moving the trigger point forward (or backward) until it is close enough to the fault point that the data capture encompasses it. The process is depicted symbolically in Figure 8-12.

In other cases, the solution is not as simple and it may be necessary to capture and analyze many samples before the user has sufficient understanding of what is going on in the target system to make an intelligent judgment and selection of a suitable trigger condition. This is one of the practical difficulties inherent in using a logic analyzer. Some practical techniques for software debugging will be explained and illustrated in Chapter 9.

Troubleshooting Using the Timing Analysis Mode

To investigate hardware-related phenomena, we can switch to the timing analysis mode. The display in this case shows activity on system buses as voltage versus time waveforms and permits the troubleshooter to look for hardware problems such as

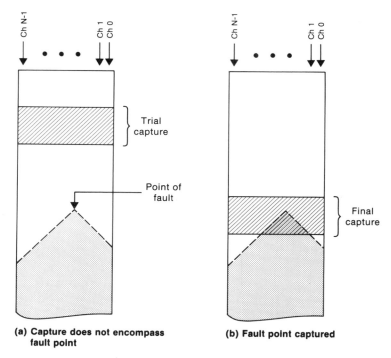

(a) Capture does not encompass fault point

(b) Fault point captured

Figure 8-12: Symbolic representation of logic analyzer troubleshooting strategy. Captured data is displayed as in Figure 8-10. Compare against documentation to reveal fault point.

stuck nodes, timing skew, noise, and other glitches that may have an adverse effect on system operation. Triggering is used here to select a small "window" of data for analysis, as depicted in Figure 8-7. This provides the user with a "snapshot" of system activity on many buses simultaneously in and about the possible fault point. Again, details are discussed in Chapter 9.

8-5 SOME PERFORMANCE AND QUALITY CONSIDERATIONS

To intelligently select a logic analyzer requires more than just an understanding of operation and troubleshooting principles as discussed above. In practice, the performance of an analyzer and how it affects the unit under test is dependent on several quality factors. An appreciation of these factors is essential if the buyer wishes to select an analyzer that suits the needs of the application without investing in sophisticated capabilities that will never be needed.

Interfacing

The interfacing capabilities of a logic analyzer should be one of the considerations when choosing a machine. The type of interface required varies with the application. Timing analysis generally requires the ability to probe anywhere in the circuit, so discrete test clips are a necessity. Groupings of about 10 clips on a pod allow this flexibility while still making the interconnection task manageable and uncluttered. State analysis, on the other hand, is usually concerned with signals at the microprocessor and so, an easy method of mass connection to all these lines is desirable. This is usually done through a probe that clips over the processor, or which plugs into the microprocessor socket as shown in Figure 8-3.

Whichever scheme is used, it is important that the probes affect the unit under test as little as possible. Good-quality probes will have high input impedance and low capacitance. Poor probes can limit the acquisition speed of the analyzer and may even affect the operation of the UUT through excessive loading or by increasing signal rise and fall times.

Speed

An important performance factor in a logic analyzer is its maximum data sampling rate. In literature, this value is usually given as a frequency. Thus a 100-MHz analyzer can sample data no faster than every 10 ns. Analyzer speeds range from 20 MHz to over 500 MHz.

Generally, timing analysis requires higher sampling rates than does state analysis. Timing analysis requires high speed to provide the necessary resolution in display of high-speed signals. This is discussed further in Chapter 9. State analysis, by comparison, need only meet the cycle time of the processor being used since it is being operated synchronously with that processor's clocking (which, by comparison, is relatively slow).

Modern analyzer design reflects the fact that the operator will generally want to use the analyzer for both timing and state analysis, sometimes interactively. Generally, applications require a greater number of channels for state analysis than for timing analysis. Thus a common practice is to provide high-speed capability on only some of the channels. This provides the operator with the resolution required for hardware analysis without inflating the cost by unnecessarily providing this capability on all channels.

Channel Width

Another criterion for consideration is the number of channels that can be supported by the analyzer. Enough capacity to monitor all address, data, and control lines are essential for effective analysis. In addition to the number of inputs available, the user must also consider the number of channels that can be displayed. The number of channels available varies from eight on very simple analyzers to greater than 64 on more elaborate machines. In general, 32 channels are suitable for analyzing 8-bit systems and 48 channels for 16-bit systems.

Trigger Complexity and Clock Qualification

Another important criterion is the available trigger and clock qualification capability. Being able to capture and display exactly what is wanted is greatly simplified if the analyzer provides powerful and easy-to-use features that let the user discriminate between what is to be recorded and what is not. Such capabilities can reduce the amount of memory needed, as much less data need be saved when it is well qualified. To effect this discrimination, many modern analyzers provide a number of clocks and qualifiers and permit the user to specify complex Boolean or other combinations across them in conjunction with sequential, multilevel occurrences of triggering conditions as discussed in Chapter 9.

Generally, requirements for timing analysis are much simpler than for state analysis. This idea is discussed in detail in Chapter 9.

Memory Depth

When selecting a logic analyzer, memory size is one of the most visible parameters. Obviously, the more memory an analyzer has, the more data that can be collected. However, as noted above, size alone is not the only criterion; the precision with which data capture and storage can be effected is also important. In general, flexibility in clocking and triggering can reduce the amount of memory actually needed, since the unit can be made more selective in what it stores.

A reasonably large memory is still desirable, though, especially in the initial stages of investigation when we are attempting to localize the problem and require data in quantity for rough analysis. Later, more selective triggering can be used to provide quality data for fine analysis. Memory sizes below 512 words are generally constrictive to most applications.

8-6 SUMMARY

Logic analyzers provide powerful test and measurement capabilities not found on other microprocessor system troubleshooting tools. Their interactive testing capability makes possible a logical process of elimination that helps distinguish between hardware and software problems, and ultimately leads to their solution. In this chapter we have introduced some of the basic ideas; in Chapter 9 we extend the details and illustrate them via selected examples.

REFERENCES

1. Pine, Ken, *A Logic Analyzer Primer,* Dolch Logic Instruments, San Jose, CA.
2. Cannon, Don L., *Understanding Digital Troubleshooting,* Texas Instruments Inc., Information Publishing Center, Dallas, TX, 1984.
3. *Hands-On Troubleshooting Microprocessor Systems* (Course Notes), Integrated Computer Systems, Santa Monica, CA.

9

TROUBLESHOOTING WITH LOGIC ANALYZERS

In Chapter 8, we looked in general terms at what a logic analyzer is and what it can do. In this chapter we expand on these ideas to give a more detailed picture of logic analyzers and how they are used to diagnose some common problems. This chapter is divided into three main sections. The first two sections will look at timing analysis and state analysis, with emphasis on practical operating details and examples of their uses. The final section shows how the logic analyzer can be used to debug some typical faults in the kernel of a microcomputer system.

The examples in this chapter were prepared using a Tektronix 1240 logic analyzer with 8085 disassembly, and a simple 8085-based microcomputer. As such, most of the details regarding setup, triggering, and so on, will be directly applicable only to this analyzer. However, most of the features discussed, or a variation of them, can be found on comparable analyzers from other manufacturers. Indeed, other analyzers may have features that allow a problem to be approached in a simpler fashion than shown here. The examples will be presented in as general a manner as possible, so that the reader can apply the underlying principles to whatever analyzer he or she may have.

9-1 LOGIC TIMING ANALYSIS

Logic timing analysis is used primarily for identifying hardware faults in computer systems at the development stage. It is here that one encounters the types of faults for which logic timing analyzers are most useful in identifying. These faults include timing problems between bus devices, noise glitches, and level-related problems. We look at each of these problems in detail shortly.

In Chapter 8 we discussed, in general terms, the ideas of clocking, triggering, and data storage. Let us now look at these items as they pertain to timing analysis.

Clocking

Timing analysis sampling is done using the logic analyzer's internal asynchronous clock to build up a picture of the signal waveform. A general rule is to use a clock rate 10 times the clock rate of the signals under test. If a slower rate is used, the resolution of the displayed waveforms suffers since the uncertainty in the position of the signal edges becomes significant. This is demonstrated in Figure 9-1. In the diagram we see that an inaccurate representation of the signals is produced when the internal sampling rate approaches the clock rate of the system under test. However,

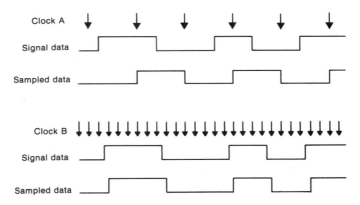

Figure 9-1:   Waveform accuracy at different clock speeds.

we must be careful not to choose too high a clock rate also. At too high a rate, the increase in resolution is offset by a reduction in the amount of data we are able to capture due to memory limitations. In practice, trial and error is often used to get an optimum balance. However, the operator should be aware that there will always be some uncertainty in the position of the signal edge.

The accuracy of the displayed waveforms is also affected by skew. Skew is caused by differences in propagation speeds between the various channels of the analyzer. This is illustrated in Figure 9-2. In the diagram, two simultaneous signal edges appear to occur at different times because of differences in propagation through the analyzer's probe set. Generally, skew is on the order of 1 to 2 ns. Because of these factors, there is an inherent possibility of a single clock period error in the position of any edge.

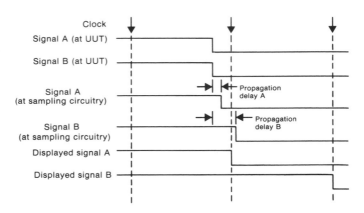

Figure 9-2: Skew in displayed waveforms.

Triggering

Triggering for timing analysis is generally fairly simple. The operator is usually looking for only one or two events to occur on the signals being monitored. Some common examples of timing analysis triggering are:

When a particular line goes high or low

When a particular pattern is detected on a set of lines

When a noise spike occurs on a particular signal

When the duration of a pulse, or the time between two signals, is too short or too long

Triggering on time faults is most easily done if the analyzer has an event timer and the ability to reset the trigger sequence. However, it can also be accomplished using delays in the triggering sequence. We will look at an example of this type of triggering in the section on signal timing analysis.

Most analyzers allow the operator to trigger on a particular pattern or sequence of patterns. Many analyzers also allow for triggering based on the length of the event. This is demonstrated in glitch triggering and filtering.

A glitch is a noise spike on the order of 3 to 10 ns. Glitches can occur asynchronously, when caused by outside activity, or synchronously when the spike is related to some aspect of system activity. Some analyzers, such as the HP 1630 A/D, allow the operator to trigger upon detection of a glitch on a particular signal. This is a useful feature when looking for noise-related problems. More will be said on this later in the example of glitch analysis.

Filtering is basically the opposite of glitch triggering, since here we are specifying that a signal must be of a minimum duration in order for it to be a valid trigger. For example, we may want to trigger when a line goes high but do not want a noise spike to give a false trigger. With filtering, we can specify that the signal must be high for a specified number of clocks before it should be considered a valid trigger.

Data Storage

Generally, data storage is always enabled during timing analysis. The main purpose of the timing analyzer is to capture the shapes of the waveforms surrounding the trigger event. You may want to use external qualifying lines for specifying the type of event (i.e., a memory read) that is associated with the signals of interest, but this is more of a trigger qualification than for control of storage. Let us now look at how we can use this tool to troubleshoot some common types of problems.

Signal Timing Analysis

Communication between devices in a system is dependent on all signals, whether they be address, data, or control information, occurring at the proper time and being of the correct duration. The timing specifications of all devices precisely define the necessary timing of each signal for correct operation of the device. If these timing specifications are not met, either because of poor design or faulty components, the system will not operate properly. In such cases, the logic timing analyzer is the only instrument that allows the troubleshooter to view these signals and identify the source of the problem.

Timing problems can occur for a number of reasons. These include:

1. Incompatible timing specifications between devices. This most often occurs when the design attempts to mix devices from different families, such as an Intel processor with a Motorola peripheral device, or when a bus device is too slow for the operating speed of the CPU.
2. Control signals are combined through random logic to produce a composite signal. Problems can result if the composite design does not take into account all possible states, or if the delay through the random logic is longer or shorter than anticipated.
3. More than one device is taking control of the bus at a time or a device is maintaining its output longer than expected. In either case, there is bus contention and the signals will be affected.
4. Components may be marginal and go out of spec with changes in operating temperature. These problems are generally intermittent and may inexplicably cause the system to "crash" after it has been operating for a while.

In the following example, we use our timing analyzer to capture a faulty control signal sequence.

Example 9-1

In our system, we wish to test the timing relationship between bus request (BREQ) and bus grant (BGNT) signals. We require that BGNT be asserted HIGH within 200 ns of BREQ going LOW.

The Tektronix 1240 has two trigger-event recognizers which can be used together to increase the triggering flexibility of the system. In this case, we will use the global event recognizer to act as a timer to measure the 200-ns maximum period between signals.

If the timer reaches this value, it will cause the analyzer to trigger and capture the data for inspection. The sequential event recognizer is set to reset the analyzer when the BGNT signal goes HIGH after the BREQ signal has gone LOW. This is illustrated in Figure 9–3(a).

Since the timer is started when BREQ goes LOW, the machine will trigger only if the 200–ns period is reached before BGNT goes HIGH and causes a reset, which restarts the sequence and returns the timer to 0. In this way, the analyzer will repeatedly test these signals until a fault is encountered, at which time the faulty data will be displayed

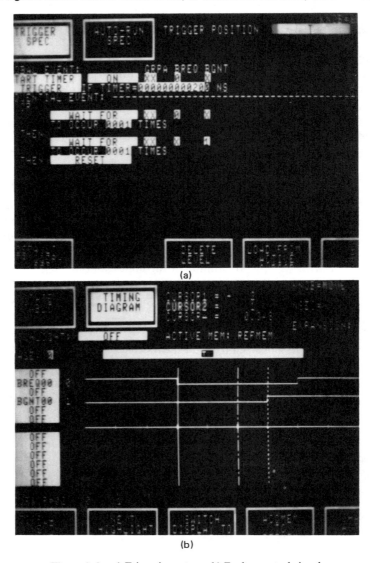

(a)

(b)

Figure 9–3:   a) Triggering set-up. b) Faulty control signals.

for analysis. A fault capture is shown in Figure 9–3(b). The cursors show that BGNT went HIGH 300 ns after BREQ was asserted. The vertical line between the cursors marks the trigger point, which occurred 200 ns after BREQ went LOW. Note that we have only identified a fault occurrence in the bus request/grant logic. Further analysis is required to determine the cause of the fault.

Signal-Level Problems

Level-related problems in microprocessor systems can be static, as with excessive loading, or dynamic, such as slow rise times. Excessive loading of outputs can cause a lowering of the output high level and/or raising of the low level. In extreme cases, the signal levels may be in the undefined region. However, even if the level is still valid, loading can reduce the signal noise margin, making it more susceptible to crosstalk or switching glitches. Slow rise times can cause an unacceptable delay in the signal or even multiple edges, due to remaining too long in the undefined region.

The major difficulty in spotting level-related problems is that most analyzers use a single threshold for differentiating between HIGH and LOW states. This level is usually set at 1.4 V for TTL. (Hewlett-Packard produces a timing analyzer with dual-threshold capability as part of their 64000 Logic Development System.) However, most analyzers offer a variable threshold mode, where the threshold level can be set to any value. Using this feature, the operator can set the threshold for defined HIGH or LOW levels. Thus, although still limited to only one threshold, the operator can now determine the times when valid levels are achieved. Consider the following examples.

Example 9–2

In this example we use the auto-run mode of the 1240 analyzer to determine the operating levels of a UUT bus signal. In this case we will depart from the norm and use an external clock that is synchronized to the bus activity. This eliminates comparison problems that may result from sampling during tri-state periods. (Technically, this then becomes a state analysis problem, but we are including it here because it is hardware oriented.)

Figure 9–4 shows a sample bus waveform as it appears during valid sampling times (i.e., not tri-stated). The signal operates at voltage levels V_{OL} (LOW) and V_{OH} (HIGH). The standard TTL threshold of 1.4 V passes through this waveform as shown. Assume that this waveform can be obtained repeatedly.

Determining V_{OL} and V_{OH} is performed as two separate operations. Let us consider V_{OH}. If we were to alter the sampling threshold of the analyzer to above V_{OH} the sampled data would always read as a LOW. Thus it would differ from the sample obtained using the TTL threshold. By repeatedly sampling the waveform at successively higher thresholds, we can find the voltage at which a difference first appears, thereby determining what V_{OH} actually is. Similarly, we can determine V_{OL} by successively lowering the threshold until the samples differ.

For our analyzer to compare acquisitions, we must sample the same data each time using an appropriate trigger event to start the capture. The trigger event chosen must provide for activity on the signal of interest which is repeatable for the length of the acquisition memory.

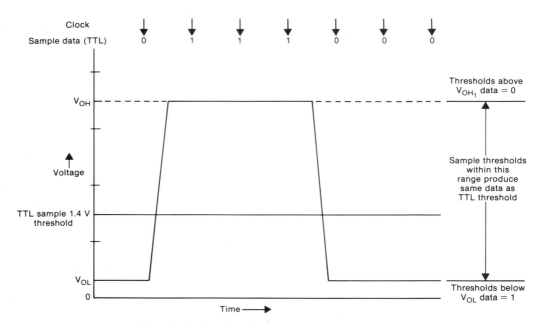

Figure 9-4: Bus signal waveform showing operating voltages.

The initial acquisition is done with the standard threshold. This capture is then stored into reference memory for comparison. Next, we set the auto-run mode of the analyzer to acquire data continuously using the previous trigger specification, until the data acquired does not match the reference data. While running in this mode, we will alter the threshold setting away from the TTL level. As discussed earlier, the threshold is increased to determine V_{OH} and decreased to determine V_{OL}. When our threshold setting moves outside the operating voltage range of the signal, the samples will differ and the analyzer will trigger.

If your analyzer does not allow the threshold setting to be varied while in auto-run mode, you can manually acquire and compare samples using different threshold values each time. Good signals will have a V_{OH} of 2.4 V or greater, and V_{OL} of 0.4 V or less. If these values are not met, the problem could be a driver with insufficient capability for the load, or a poor system ground.

Note that this test can be applied to a group of related signals, such as a data bus, instead of just the single line as shown here. If even one line has a level problem the analyzer still detects it since the bus pattern is altered. A comparison of the captures will show which bit has changed, thereby identifying the faulty line.

Example 9-3

All CPUs require a minimum delay period between application of power and start of execution. This is accomplished by providing a slow-rise-time signal on the RESET input which inhibits execution until a valid HIGH (2.0 V) is reached. If the rise time of this signal is too fast, the specified delay is not met, and the CPU is not guaranteed to function properly. We wish to measure this rise time to ensure that the CPU is being properly powered up.

We will do this by capturing the reset signal using two different threshold settings. The first capture uses a threshold of 0.4 V to determine the approximate time that the reset signal begins rising (i.e., the moment that power is applied to the system). This capture is stored into the reference memory. The second capture uses a threshold of 2.0 V, at which time the reset circuitry of the CPU recognizes a valid HIGH and begins execution. By comparing the times at which each threshold is reached, we can determine the time it took for the reset signal to reach a valid HIGH, and hence the delay time between power-up and start of execution.

Note that we cannot use the reset signal as a trigger, since this will place the trigger point at the same relative position in the capture memory, eliminating the time displacement we wish to see. The trigger must come from an event that is dependent on the signal of interest. In this case, we use the synchronous time base of the analyzer to detect the initial instruction fetch. Meanwhile, we use the other time base to asynchronously sample the reset signal at 200-μs intervals. The analyzer display is time-aligned, so each threshold crossing will be seen relative to the instruction fetch. These ideas are illustrated in Figure 9–5(a).

Figure 9–5(b) shows the second capture of the reset signal, using the 2.0-V threshold. The instruction fetch trigger event is marked by the dash-dot vertical line at the right. The shaded area shows the period where this capture differs from the initial capture in reference memory. The dual cursors are placed on the boundaries of this area and show a rise time of 12.8 ms, which is a more-than-adequate delay for the 8085 processor in our example system.

Note: If you have access to a storage oscilloscope, this measurement can be performed more simply by capturing and analyzing the actual reset signal waveform.

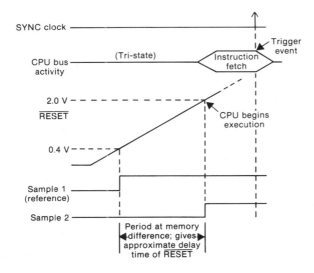

Figure 9–5: a. Reset signal sampling.

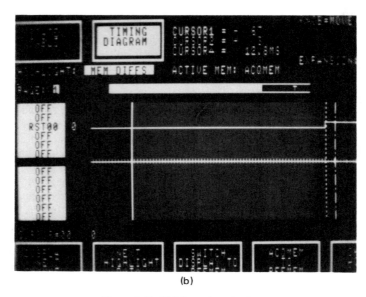

(b)

Figure 9-5 b) Measuring risetime.

Glitch Analysis

Effective glitch capture and display is an important feature of timing analyzers. Glitches occurring at inopportune times can cause incorrect bus information or false clocking. The effectiveness of an analyzer for glitch analysis is based largely on three factors:

1. The ability to capture very short glitches occurring between clocks. Many analyzers will detect glitches as short as 5 ns. The HP 64000 can detect glitches of 3.3–ns duration. This is generally not a problem for any good-quality analyzer.

2. The ability to trigger on glitch occurrence. Hewlett-Packard and Tektronix offer analyzers that can trigger on glitches, either unqualified or when they occur in relation to some other event. The latter is useful for capturing glitches only when they occur close to some critical point where they are most likely to have a detrimental effect.

3. The glitch should be displayed in a unique and easily identifiable manner. The ability to capture a glitch is wasted if the operator cannot find it among the other transitions or if, as can happen, it does not get displayed at all.

The latter point has split the majority of the logic analyzer industry into two camps.

The first group uses the latching method to store and display glitches. With this method, detected glitches are "stretched" and displayed as a single-clock-width pulse at the next sampling edge. The stretched glitches are stored in the same memory as the other data.

The second method uses a separate memory to store glitch information and displays them in a different manner from regular data, such as a vertical line or solid block. Hewlett-Packard and Tektronix are among those who use this method. Although it requires twice the memory of the first method, this technique is preferable since glitches can be distinguished from other data readily. In addition, latching will not display glitches that occur in the same sampling period as a valid edge. A comparison of the two methods is shown in Figure 9–6.

Glitches are not necessarily detrimental to the system operation. However, one should be wary of noise spikes that occur on the following:

Clock signals

Gating strobes, such as $\overline{\text{RD}}$ or $\overline{\text{WR}}$, or chip selects

Address or data lines during the setup and hold periods around a strobe edge

Using the timing analyzer, we can determine if the glitch is in one of these critical areas and take corrective action to eliminate the noise.

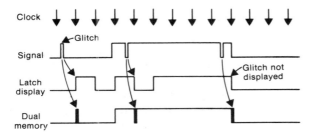

Figure 9–6: Comparison of glitch display methods.

9–2 LOGIC-STATE ANALYSIS

Logic-state analysis is the study of system events that occur synchronously to the system's clock activity. This includes address and data bus information and synchronous control signals such as chip selects and read/write strobes. Consequently, the main use for state analyzers is in software development, since it allows the operator to trace the flow of execution and determine where problems are occurring. We will examine software analysis a little later. However, the state analyzer can also be useful for locating certain hardware faults, by acting as a multichannel "synchronous probe." This idea will be discussed in the next section, on kernel troubleshooting. First, we will look at the clocking, triggering, and data storage parameters for state analysis.

Clocking

State analysis always uses synchronous clocking since bus sampling should occur only during times when information is valid. This is done by connecting the external clock probe inputs to a suitable signal or signals and defining the synchronous clock(s) in terms of rising or falling edges on these inputs. For example, in a 6809 system, address and data are valid on the falling edge of the E clock. Thus we would connect a clock probe onto the E clock line and set the analyzer to sample on the falling edge of this clock input.

Multiplexed buses complicate the problem since one set of lines contains both address and data information at different times. Some analyzers, such as the Tektronix 1240, allow the analyzer to be set for a demultiplexing clocking scheme by defining two synchronous clocks that alternate; the first samples the lines when they contain address information, the second when they contain data. Other analyzers use two separate time bases for obtaining information off a multiplexed bus or have an intelligent interface pod which performs the demultiplexing for the analyzer.

If a dedicated interface pod is used, such things as clock definition, probe assignments, and display formatting will probably be taken care of by built-in firmware, so the operator need not worry about them. The analyzer will set up its own parameters to suit the microprocessor in use. For example, in our setup, a special ROM cartridge defines the clocking scheme for our 8085 system as follows:

> *Low-order address lines:* Falling edge of ALE strobe
>
> *High-order address,*
> *data, and control lines:*   logical OR of the rising edge of $\overline{\text{RD}}$, $\overline{\text{WR}}$, $\overline{\text{INTA}}$, and ALE

The OR'ing of the signals is required so that a clock will occur no matter what type of cycle the processor is in.

In cases where the CPU provides status outputs, the analyzer should be connected to these so that it can determine the type of execution cycle (i.e., instruction fetch, I/O write, interrupt acknowledge, etc.) and use this information for triggering or storage purposes.

Triggering

State analyzers require a great deal of triggering flexibility since they are often required to trace long, complex software sequences. It is in this area that the greatest diversity between various analyzers exists. Each manufacturer has its own unique construct for defining tracing and triggering parameters. It is beyond the scope of this book to familiarize the reader with specifics for all analyzers. However, the following capabilities are essential to proper state analysis and are provided on many analyzers in one form or another.

1. *Sequence tracing.* This allows the operator to define a sequence of events that the analyzer will look for. (An event is simply the pattern of 1s, 0s, and don't cares that the analyzer has been programmed to look for, and which may include time-duration qualification before the analyzer will recognize it.) When the first event is found, it will proceed to the second event, and so on. Various actions may be taken upon recognition of an event. The maximum length of the sequence will vary between analyzers. This feature allows tracing of long software sequences by picking out key "signposts" along the way.

2. *If-then-else constructs.* This construct means that if the defined event occurs, the analyzer will perform a particular action. Otherwise, a different action will be taken. Examples of useful actions would be to trigger the analyzer, to reset the analyzer and start from the beginning of the sequence, to jump to a particular level within the sequence, or simply to wait for the next defined event to occur. This feature allows the operator to control the trace dynamically, based on events encountered.

3. *Timing capability.* In many instances, the execution time of a software routine is critical. The state analyzer should provide some means for determining execution time.

Figure 9-7(a) illustrates some of these ideas. Here, we wish to wait for event A to occur twice, wait for event B. When B occurs, if the next sample is not event

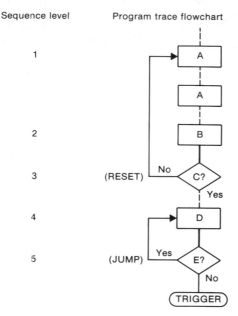

Figure 9-7:   a) Desired trigger sequence.

C, we reset the sequence and start again. If it is C, we wait for event D. If the next sample is event E, we return to the previous level to wait for D again. When the sample immediately after D is not E, the analyzer will trigger. Figure 9-7(b) shows how this trigger sequence is implemented on the Tektronix 1240 analyzer.

Data Storage

State analysis requires the ability to control what information is stored in memory in order to present only useful data for analysis. Often, the operator does not need to see all the information sampled through the trace sequence, even assuming that the analyzer has a large enough memory to hold such quantities. The greater the selec-

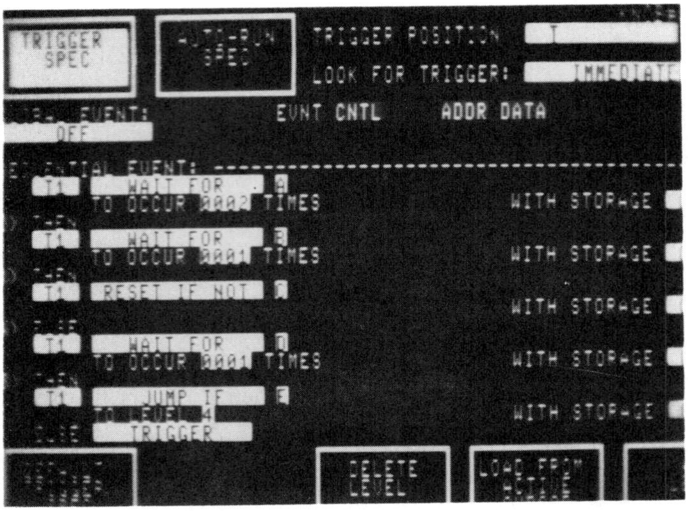

Figure 9-7: b) Tektronix 1240 implementation.

tivity, the more easily the data are analyzed. Some useful capabilities include the ability to turn storage on and off for particular portions of the trace sequence, and to store only a specified event or event type.

Software Analysis

Software analysis can be divided into two main categories: code debugging and performance analysis. It is beyond the scope of this chapter to discuss either topic in any but the most general terms. Unlike hardware, for which there are a number of basic principles which are almost universally applicable, software has an endless variety of forms. Each program is a unique creation, and any specifics presented here would likely be of little value in terms of software that you may encounter. This chapter presents only an overview of how a state analyzer can be applied to software analysis.

Code debugging involves tracing the flow of execution in order to locate faulty routines and ascertain the nature of the fault. The task of such debugging can be greatly simplified if the programmer takes a "building-block" approach to the software. The initial stages of coding should involve basic routines that can be individually tested for their functional correctness. These routines can then be used by higher-level modules, whose own functionality can then be tested without having to worry about whether the lower-order routines are executing properly. In this way, software can be built up level by level until the final program is assembled. This method, of course, requires a well-structured design.

Even with this approach, you may still encounter problems with software modules interacting in unexpected ways. Here is where a powerful and flexible sequential trace capability is needed, for we must observe not only the final "crash site" but also the route by which our program arrived there. A routine may operate normally when called from one area, yet fail when called from another. Through selective tracing, we can observe various routes until the one that leads to the failure is obtained.

Often, the most difficult part of code debugging is determining the trace specifications required to capture the fault. The following are some commonly used tracing techniques and how they can be implemented within the state analyzer.

1. *Controlling the trace path according to the value written to or read from a device.* During product development, it is not always evident whether a problem is due to a hardware fault or an error in the software that handles the device. This technique allows us to monitor the interaction between the two and capture any unexpected events, such as the device returning incorrect data or the software sending faulty information to the device.

    In this example, we will reset when the value 00 is read from a memory-mapped input port at address 3000. If the value read is not 00, we will trigger the analyzer. Figure 9-8(a) shows the sequence of bus events that takes place to execute this read. Notice that in this example, the addressing scheme requires two memory reads to get the port address before the memory read to acquire the port data. Figure 9-8(b) shows the trace specification that we will use. The

Address	Data	Control
0500	rr	\<instruction fetch\>
0501	30	\<memory read\>
0502	00	\<memory read\>
3000	nn	\<memory read\>

where rr = hex code for "read"
              instruction (e.g., LDA)
    nn = data from input port

(a)

```
WAIT FOR addr = 0500 cntl = inst. fetch
DELAY 2 CLOCKS
RESET IF data = 00
ELSE TRIGGER
```

(b)

Figure 9-8:   a. Instruction execution sequence.
                    b. Trace specification.

first step causes the analyzer to wait until the instruction is encountered. Next, we must wait two clocks for the port address to be fetched, using the delay feature. Finally, we test the read statement to see if the value 00 was placed onto the data bus and, if so, we reset the analyzer. Otherwise, the analyzer is triggered. Note that if the addressing method chosen did not require the port address to be fetched over the bus (e.g., the port address is obtained from an internal CPU register), we would eliminate the delay statement.

2. *Eliminating storage of subroutines to allow easy analysis of main routine.* This is often required since a long subroutine can take up most of the memory, thereby preventing us from following the flow of the main routine. Figure 9-9(a) shows a subroutine call from within another routine. Figure 9-9(b) shows how the analyzer could be set up to eliminate the subroutine code. The analyzer waits for the start address of the subroutine with storage on. When the subroutine

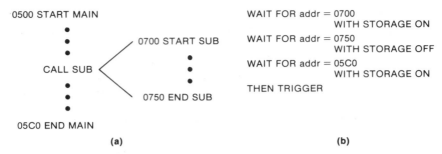

Figure 9–9:   a) Subroutine call. b) Trace specification.

is entered, the analyzer waits for its end address with storage off. Finally, it waits for the end of the main routine with storage on before triggering to end the capture. Thus the subroutine code is not stored.

Note that this method can become impractical if the main routine has many subroutine calls, since each call requires a pair of statements to turn storage off, then on again. An alternative, if your analyzer is capable of it, is to specify storage only over the address range of the main routine. Any instructions outside this range, as in the subroutines, will not be stored. If your analyzer cannot specify address ranges, you can approximate using don't cares in the lower-order address bits. In this case, our routine ranges from address 0500 through 05C0, so we could set the analyzer to STORE ON address = 0000 0101 xxxx xxxx. However, this will store extraneous data if any subroutines called reside in addresses 05C0 through 05FF.

3. *Storing reads and writes to stack memory.* The most common uses for stack memory are context saving during subroutines and interrupts, and parameter passing to subroutines. In either case, the stack should exhibit a nested pair structure, where data are restored in the reverse order to its saving. By observing stack activity alone, we can identify RAM problems, which alter the data that is saved, or code problems that make incorrect use of the stack and disrupt the nested pair structure. As in the last example, we can use global storage qualification only to store reads and writes to the stack address range, or its approximation using don't cares.

There are a couple of factors that can complicate the debugging task. The first is software dependence on hardware conditions. The software path we wish to observe might be taken only if certain external conditions are met. This could range from a certain switch being operated to having a particular voltage on the input of an analog-to-digital converter. The operator must make sure that these conditions are provided, and this may involve adding test hardware to simulate a particular condition.

The second complicating factor is the language used to code the program. Almost all analyzers go no higher than assembly code instructions. (Hewlett-Packard offers a high-level language state analyzer for their 64000 Logic Development System.) If the program was written in a high-level language, the code being observed will have been produced by a compiler. This adds a level of unfamiliarity which certainly does not make the task easier. The best approach here is initially to trace the flow of high-level statements, while ignoring the actual code of each. Use the addresses equated to each statement by the compiler in the event sequence. When the fault location has been roughly isolated, you can backtrace from that point to observe what is happening at the code level. This is analogous to our hardware approach, where we begin with functional testing to isolate the faulty block, then delve into that block ever deeper until the fault is pinpointed to a particular device.

Performance analysis tests the efficiency of the software by providing the operator with an overview of software activity. Typically, the software is divided into functional modules, which are specified to the analyzer as address ranges. The analyzer then monitors the software as it is executing, keeping track of how much time (relatively or absolutely) is spent in each module. This information is presented as a continuously updating histogram display which the operator can use to detect bottlenecks, or code that is consuming far more CPU time than it should. This code can then be optimized, or the program structure altered, to improve the software efficiency. Figure 9-10 shows a typical histogram display.

Unfortunately, only a few analyzers have such performance analysis capability. However, we can still evaluate the execution times of software routines using a basic state analyzer with timing capability, as shown in the following example.

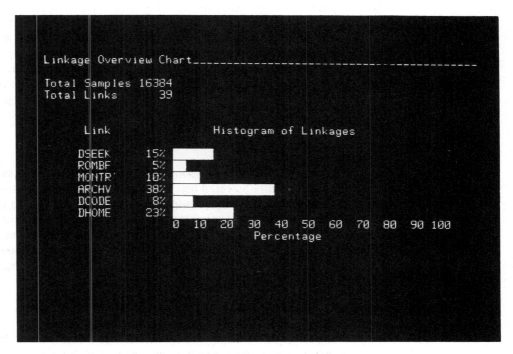

Figure 9-10: Performance analysis histogram display. Photo courtesy of Hewlett-Packard Company.

Example 9–4

Our software contains a task handler module whose execution time will vary, depending on parameters that are passed to it. We require that its maximum execution time does not exceed 10 ms. In this case we will set up the analyzer timer to start on the beginning of the task handler, and to cause a trigger if it reaches 10 ms. Meanwhile, the sequential event recognizer is programmed to wait for the start of the handler, then to reset the analyzer upon detection of the end of the handler. With this setup, the analyzer will trigger only if the execution time of the handler exceeds 10 ms. The code can then be analyzed to determine why it took so long to execute and where improvements can be made.

9–3 TROUBLESHOOTING THE KERNEL HARDWARE

In previous chapters, we looked at the variety of faults that can prevent the kernel from operating properly. These faults included bad buffers, shorted or open traces, wiring errors, and faulty devices. Although not ideally suited for finding such faults, the logic analyzer can track down such problems. As we will see, the majority of these problems will affect the natural flow of activity within the system. With the proper techniques and a bit of intuition, an experienced operator can quickly isolate the problem.

Most problems can be found using the state analysis mode of operation. This allows the analyzer to act as a "synchronous probe," much as on the Fluke 9010A. However, instead of using an external instrument to stimulate the system, we rely on the natural activity of the system to provide clues as to the nature of the fault. In some cases, we may have to use the state and timing modes interactively to determine the nature of the problem. We will see examples of both types of troubleshooting a little later. First, we will look at some basic techniques that we can apply to a system under test.

Tracing from Power-Up

With this technique, we are doing nothing more than using the analyzer to capture all bus activity after the system is powered up. This is a good first step in troubleshooting most problems, since power-up provides us with a known starting point. The system will always attempt to begin execution from its reset address. By observing how and where execution deviates from the norm, we can draw conclusions as to the possible nature of the problem. It is important that this trace be taken more than once. By comparing the traces, we can see whether the fault point is the same each time or is different, thereby indicating a fixed or intermittent fault.

Testing for Stuck or Shorted Bus Lines

A stuck line will manifest itself by displaying no activity. It will always be HIGH or LOW. However, before proclaiming any inactive line as bad, be certain that the natural system execution requires activity on the line. Shorted lines may have identical activity on them or the short may prevent any activity from happening, in which case both lines will appear to be stuck. It is often useful to display the state activity from the buses in a timing display format. This provides a "horizontal map" of the activity on each line, which makes the task of identifying stuck or shorted lines somewhat easier.

These problems will not always appear at the microprocessor, where the state analysis probes are attached. There may be intervening buffers and latches between the fault site and the probe set. In such cases, additional probing will be required to sample lines beyond these buffers. This is analogous to the Fluke 9010A, where the built-in bus test only checks up to the first set of buffers. Beyond that point, manual probing is required with the Fluke's synchronous probe. If the buffer is not always enabled, we must qualify our sampling clock with the buffer enable signal, so that we only observe the buffer outputs when they are valid. Alternatively, a simple logic probe or scope can provide a quick test to see if a buffer output is stuck in one state. However, these tools cannot determine the correctness of any activity observed.

Testing for Open Traces

Another common fault is where a signal is good but is not reaching a device because the trace is open for some reason. To detect such faults, we must probe directly at the device in question, to see if the signals from the microprocessor are reaching it. The corollary to this is that the device may be outputting good signals but they are not appearing at the CPU due to some intervening discontinuity. A logic probe or scope are of limited usefulness here, depending on the location of the discontinuity and the type of line being tested. For example, on a data bus line there will probably be activity on both sides of a break because it is bidirectional and so can be driven by both the isolated device and the CPU. Also, systems with multiple-bus controllers may show activity at all devices if the discontinuity only prevents one controller's signals from reaching a device. With remote probing by the logic analyzer, we can differentiate between activity from the source under investigation and other sources, thereby identifying missing signals due to trace breaks.

Combining Functional Testing with Logic Analysis

Normal system operation may not always provide sufficient stimulus for the logic analyzer to identify the problem. The system may appear to operate normally because the problem area is not being utilized for some reason. This is where some simple functional test software can assist the logic analyzer by forcing the bad device to manifest its fault. This requires that enough of the kernel is operational to allow software to be executed. As discussed in Chapter 7, the functional test software can be part of a system ROM, or contained in a separate ROM which is inserted for testing purposes.

Functional tests assist in troubleshooting in two ways. First, they can test a device and its associated circuitry to see if they are functioning correctly. Here, the logic analyzer acts mainly as a display for showing where the test failed and why. For example, we may have routines to perform a checksum on the system ROMs and a pattern sensitivity test on the system RAM. On detection of an error, the routine enters an error handler whose address is used to trigger the analyzer. By triggering on the error and using the analyzer to trace backwards, we can find where in memory the fault occurred and what the fault was. This information will probably provide clues as to the physical cause of the fault to assist us in further troubleshooting.

The second benefit obtained from functional testing is that it provides a source of stimulus for the circuitry being investigated. Such stimulus is not always easily obtained through normal system activity. The software does not need to be able to detect the fault, only provide sufficient activity for the logic analyzer to do so. For example, the software may write a series of patterns to a port, while the analyzer monitors its outputs to see if the correct value is appearing there. In some cases, it is enough simply to access a device so that the analyzer can check for correct control signals at the device, or see if interface circuitry associated with the device is functioning properly.

Waveform Capturing

Some problems may require us to see the shapes of the signals in order to determine the nature of the fault. Most good analyzers allow for interactive operation between state and timing analysis modes. A common technique is to use a particular state event to trigger the capture of asynchronous data, or vice versa. You may also encounter cases where it is necessary to observe the exact shape of the signal. This can be done by connecting the trigger output of the analyzer to a device such as a storage oscilloscope. When the trigger event is reached, the analyzer will trigger the scope to store the signal(s) of interest.

Let us now look at some examples where we apply these techniques to actual hardware problems. The system used in these examples has a power-up self-test which checks various devices. Unless stated otherwise, the system is unable to execute even this much of its software. Also note that analyzer hardware limitations prevented probing of more than nine lines at a time, away from the CPU. The procedures used in these examples reflect this limitation.

Example 9–5

The power-up, or reset, trace test shows that the system is reading and executing instructions normally until it jumps to address 0447. Here we seem to encounter a string of CMP E instructions, as shown in the disassembled display of Figure 9–11(a). One possibility is that the ROM data have been corrupted so that all these locations now contain the CMP E instruction. However, as we saw in earlier chapters, we must first check the buses and control signals before we can conclude that the device is at fault.

It is unlikely that there is a problem with the data bus since the first few statements were read properly. A more likely possibility is an addressing problem that is causing the CPU to access a location other than the one specified by its address outputs. The system contains a buffer and address latch, so our next step is to check the address lines on the outputs of these devices. An additional probe set is attached to the outputs

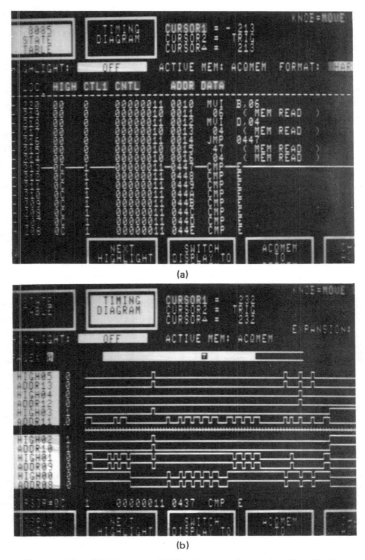

(a)

(b)

Figure 9-11   a) State trace. b) Signal comparison using time display.

of the high-order address buffer and the reset trace is repeated. The buffered addresses are displayed in Figure 9-11(a) in the column second from the left labeled HIGH. Here we see that the buffer outputs are correct when the high-order address lines are all LOW but that address line 11 is going high when the address 04xx is presented, causing an address of 0Cxx to appear on the outputs. Since a 4 in that position is caused by address bit 10 going HIGH, we can suspect that address bit 11 is following bit 10. This is confirmed by the display in Figure 9-11(b). Here we have displayed six of the CPU address lines (ADDR08 to ADDR13) next to their buffered counterparts (HIGH00 to HIGH05), using the timing display format for easy comparison of state activity. The display clearly shows that the buffered address 11 (HIGH03) is identical to the buffered and unbuffered address 10 signals. The problem was traced to a wiring error on the PCB where the buffer input for address 11 was incorrectly connected to address 10 at the CPU.

Example 9-6

On power-up, the self-test software indicates a problem in the system RAM but provides no information on the nature of the fault. As before, this does not necessarily imply that a RAM chip is bad. The problem could be faulty address or control inputs, or there may be a problem on the data bus which prevents data from being written or read properly.

Our task is simplified by the fact that the kernel is able to execute the RAM functional test. We can use this as a stimulus source for accessing the RAM while using the logic analyzer to observe the activity that results. Each of the potential fault sources can now easily be tested using standard observation techniques.

The first step is to observe the point at which the RAM test fails. This will indicate where in RAM the first error occurs and why the test failed. The RAM test stores an incremental pattern into each RAM location, then tests each location to see that the data were stored properly. When the data do not match, the software enters an error-handler routine which terminates the test and displays a RAM error message on the system display. The analyzer is set to trigger on entering this error routine and the system is powered-up. The resulting capture shows that the RAM test failed at the first location it attempted to read from. In a system with multiple RAM chips, the failure address will indicate on which chip, or bank of chips, the error occurs. If your system uses banks of RAM to store a byte or word, a comparison of the expected and actual data could further isolate the problem by noting which bit or bits are different.

The next step is to observe bus activity at the RAM chip in question. We may have to perform these tests on more than one chip if our initial test was unable to isolate the problem to a particular IC. Our first test will check the low-order address lines at the RAM. To simplify analysis, we set the analyzer to trigger on the start of the RAM test (address 005E), with posttrigger storage of RAM accesses only, as specified by the RAM address range 0800 to 08FF. The set up for this is shown in Figure 9-12(a). This will eliminate the ROM instruction fetches from our capture, so that we can concentrate on RAM-related events only. The trace obtained is shown in Figure 9-12(b). The listing shows the routine storing the incremental pattern into RAM. In the second column from the left, labeled LOW, we have the low-order address lines as sampled at the RAM. Here we see a discrepancy, in that address bit 7 is always HIGH. Thus address 0800 is actually accessing RAM location 0880, and so on. The problem was traced to an opened trace between the RAM chip and the address latch, causing the RAM address input to float HIGH.

If this test had not found the problem, we could have proceeded to check the upper address lines and the chip select and write strobe lines. Data bus testing would involve comparison of data being read and written at both the CPU and the RAM. If these tests showed no external problems, we could conclude that the RAM is bad and replace it.

Example 9-7

The initial trace of activity from power up shows that the first ROM location is reading correctly, but that every location after that returns a value of 00, which the processor

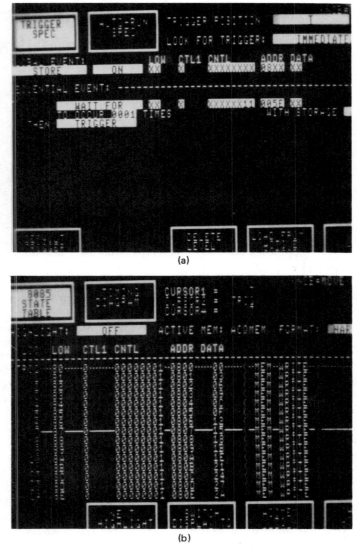

Figure 9-12 a) Analyzer set-up. b) RAM access trace.

executes as a NOP (No OPeration). Applying our usual tests, we find that address and data information is the same at both the ROM and CPU, but the ROM chip select line is HIGH when data are being read. The next logical step is to examine the decoding logic.

The nine analyzer probes are attached to the three addressing inputs and to the lower six decoder outputs. We will format our display to show each line individually. The decoder inputs will be grouped under the display label CBA (corresponding to the names of the inputs) and the outputs will be grouped under the label CSEL. The power-up trace is repeated and the results are shown in Figure 9-13.

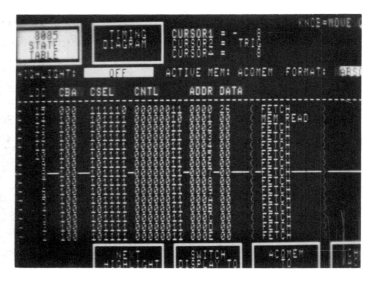

Figure 9–13:   Software trace showing decoder levels.

The trace shows us that the proper chip select (the rightmost one in the CSEL group) occurs only on the first read. After this initial read, decoder input C inexplicably goes HIGH (as shown in the second column from left), causing decoder output 4 to go LOW instead of output 0. Output 4 is used to select an input port that currently is reading a value of 00. Thus the processor is interpreting this read as an instruction fetch and executing NOPs. Using our probe lines and repeating the measurements, we backtrace the C signal to find an opened trace between the decoder input and the address buffer feeding it. This caused the input to float HIGH, preventing the ROM from being selected.

Example 9–8

The power-up trace shows some ROM locations being read correctly while others are not, based on ROM listings which show the expected data for each ROM address. Furthermore, repeating this trace shows that the faulty reads do not always occur at the same addresses. An examination of the ROM inputs shows that the faulty reads are usually associated with a missing ROM chip select, although in some cases the data are incorrect with the select signal present. The decoder inputs are tested and appear to be correct. However, replacing the suspected bad decoder does not correct the problem.

Faced with such an intermittent fault, we will use the full timing and state analysis capabilities of the analyzer to examine the ROM control signals in detail. Two of the probe inputs are connected to the read strobe and chip select signals of the ROM. For display purposes, these signals are labeled READ and ROM, respectively. However, rather than sampling these lines synchronously as we have been doing, we will use an asynchronous time base (20-ns sampling interval) with glitch capture enabled. This will allow us to see the waveforms of these signals.

The probe connections at the microprocessor will remain in synchronous mode so that we can continue to monitor state activity. Since the majority of faulty reads return a value of FF on the data bus, we will use the first occurrence of this value to trigger the analyzer. In effect, we are using state information to provide the trigger for capturing the timing information of interest. Running this test yields the timing display shown in Figure 9-14. In the photograph, we see glitch activity occurring on the chip select, especially toward the end, where stability is critical. The cursor is positioned at the moment of state sampling, as shown by the single line of state information displayed beneath the timing display. We can conclude that this noise on the chip select is interfering with the ROM accesses. In addition to a bad device, noise of this nature can be caused by inadequate decoupling of devices. In this case, replacing a faulty decoupling capacitor corrected the problem.

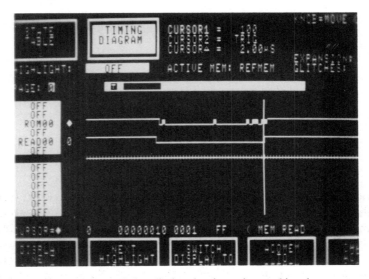

Figure 9-14:   Timing display showing noise on chip select.

9-4 SUMMARY

In this chapter we looked at some basic techniques for applying logic analysis to a variety of hardware and software problems. It is hoped that the examples dealt with here have provided some insight into what is, perhaps, the most difficult aspect of logic analysis: how to apply the analyzer's capabilities to reveal the nature of the fault. Of course, due to the operational diversity of different analyzers, the chapter should be viewed as a general guide, not an explicit how-to manual.

Although not the best tool for troubleshooting every problem, the logic analyzer is certainly the most versatile one. Almost any fault, whether hardware or software related, can be diagnosed using this instrument. Some faults, such as timing problems, can be identified only with a logic analyzer. However, full utilization of the logic analyzer's capabilities can be achieved only with a skilled user. The user requires an intimate understanding of the hardware or software being investigated, familiarity with the operation of the analyzer being used, and expertise in logic analysis techniques. In the right hands, though, the logic analyzer can be the single most useful tool on the troubleshooter's workbench.

10

NODAL TESTERS

In previous chapters we looked at different instruments that troubleshoot down to the node level. However, the task is not complete until the nature of the fault within the node has been identified and, of course, corrected. These faults can range from solder bridges and open traces to faulty IC inputs and outputs.

Correctly identifying the fault can be a difficult process, since different faults can produce similar symptoms on the surface. Since we have employed a systematic approach to troubleshooting this far, it would be unproductive to revert to tactics such as trial-and-error component replacement which may or may not work. This is where a group of hand-held instruments known collectively as *nodal testers* become extremely useful. This group consists of the current tracer, logic pulser, and logic probe. With these tools and an understanding of the circuitry involved, the trouble-shooter can pinpoint the cause of the fault with a high degree of certainty.

In the rest of this chapter we take a detailed look at each of these devices and how they can be used to identify a variety of faults.

10-1 THE CURRENT TRACER

As noted in Chapter 1, the *current tracer* is a handheld device used to trace current flow in electronic circuits. It permits the troubleshooter to identify fault current paths on circuit boards and hence, nondestructively, to locate bad devices causing stuck nodes and to find foil shorts, solder bridges, shorted power supply lines, and similar problems. Figure 10-1 shows a typical current tracer.

A typical instrument is the HP 547A current tracer. It detects alternating current in the trace it is placed over by sensing the magnetic field induced by the current. A sensitivity control allows the operator to select a range of currents that the probe is able to detect.

Figure 10-1   A current tracer being used to trace a fault current path in a microprocessor system.

Since the probe can detect only alternating current, it is necessary for the node to be stimulated in such a way as to produce high–low and low–high transitions. This stimulus can come from the natural activity of the node, if available, or from a logic pulser, which will be discussed shortly.

The current tracer is the most difficult of the nodal testers to use since effective tracing is dependent on two factors: tracer orientation and sensitivity setting.

The sensing tip of the tracer is highly directional to minimize crosstalk interference from nearby traces. As a result, the operator must be very careful to maintain proper probe orientation. The index mark on the plastic tip must be aligned in the direction of the trace. The probe must also be placed directly over the trace and held perpendicular to the board. These three aspects of orientation are illustrated in Figure 10-2.

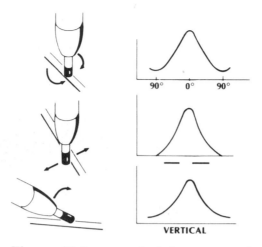

Figure 10-2 Proper current tracer orientation. Courtesy of Hewlett-Packard Company.

The sensitivity control of the tracer varies the current window that we can observe. This is illustrated in Figure 10-3. Within the current window, the relative strength of the current is indicated by the brightness of the lamp. For example, at one setting, a current of 10 mA barely lights the lamp, 30 mA produces half brilliance, and 50 mA or greater fully lights the lamp. The tracer has a fairly wide dynamic range, with the current needed to turn on the lamp being only 300 μA at maximum sensitivity, and 300 mA at minimum sensitivity. The sensitivity control is set at the point of stimulation for the node. This is either the node driver pin or the tip of the

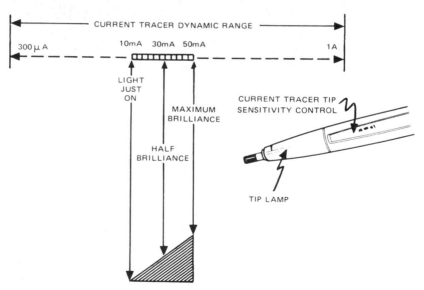

Figure 10-3 The sensitivity control selects the range of currents which the tracer will detect. Courtesy of Hewlett-Packard Company.

logic pulser, as shown in Figure 10-4. The setting should be such that the lamp is dimly lit. The tracer is now set for that node and normally should not be changed. The exception to this is ground nodes, where the trace width can vary greatly. It may be necessary to adjust the sensitivity to account for variations in the flux density. The path of current flow is traced by observing the lamp as the tracer is moved along the PCB trace. Using the tracer to find faults is discussed in detail in later sections.

Figure 10-4   Setting tracer sensitivity at tip of pulser.

10-2 THE LOGIC PULSER

The logic pulser is a hand-held device which injects HIGH and LOW pulses into normal and stuck nodes. A photo of a logic pulser is shown in Figure 10-5. A typical device is the HP 546A logic pulser, which is programmed through a simple pushbutton code to provide a variety of stimuli. These include single pulses, pulse bursts, and continuous pulse streams at 1, 10, or 100 Hz. Figure 10-6 shows how the pulser is programmed for the various modes. In addition to simple stimulation, the pulser can be used to output a precise number of pulses, as might be used to load a counter with a specific value.

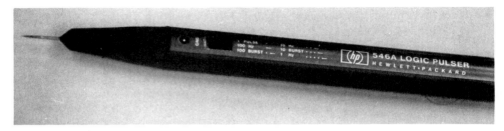

Figure 10-5 A logic pulser. Photo courtesy of Hewlett-Packard Company.

PRESS AND RELEASE CODE BUTTON	o			
PRESS AND LATCH CODE BUTTON	o⌐			
OUTPUT MODES:		TO OUTPUT EXACTLY 432 PULSES:		
o	SINGLE PULSE	1. 100 Hz BURST	oo⌐	98
				100
o⌐	100 Hz STREAM			100
				100
oo⌐	100 Hz BURST			400
		2. 10 Hz BURST	ooo o⌐	6
ooo⌐	10 Hz STREAM			10
				10
oooo⌐	10 Hz BURST			430
		3. SINGLE PULSE	o	1
ooooo⌐	1 Hz STREAM	SINGLE PULSE	o	1
				432

Figure 10-6 Programming the HP 546A logic pulser. Courtesy of Hewlett-Packard Company.

Regardless of the output mode, the pulser produces a dual polarity pulse, first going low and then high. The amplitude of the high level is determined by the supply voltage that the pulser is using. Therefore, the pulser should be connected to the UUT's power source or one of equivalent voltage. If connected into an open circuit, the pulser's output will appear as shown in Figure 10-7. If connected to a node that is low or high, the pulser will only force the node into its opposite polarity. A node that is high cannot be driven any higher, and similarly, a low node will not be pulled lower.

Notice that the high-level pulse width is less for TTL than for CMOS. This is because TTL requires a high current to overcome the low level. However, this high current, if sustained for a sufficient period of time, can destroy the output driver of the node. The pulser accounts for this by sensing the current draw and limiting the pulse width to about 500 ns. In the case of CMOS, which draws little current, the pulse width is wider. This feature eliminates the need to desolder and lift out the output on the node, as was necessary when simple function generators were used as stimulus sources for IC inputs.

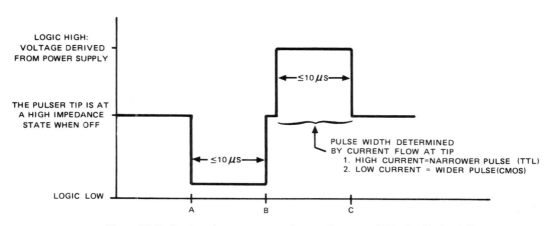

LOGIC HIGH:
VOLTAGE DERIVED
FROM POWER SUPPLY

≤10 μs

THE PULSER TIP IS AT
A HIGH IMPEDANCE
STATE WHEN OFF

PULSE WIDTH DETERMINED
BY CURRENT FLOW AT TIP
1. HIGH CURRENT=NARROWER PULSE (TTL)
2. LOW CURRENT = WIDER PULSE(CMOS)

≤10 μs

LOGIC LOW

A   B   C

Figure 10-7 Logic pulser output waveforms. Courtesy of Hewlett-Packard Company.

10-3 THE LOGIC PROBE

Logic probes are the simplest of the nodal testers and are used to indicate the logic level of the node voltage and whether that node is in a steady state or contains pulse activity. A typical probe, the HP 545A, is shown in Figure 10-8. This particular probe has a lamp near the tip which is off for a logic low and on for a logic high. If the node is at an undefined level, the lamp will glow dimly. When the lamp is flashing there is pulse activity on the node. Pulses as short as 10 ns can be detected, then "stretched," to produce a short lamp flash. Pulse streams will appear as a rapid, steady flashing of the lamp. A TTL/CMOS switch allows the probe to be used on both logic families.

Logic probes from other manufacturers are the same in principle but may differ in detail. For example, some probes have three indicator lamps—a red for high,

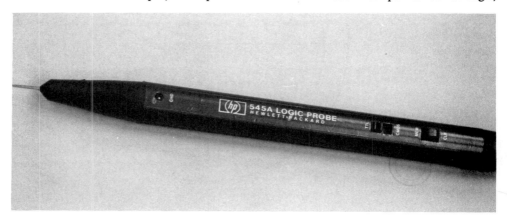

Figure 10-8 A logic probe. Photo courtesy of Hewlett-Packard Company.

a green for low, and an amber for indeterminate (or floating) state. Regardless of their detail, however, all perform basically the same function and are used in the same way.

In the next section we examine the different faults that can occur in a digital system, and how these faults can be tracked down using a combination of these three instruments.

10-4 NODAL FAULT DIAGNOSIS

For effective node-level troubleshooting, it is insufficient merely to understand how the various nodal testers operate. To diagnose a nodal fault, the troubleshooter requires a good knowledge of the types of faults which can occur and how these faults manifest themselves. Figure 10–9 shows the six major fault types found in digital circuitry and the relative frequency of occurrence.

In the majority of cases, voltage-based testers such as the pulser and logic probe will be sufficient to pinpoint the problem. For this reason, fault investigation usually begins with these testers. Even in the remaining cases, which require current tracing, starting with the pulser and probe will quickly identify whether a node is stuck due to an internal or external short to V_{cc} or ground. In such a case, pulsing the node will have no effect on the node voltage level, and the logic probe will not show any

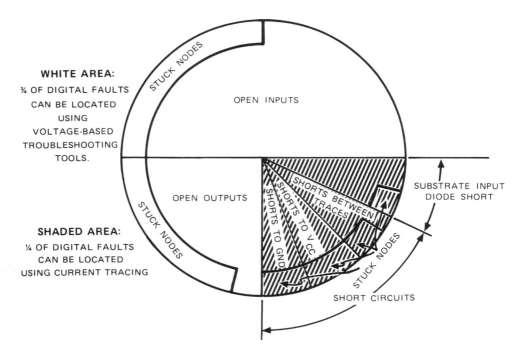

Figure 10–9 Fault types in digital circuits. Courtesy of Hewlett-Packard Company.

activity. This is an important first step in that the fault has now been categorized into one of the two fault groups.

Observation of current activity in the node can also provide valuable clues to the nature of the fault. Consider a standard TTL circuit, as in Figure 10-10. With a fanout of 1, the driver will source 40 μA in the high state and sink 1.6 mA in the low state. Even at maximum fanout, the current in the node will not exceed 16 mA. However, if the node is shorted to ground, up to 55 mA can be sourced by the driver [1]. This excess of current is found in other families as well. In general, a grounded node will carry current at least an order of magnitude higher than a normal circuit. This also easily allows the troubleshooter to trace the current from the stimulus source to the point that is holding the node stuck.

Absence of current activity can also be indicative of the fault, assuming of course that the node should contain activity. In cases where both voltage and current activity are absent, one can usually suspect an open or dead node driver. If there is normal voltage activity at the driver but no current is flowing, the problem is probably due to a broken trace between the driver and the device(s) being driven. Note, however, that all inputs must be isolated from the driver for there to be no current flow. A quick pin-to-pin check of the inputs will confirm if the signal is reaching all devices, though.

The troubleshooter should keep in mind that the foregoing are intended merely as guidelines. Not all faults will produce symptoms as clear as these. In many cases, intuition and experience will largely determine how quickly the problem can be tracked down. But with these basics in mind, a careful and systematic approach will yield positive results fairly quickly. Let us now look at how we can use our knowledge of circuitry and tools to troubleshoot various types of faults.

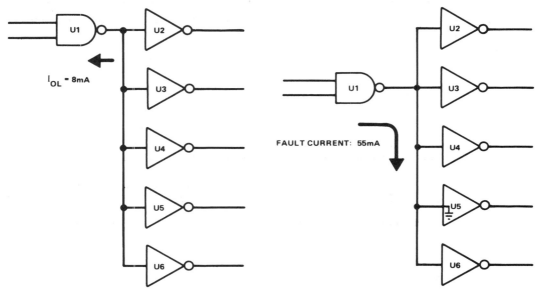

Figure 10-10 a. Current flow in normal node. b. Current flow in faulty node. Courtesy of Hewlett-Packard Company.

10–5 V_{cc}-TO-GROUND SHORTS

This is an appropriate fault to start with since if it exists, it will have to be fixed before anything else can be done. In most cases, a V_{cc}-to-ground short will be caused by a shorted decoupling capacitor, usually due to a fault in the capacitor itself, as indicated in Figure 10–11. Rather than remove capacitors until the problem goes away, we can trace the short in a manner similar to tracing any stuck node. There are, however, some special considerations for dealing with power traces.

To begin with, one side of all electrolytic capacitors on the supply bus should be lifted. This will greatly reduce the time needed to find the short since electrolytics "eat" current pulses, thereby creating many different current paths [1]. Second, the current may seem to go away even though the tracer has not located the short. This can be caused by several things. Power and ground traces generally vary in width, causing the current's field density to fluctuate. If the variation is too great or the tracer sensitivity is set too low, the tracer will lose the signal. This can also happen when the signal branches out over several current paths, causing a current drop in the path being traced. A slight adjustment to the sensitivity control should remedy the problem and tracing can continue.

To trace the fault, remove power from the board and attach the pulser at the power supply pins or across components in the corners. If the board has more than one power connector, parallel current paths can exist. In such cases, it may be necessary to move the pulsing point around to locate the short.

When the short is passed, the current will disappear. To confirm that the short has indeed been found, attach the pulser directly across the suspected short. If it is the short, the tracer will not detect current anywhere else on the board.

The component or solder bridge causing the short can now be removed and the supply traces checked with an ohmmeter to verify that the short is gone. Remember to reattach the electrolytics that were previously lifted.

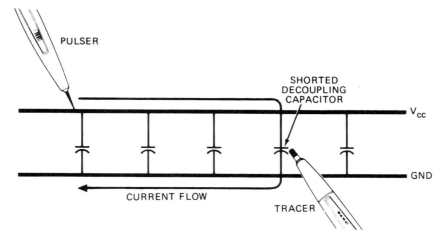

Figure 10–11 Vcc-ground short through capacitor. Courtesy of Hewlett-Packard Company.

10-6 SOLDER AND COPPER BRIDGES

As the density of PC boards has increased, so have occurrences of shorts between traces. These shorts can result from manufacturing errors where the copper has not been properly etched away, and from solder bridges when the boards are assembled. As shown in earlier chapters, identifying two shorted nodes is fairly simple, whether done by stimulus testing or by signature analysis.

The problem now is to locate the bridge if it cannot be found simply with a magnifying glass. The tracer allows us to do this, even if the short is hidden under an IC or other installed components. Figure 10-12 illustrates the process involved. The pulser is placed at the driver end of the node and the tracer sensitivity is set at this point to produce a dim glow. The tracer is then moved along the traces until the lamp goes out, indicating the location of the bridge. A visual inspection should confirm the fault. Solder bridges can be removed by heating with a soldering pencil and sucking off the solder with a desoldering tool. Copper bridges can be removed by scratching the copper with a sharp knife until the traces are separated.

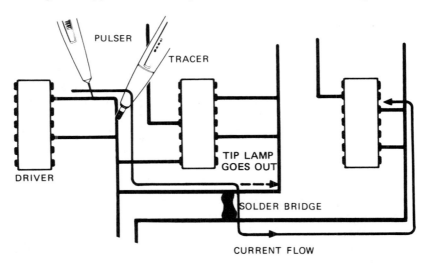

Figure 10-12   Locating a solder bridge with the tracer. Courtesy of Hewlett-Packard Company.

10-7 STUCK NODES

Stuck nodes are a frequently occurring problem in troubleshooting and are a symptom for a group of faults rather than being faults themselves. Simply put, a *stuck node* is a node that should show activity but doesn't. This can be caused by a faulty driver chip or by an internal or external short clamping the node to a fixed level.

The first step in troubleshooting a stuck node should always be to determine if the node is clamped. As indicated earlier, a logic probe will not show any activity if a clamped node is stimulated by a pulser. Based on the results of this test, further investigation will proceed along one of two paths.

Clamped Nodes

If this initial investigation shows the node to be clamped, the next step is to determine what is clamping the node. The problem could be caused by an internally shorted input, an internally shorted driver output, or an external short to V_{cc} or ground due to a solder or copper bridge. Again, the pulser and tracer can be used to locate the short.

Consider the following example, illustrated in Figure 10–13. Here the node is being clamped low through an internal short to ground at one of the gate inputs. As before, the pulser is placed at the driver output and the tracer sensitivity is set at this point just to turn the lamp on. Only the faulty input will have current flowing into it. Thus we can simply touch the tracer to the input pins on the node. The bad input will cause the tracer lamp to be on.

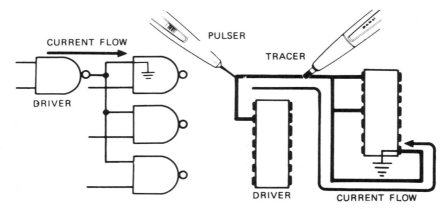

Figure 10–13   Tracing current to faulty input. Courtesy of Hewlett-Packard Company.

What would have happened if it had been the driver output that was clamping the node to ground? In that case, the tracer would have shown no current activity anywhere on the node since the pulser was pulsing directly into the short.

If the node was clamped due to an external short, none of the inputs would have lit the lamp but there would be activity in the trace away from the driver pin. In this case, the fault can be found the same way as for two nodes shorted together. As the tracer is moved past the short, the lamp would go out and a visual inspection would confirm the diagnosis.

Open IC Inputs and Outputs

If the earlier test shows that the node is stuck but is not being held at a fixed level, there is a good possibility that either the node output or one of the IC inputs has opened up internally. In either case, the IC will have to be replaced.

However, a word of caution. Many ICs have control inputs such as enables, resets, and so on, which must be at the proper level for the chip to function. Although these should have been checked earlier in the troubleshooting process, oversights do happen and it does not hurt to double check these inputs with a logic probe. There is a very real risk of damage to the PC board whenever an IC is removed, so one should be very certain that the chip is at fault before performing radical surgery. In Section 10-10 we look at methods for removing IC devices with minimal risk to the board.

10-8 FAULTS ON BUS STRUCTURES

Although placing bus structures under a separate heading would seem to imply a unique set of faults for such circuits, this is not the case. Bus structures are subject to exactly the same types of failures noted earlier. They are simply more difficult to troubleshoot because of their complexity.

The three-state output structure allows more than one driver to be placed on the bus, as shown in Figure 10-14. Indeed, many devices can be both drivers and listeners, depending on how they are enabled.

As with simple node structures, it is important to learn as much as possible about the nature of the fault from the higher levels of investigation before proceeding with low-level tracing. Preliminary and intermediate testing should show not only the faulty node, but whether this fault interferes with only one device or the entire bus line is affected. Such clues are especially invaluable when dealing with a complex bus structure.

In many cases, fault tracing will proceed in a manner similar to that used on single-driver nodes. If the node shows a lack of activity, it should first be checked

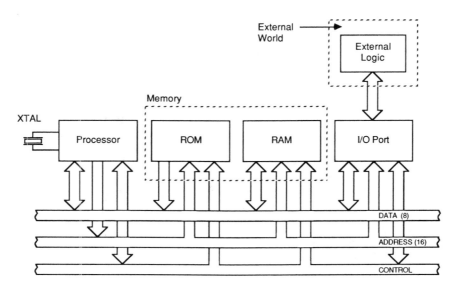

Figure 10-14 A typical microcomputer bus structure.

for clamping using the probe and pulser. If clamped, the pulser and tracer will locate the source of the problem, as before.

Checking drivers for open input and outputs becomes slightly more difficult since we must ensure that only the driver under test is enabled. When testing drivers, be certain that they can be enabled and disabled without stressing them physically or electrically. Also, check multiple inputs to drivers to be sure that you have control when you want to stimulate the circuit. This is not always possible, in which case the bus listeners should be checked first for possible faults.

Ultimately, there are no hard-and-fast rules set out to cover the myriad of problems that can occur in the many diverse bus structures possible in today's digital systems. Rather, the troubleshooter must use a combination of system awareness, knowledge of basic troubleshooting principles, and deductive reasoning to solve each fault occurence. In the next section we will see how the Fluke 9010A can be used to aid in finding difficult bus faults.

10-9 BUS TROUBLESHOOTING USING THE FLUKE 9010A

In conjunction with the current tracer and logic probe, the Fluke 9010A can be an effective tool in troubleshooting node-level faults in bus structures. The key to the Fluke's effectiveness is its ability to control the system's bus structures precisely and to synchronize its stimulus probe to specific periods of the bus cycle [2].

Sometimes, a bus problem may manifest itself only when a device is accessed in a certain way. In such a case, the fault may be difficult to locate using the basic nodal testers if the system cannot be exercised in the manner that induces the fault. The Fluke gives us that necessary control. Let us look at an example to see how the Fluke and a current tracer work together to trace a fault.

The Fluke has just performed a RAM test and has determined that data bits 3 and 4 are tied together. Now that the specific node at fault has been identified, we can use the Fluke to provide the required stimulus for tracing the short.

First, since we are dealing with the data bus, the stimulus probe is set to DATA SYNC mode. Set the probe for HIGH and LOW stimulation and locate it as close as possible to the node source.

Repeat the test that caused the error and instruct the Fluke to LOOP on the error. The probe's red and green lights should now be on, indicating stimulus activity.

As with the logic pulser, set the tracer sensitivity at the tip of the Fluke probe. The tracer can then be moved along the trace as before, until the short is located.

Procedurally, we are doing nothing more complicated than combining the node identification process discussed in Chapter 5 and the current tracing explained earlier in this chapter. The advantage of this method (other than eliminating the cost of purchasing a separate logic pulser) is the added control of the system it provides. Recall the problem discussed earlier regarding the enabling and disabling of multiple node drivers. This can be done easily through the Fluke's control over the device selection logic.

Of course, the Fluke can also be used for simple stimulation of random logic nodes by setting the probe synchronization to the FREE RUN mode and using it as you would a normal logic pulser.

10–10 PROPER REMOVAL OF DIP ICs

It is an unpleasant fact of life that ICs do fail and have to be replaced. If not done properly, the PC board can easily be damaged. Here are two ways in which ICs can be safely removed.

If you are fortunate enough to possess a hollow tip, vacuum-equipped desoldering tool, IC removal is quite simple. The hollow tip is placed over the IC lead until the solder becomes molten. The operator then moves the tip and lead in a circular motion while applying the vacuum suction for about a second. The vacuum not only removes the solder, but also cools the lead and pad area so that they do not reform a solder bond when the heat source is removed. After desoldering all the leads, the IC can be pried out whole. Incidentally, such a tool is an absolute necessity if you are required to desolder chips from multilayer boards.

If you are equipped only with a soldering pencil and hand-held suction device, this method cannot be used since enough solder remains to hold some of the pins to the inside of the hole when the heat is removed. Prying the chip will probably result in some of the pins breaking off inside the hole (and they are not easy to get out!), or in the worst case, causing the pin to pull pad and trace off the board.

To avoid such needless destruction, the following method of IC removal is recommended:

1. Using wire cutters, cut each IC pin where it enters the body of the chip. Keep the body for your dead chip collection.
2. Grip the IC pin with a pair of needle-nose pliers. Heat the IC pad to melt the solder and pull the pin free. Repeat until all pins are removed.
3. Clean out the holes using a desoldering tool and, if necessary, copper braid.

Such treatment will go a long way toward providing a long and productive life for your PC board.

10–11 SUMMARY

Nodal fault diagnosis is accomplished using three tools: the logic pulser, the current tracer, and the logic probe. The logic pulser provides stimulus for the node, while the current tracer and logic probe monitor the current and voltage responses, respectively, to the stimulus. Through proper use of the tools and an understanding of the symptoms displayed, nodal faults can now be pinpointed as to location and cause, drastically reducing the amount of guesswork and, consequently, time necessary to debug digital circuitry.

REFERENCES

1. *The IC Troubleshooters*, Application Note 163–2, Hewlett-Packard Co., Palo Alto, CA.
2. Kaplan, Howard, Find That Bus Short, *Fluke Troubleshooter*, No. 4, October 1983, John Fluke Manufacturing Co., Inc., Everett, WA.

11

UNDERSTANDING THE TROUBLESHOOTING ENVIRONMENT—GROUNDING AND NOISE CONSIDERATIONS

Systems that are logically correct may fail due to poor power supply and ground distribution practices. Such failures may result in intermittent operation with problems that seem to come and go inexplicably. Although essentially design related, troubleshooters should be aware of such problems and be able to recognize them as possible sources of system malfunction.

11-1 POWER AND GROUND DISTRIBUTION SYSTEM CONSIDERATIONS

For reliable circuit operation, voltages at device power pins must meet defined specifications, typically 5 V ± 5 percent. However, voltage drops are created when currents flow through power/ground distribution impedances. To keep the resulting voltage excursions within bounds, we must keep the impedance of the distribution system low. Low resistance is not enough, since even moderate inductance can result in appreciable voltage swings due to the abrupt current changes found in digital systems.

To understand the nature of the problem, consider a set of buffers driving a multiline bus. Under worst-case conditions, surprisingly large rates of change of currents can occur. Because of the inherent inductance in the power/ground distribution system, these can cause significant voltage drops along the conductor paths, resulting in voltage dips and rises as the current is switched on and off. For example, suppose that the buffer pair illustrated in Figure 11-1 switches a total of 16 lines from all 1s to all 0s simultaneously. If each line drives two TTL loads, the current change is 3.2 × 16 lines, or about 50 mA. Assuming a fall time of about 10 ns, we

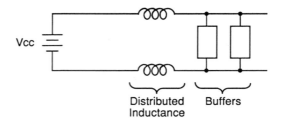

(a)

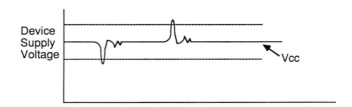

(b) Without decoupling capacitors

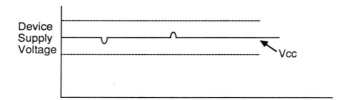

(c) Properly decoupled

Figure 11-1   Distributed inductance of power and ground system results in voltage excursions due to current switching.

see that the rate of change of current is about 5 million amperes per second. This is a massive shock to the system. Since the voltage drop in the inductance of the distribution system is equal to its inductance times the rate of change of current ($v = L \, di/dt$), we see that even a modest amount of inductance in the distribution system poses a problem. A similar effect occurs when all lines are simultaneously switched in the opposite sense. The resulting noise voltages on V_{cc} are illustrated in Figure 11-1(b). If these voltage excursions exceed device limits ($\pm$ 5 percent for TTL and most microprocessor components), the affected devices may malfunction, resulting in intermittent operation.

One very effective way to minimize such noise is to use power and ground planes for supply distribution. However, in most industrial and commercial designs, this is too expensive and thus is not widely used. Fortunately, however, a fairly effective low-impedance distribution system is formed by the grid of power and ground conductor traces that is commonly used on printed circuit cards. This, coupled with suitably placed decoupling capacitors, can go a long way toward creating a quiet power/ground distribution system.

In setting up this power/ground system, proper layout is essential, with decoupling capacitors properly positioned between V_{cc} and ground, close to the device pins. This is illustrated in Figure 11-2. The layout of part (a) is ineffective, as it results

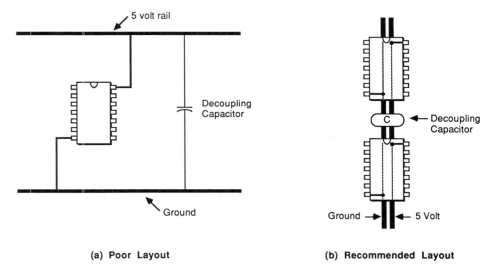

(a) **Poor Layout**   (b) **Recommended Layout**

Figure 11-2   Layout (a) has high series inductance because traces are too far apart and capacitor leads are too long. The recommended layout at (b) dramatically reduces the inductance and shortens the capacitor leads.

in prohibitively large inductance between the capacitor and the worst-positioned IC and will likely fail. The recommended layout of part (b) greatly reduces the track inductance. With this layout, the transient current demand is satisfied locally by the capacitor (rather than from the supply through the power/ground inductance), and thus the voltage dips and rises are minimized, as indicated in Figure 11-1(c). When we consider that the function of the decoupling capacitor is to satisfy the large instantaneous current demand of the device being switched, we see that the safest course is to put one capacitor directly adjacent to each pair of ICs, as illustrated. Note also that to lower the impedance further, the power and ground traces should be made as wide as practical.

Over the years, ceramic disk, tantalum bead, and similar types of capacitors have been used for decoupling. In newer designs, monolithic ceramic types are taking over. The capacitance value to be used depends on the device being decoupled. For small-scale logic devices such as decoders, 0.01 μF is typical.[1] However, some circuits need considerably more. For example, dynamic RAM is sensitive to decou-

---

[1]Even the adequacy of this is now being questioned [1].

pling-induced "soft" errors (i.e., random loss of data due to noise voltages), and larger capacitor values are needed to protect them. Test results [2] have shown that while 0.1 μF directly adjacent to 64K DRAMs is adequate, 0.33 μF is needed to obtain the same level of performance with 256K devices.

If the system under test is "glitching" intermittently for no apparent reason and too few decoupling capacitors are installed, try tack soldering a few in place. In keeping with the principles described above, position them as close to device V_{cc} pins as possible, with leads as short as possible.

11-2 NOISE CONTROL IN ELECTRONIC SYSTEMS

The term "noise" when used in an electrical sense refers to any unwanted signal or disturbance. The V_{cc} voltage excursions described above are examples of noise. Noise signals may be steady state or transient and may contain significant frequency components, ranging from dc to several megahertz and higher [5]. The effect of such noise is insidious and difficult to quantize. There is seemingly an art as well as a science to noise control. Nonetheless, there are some general principles that we can describe and some ensuing practices to which we can routinely adhere to ease the problem.

There are many sources of noise and several ways in which such noise can be coupled into a system. Possible sources include commutator hash (sparking at brushes) from dc motors, heavy load currents flowing in logic grounds, voltage spikes across nonsuppressed relay coils, solenoids and other inductive devices, switched high-energy circuits, ground loops, and current spikes in the logic system itself. Noise may be coupled into a system through conductive paths, by electrostatic or electromagnetic induction or by radiation. Here we limit our attention to conductively coupled noise and its control.

Signal Ground Considerations

In microprocessor systems, as in other electronic systems, a "common" or signal ground is used as the reference from which voltages throughout the system are specified and measured. It is assumed that this ground is everywhere at the same potential—that is, that there are no voltage differences between points on it. In a well-designed system, this is so (or nearly so) and any differences that do exist are so small as to be negligible. However, this may not always be the case; in fact, many real-world circuit malfunctions can be traced to an inadequate ground system. To keep these noise voltages under control requires careful ground current management. This is described next. In addition, keeping distribution system impedance low as described in Section 11-1 is essential.

Conductive Coupling of Noise

Conductive coupling occurs when noise currents (from whatever source) flow through impedances that are common to both the noise source and the logic system. This is illustrated in Figure 11-3. Here the noise voltage caused by stray currents flowing

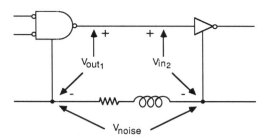

Figure 11-3 Noise voltage is superimposed on signal output.

in the ground impedance is superimposed on the legitimate signal. Thus

$$V_{\text{in}_2} = V_{\text{out}_1} \pm V_{\text{noise}}$$

If the noise is severe enough, it can completely mask the signal. To illustrate, consider Figure 11-4. Assume that the output of gate 1 is logic low, as illustrated in part (a) at its maximum permissible value of 0.4 V. If a noise voltage exceeding 0.4 V is superimposed on this low output, it will drive the input of gate 2 into its undefined region, resulting in a possible "glitch" on its output. Conversely, if the output of gate 1 is high and the noise is negative going, a glitch as in part (b) may result.

This problem can become especially severe if heavy load currents flow through the logic ground as depicted in Figure 11-5. Problems arise due to both resistance and inductance in the ground path. In fact, inductance is usually the dominant factor. However, to simplify the presentation, we will initially ignore the inductance and concentrate on the resistance. Although the details are incomplete, this simplified approach lets us easily visualize the nature of the problem.

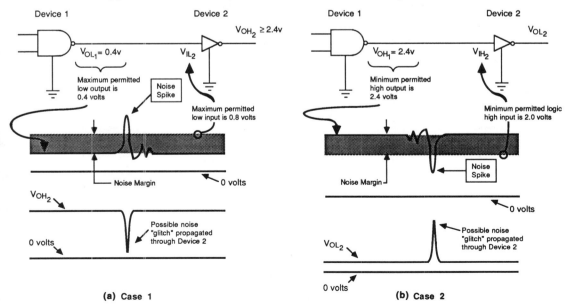

Figure 11-4 If noise exceeds the allowable noise margin, it may propagate throughout the system.

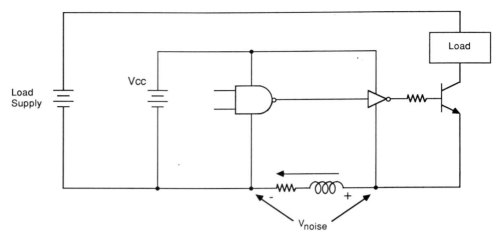

Figure 11-5   Noise caused by conductive coupling.

To illustrate, assume a load current of 10 A and a ground resistance of 0.08 ohm between the two devices indicated. This causes a drop of $10(0.08) = 0.8$ V— thus the second IC will have only 4.2 V between its V_{cc} and ground pins—not enough to guarantee proper operation. Even if the resistance were 0.04 ohm, there would still be a 0.4 V drop, and we would be left with no noise margin on the logic signal.

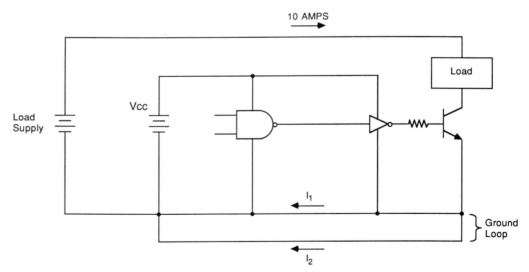

Figure 11-6   Ground loop.

Ground Loops

As a first attempt to solve this problem, one might be tempted to add a low-impedance conductor in parallel with the existing ground as in Figure 11-6. However, this only partially removes the load current from the logic ground. Experience has shown that it does not solve the problem, as it is not possible to predict how the current will divide. Thus, instead of solving the problem, we have created a circuit loop with currents in both conductors. This is referred to as a "ground loop."

11-3 GROUND CURRENT MANAGEMENT

A more suitable approach to solving the problem is to revise the circuit in such a fashion as to steer the load current away from the logic ground entirely. This is known as ground current management and is illustrated in Figure 11-7. Note that the load current no longer flows through the signal ground—thus it cannot create a voltage drop as described earlier. Note also that the grounds now connect at one point only.

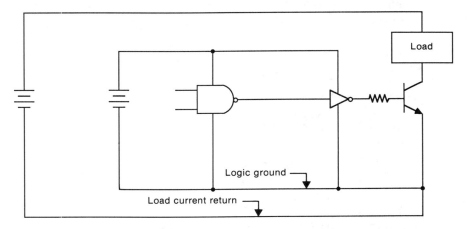

Figure 11-7 Noise currents steered out of the logic system ground.

This is referred to as "single-point" grounding. With single-point grounding, the load current is carefully steered away from the logic ground. Single-point grounding is a fundamental tenet of conductive noise control in electronic systems.

When dealing with ground current management, you need pictorial representations so that you can see clearly the various current paths. Schematics are inadequate because they do not show the physical orientations. To illustrate, the previous diagram is repeated below in schematic form (Figure 11-8). Note that the current steering nature of the circuit is completely obscured in this representation. In contrast, the pictorial representation of Figure 11-7 shows clearly the current management aspect of ground system design.

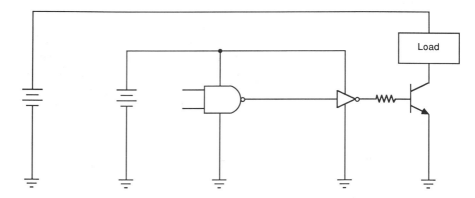

Figure 11-8 Schematic does not adequately show ground current management aspect of the ground system.

The stray inductance that we have ignored adds greatly to the problem. In fact, as noted, its effect is usually far more severe than that of the resistance. Thus the observations noted above are quite on the conservative side.

11-4 GROUNDING PRACTICES

In any given installation, there may be up to four ground systems. These are:

1. The logic system ground
2. The analog system ground
3. The power supply ground
4. The safety (true earth) ground

Note that all of these are not necessarily present in any given system. For example, in portable battery-operated equipment, there will be no safety ground; in purely digital systems, there will be no analog ground.

Because the various elements of the system must work together, all grounds must ultimately be tied together. To do this in a manner such as to avoid conductive noise problems, a clear understanding of the nature of each is essential. The overriding principle here is to set up all return paths such that currents do not flow where they can introduce noise voltages into susceptible areas.

Logic System Ground

The logic ground has already been dealt with. As noted, it is the reference for logic signals in the digital portion of the system. Thus it is the circuit common for the μP chip, the memories, the decode logic, the I/O ports, and so on.

Analog System Ground

In systems incorporating analog gear, a separate "analog" ground may be required—for example, in high-precision systems or systems with low analog voltage ranges. Since both suffer loss of accuracy for even small noise voltages, a highly stable ground reference is necessary. To understand why, consider Figure 11-9. Part (a) shows a system where ground currents from the digital subsystem flow through the measurement portion of the analog subsystem ground, causing a voltage drop that is superimposed on the legitimate analog input as illustrated in part (b). In high-level and low-resolution systems this noise is negligible; in low-level and high-resolution systems, it is not. In low-level systems, the noise can completely mask the input, whereas in high-precision systems, it can completely rob the result of its significance.

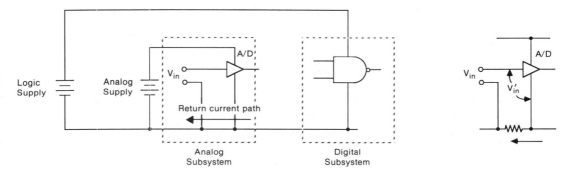

(a) Digital subsystem currents flow through analog ground.

(b) $V_{in} \neq V'_{in}$ because of superimposed noise.

Figure 11-9   Improper grounding can cause problems with analog subsystems.

For critical applications, one may separate the analog and digital grounds as indicated in Figure 11-10. This scheme keeps the digital ground return currents out of the analog ground circuit, avoiding the generation of a noise voltage as noted above. Note, however, that the two subsystem grounds must come together at some point, since the A/D converter supplies digital information to the logic subsystem. Note also that a pictorial representation is necessary, as described previously, to show the current management details.

Power Supply Ground

The power supply ground must connect to both the analog and the digital grounds. As noted above, currents may have to be carefully steered out of the analog portion (high-resolution or low-level systems). Often, however, power return is common with the digital ground. This generally poses no problem as long as the ground impedance is kept low and heavy load currents are prevented from flowing in this return.

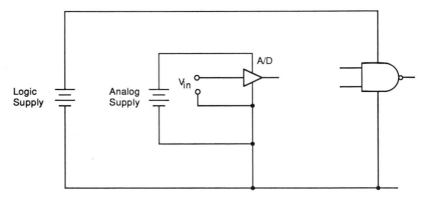

Figure 11–10   Improved grounding to keep noise currents out of analog subsystem.

Safety Ground

The fourth ground is the safety or frame ground. It is used to protect personnel from the hazards of electric shock and is a true "earth" in the sense that it actually connects to earth at some point. This ground is connected to frames, cabinets, panels, and other exposed metallic parts of the system. Requirements here are governed by national and local electrical safety codes. Unfortunately, these codes sometimes conflict with good noise-control principles.

11-5 ILLUSTRATIVE EXAMPLES

We will illustrate two examples of improper grounding practices that can result in deviant system behavior. Although the designs are logically correct, these practices can cause them to malfunction and hence be passed to the troubleshooter for attention.

Example 11-1: A Backplane Problem

A common electronic packaging scheme is the multiboard arrangement depicted in Figure 11–11. As illustrated, a motherboard distributes power, ground, and logic signals to individual boards. Care must be exercised here to avoid creating noise problems. Here the indicated driver on card A drives logic circuits on several cards via the backplane. Considerable capacitive load exists due to the stray capacitance of the long conductor run and the input capacitance of the devices driven. As a result, the driver must switch considerable transient current. This current flows through the impedance of the ground paths, and because of the fast rate of change of current and the inherent inductance of the path, considerable noise voltage may be created. This means that the "ground" connection between the various gate grounds is not solid and there is a momentary difference of potential (a "glitch") between the ground pin of the driver and the ground pins of the driven gates. This noise voltage is superimposed on top of the legitimate

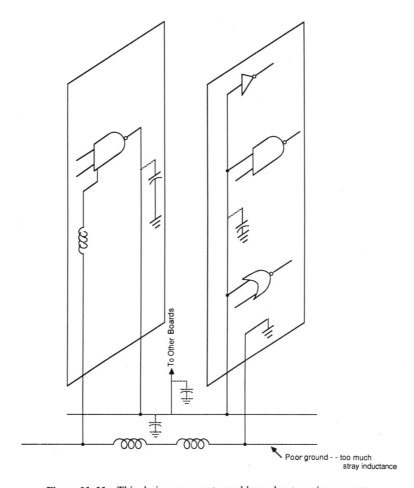

Figure 11-11   This design can create problems due to noise currents.

signal, and if severe enough, can propagate through the driven gates, resulting in glitches in their outputs as described earlier.

The way to avoid this problem is to utilize a properly designed ground system [4]. As noted previously, low resistance is not enough since the principal culprit is the inductance. Thus a low-inductance system must be created. This is shown in Figure 11-12. Note that good ground current management techniques plus several other noise reduction techniques are employed here. For example, the ground path for the driver on card A has been separated from the rest of the logic ground on card A to ensure that no driver current flows through it. In addition, the driver has been physically relocated near the edge of the card to shorten its ground path and hence lower its impedance. To further lower the impedance of the ground system, the original ground interconnection on the backplane has been replaced by a heavy ground trace. This helps ensure a "solid" ground system with acceptably low voltage difference between all card grounds. A fur-

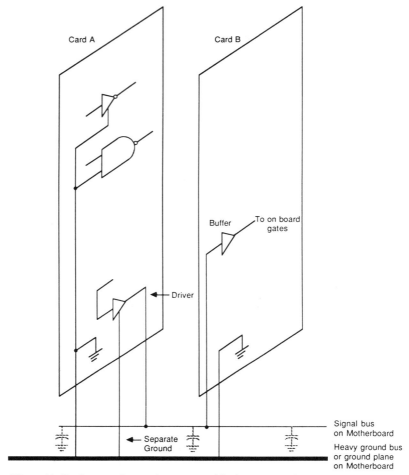

Figure 11-12   Improved ground system provides better ground current management.

ther refinement is the addition of a buffer on each driven card. This helps lower the capacitance seen by the driver. (It now only drives one capacitive input per card, instead of several. In addition, it has less stray capacitance to drive.) All these techniques help reduce noise and go a long way to ensuring a quiet bus.[2]

Example 11-2: A Problem Due to a Safety Ground

As noted earlier, improper grounding practice can result in ground loops. As illustrated in this example, this can permit coupling of noise into the system from external sources. A particularly easy trap to get caught in is the one created by connecting two or more signal grounds to the green wire safety ground of the power system [6] as illustrated in Figure 11-13. If both ends are "grounded" to this line as shown, noise currents from external sources such as motors will flow through this signal ground, creating noise volt-

[2]Note that each buffer adds a delay of typically 10 ns maximum. The effect of these delays should be evaluated with respect to timing margins.

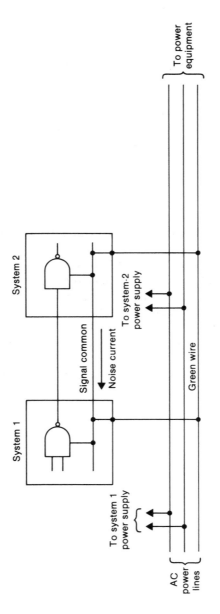

Figure 11-13 Ground loop created by connection to green wire ground.

ages as described earlier. However, if one end or the other is disconnected, the ground loop is eliminated. The metal cabinets can still remain attached for safety purposes—only the signal ground connection needs to be broken. Always comply with safety code requirements.

11-6 SUMMARY

The problem with noise control is that it is an imprecise science—although we can enunciate basic principles, we cannot quantize effects, and hence we cannot analyze their interrelations. Because of this, we must sometimes resort to a "cut and try" approach. A good understanding of basic principles, however, provides us with valuable insights and a resulting set of guidelines to follow.

REFERENCES

1. Catt, Ivor, Walton, David, and Malcolm Davidson, *Digital Hardware Design,* Macmillan Press Ltd., London, 1979.
2. Martin, Arch G., *Decoupling 256K DRAMs,* AVX Corporation, Myrtle Beach, SC.
3. White, Donald R., *EMI Control in the Design of Printed Circuit Boards and Backplanes,* Don White Consultants, Inc., Gainsville, VA, 1982.
4. Fichtenbaum, Matthew L., Circuit Layout Minimizes Noise in Digital Systems, *Electronics,* August 19, 1976.
5. Harrison, Thomas J., Handbook of Industrial Control Computers, Wiley-Interscience, New York, 1972.
6. Hall, Douglas V., Microprocessors and Digital Systems, McGraw-Hill, New York, 1980.

Appendix A

THE MOTOROLA MC6809
SYSTEM

THE 6809 CPU

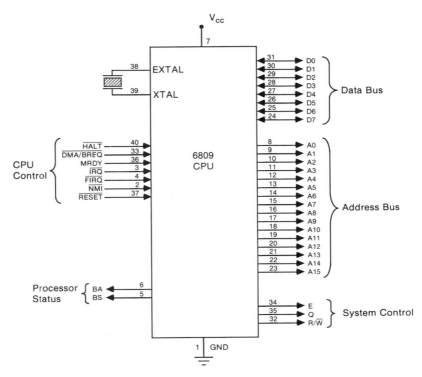

Figure A-1: 6809 CPU signals, functional assignments and pin-outs.

Address bus: a standard 16-bit, tri-stateable address bus, able to access directly 64K bytes of memory and I/O using memory-mapped techniques.

Data bus: a standard 8-bit, bidirectional data bus.

Clock (E): the primary timing reference for the system. Most bus transactions are keyed to its falling edge.

Secondary clock (Q): the quadrature clock. It is used to simplify the design of some types of interfaces.

Read/Write (R/$\overline{W}$): the direction control line. When high, it indicates that a read cycle is in progress; when low, it indicates a write cycle.

Memory ready (MRDY): stretches the E and Q clocks to permit interfacing of slow peripheral devices. It is also used to extend the access time in multiprocessor applications when shared memories are used.

DMA/Bus request ($\overline{DMA/BREQ}$): an input line used to alert the processor when a DMA transaction or a refresh operation is required.

Bus available (BA): an output line that indicates to external logic that the system buses have been tri-stated.

Bus state (BS): output line that, in conjunction with BA, provides information about the internal state of the processor.

$\overline{HALT}$: an input line used to suspend operation of the CPU and tri-state the buses.

Non maskable interrupt ($\overline{NMI}$): a nonmaskable interrupt request input; has the highest priority.

$\overline{IRQ}$: the standard maskable interrupt request input.

$\overline{FIRQ}$: $\overline{FIRQ}$ is a maskable, fast interrupt request input.

$\overline{RESET}$: used to reset the CPU. Incorporates an internal Schmitt trigger to permit usage of a simple *RC* network.

$\overline{XTAL/EXTAL}$: accepts a frequency-determining element such as a crystal or TTL-level clock. Because the internal oscillator contains a divide-by-4 circuit, the frequency of the source must be four times the desired bus frequency.

TIMING WAVEFORMS

See Figure A–2.

SOME FAMILY DEVICES

A number of parallel, serial, and other devices are available. These include parallel ports (standard and industrial versions), serial ports (synchronous and asynchronous), CRT controllers, programmable timers, video display generators, an advanced data link controller, a DMA controller, a memory management unit, a floating point ROM, and so on.

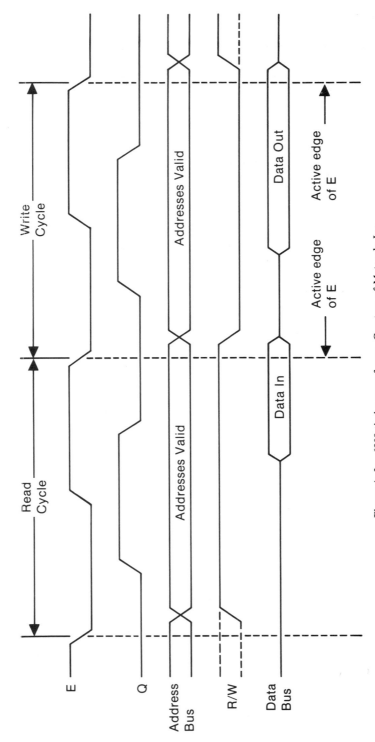

Figure A-2: 6809 timing waveforms. Courtesy of Motorola Inc.

Example A-1: The 6821 Peripheral Interface Adapter (PIA)

A universal parallel I/O port with handshake features. Incorporates two 8-bit bidirectional ports and four peripheral control lines (Figure A-3). Each of its 16 peripheral data lines may be configured as either an input or an output and its four I/O control lines may be used in simple flag polling operation, interrupt-driven operation, handshake operation, or combinations thereof.

From a software point of view, a PIA looks like a set of six registers, as depicted in Figure A-4. To configure a line for output, set its corresponding bit in the data direction register = 1; to make a line an input, set the bit to 0. To define the operating characteristics of the port, consult Table A-1.

In each port, the data register and the data direction register share the same address. A pointer bit in each control register (bit 2) determines whether the address refers to the data register or the direction register. With port A, for example (Figure A-4), if the pointer = 0, address 8000 accesses the direction register; if the pointer = 1, address 8000 accesses the data register.

To configure the PIA with all side A as output and all side B as input, write FF to direction register A and 00 to the direction register B. Control options are summarized in Table A-1. If no control or handshake is required, we need only set the pointer bit (bit 2) to 1. A suitable initialization sequence for this case is:

1. Clear the PIA using reset (a hardware operation).
2. Write FF to direction register A.
3. Write 04 to both control registers.
4. Perform the required test.

If control or handshake is needed, consult Table A-1.

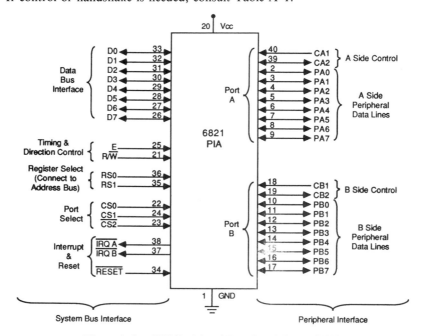

Figure A-3: 6821 Peripheral Interface Adapter (PIA).

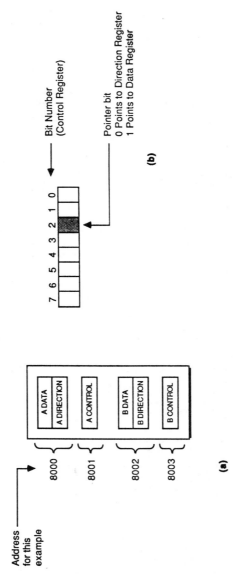

Figure A–4: PIA looks like six addressable registers. The example shown has been assigned addresses 8000 to 8003.

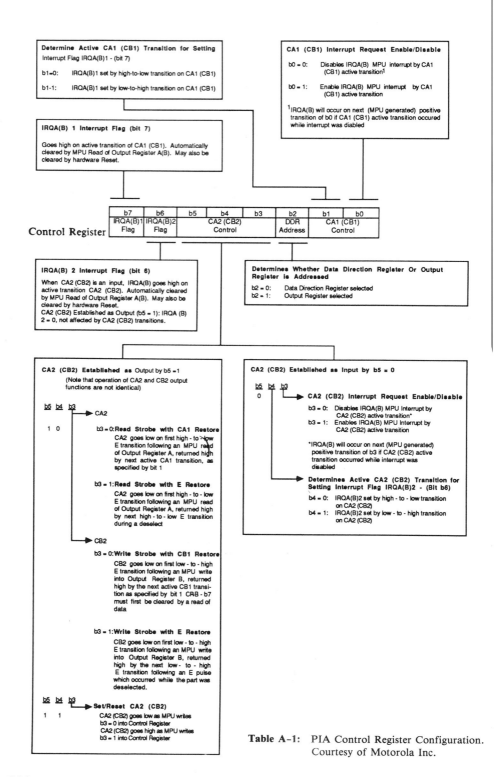

Table A-1: PIA Control Register Configuration.
Courtesy of Motorola Inc.

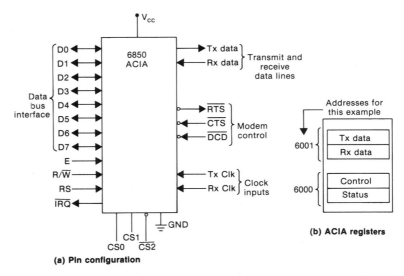

(a) Pin configuration

(b) ACIA registers

Figure A-5: 6850 Asynchronous Interface Adapter (ACIA). Hardware and software model. Each register consists of one read-only register and one write-only register sharing the same address.

Example A-2: The 6850 Asynchronous Communications Interface Adapter (ACIA)

The 6850 ACIA (Figure A-5) is one of several asynchronous serial I/O ports available to interface serial devices (such as CRT terminals) to the 6809. It is programmable and must be software configured to match the needs of the application. Included are a number of sense and control lines that permit it to couple via a modem to telephone lines for

COUNTER DIVIDE SELECT BITS

CR1	CR0	Function
0	0	÷ 1
0	1	÷ 16
1	0	÷ 64
1	1	Master Reset

WORD SELECT BITS

CR4	CR3	CR2	Function
0	0	0	7 Bits + Even Parity + 2 Stop Bits
0	0	1	7 Bits + Odd Parity + 2 Stop Bits
0	1	0	7 Bits + Even Parity + 1 Stop Bit
0	1	1	7 Bits + Odd Parity + 1 Stop Bit
1	0	0	8 Bits + 2 Stop Bits
1	0	1	8 Bits + 1 Stop Bit
1	1	0	8 Bits + Even Parity + 1 Stop Bit
1	1	1	8 Bits + Odd Parity + 1 Stop Bit

TRANSMITTER CONTROL BILLS (MODEM CONTROL)

CR6	CR5	Function
0	0	$\overline{RTS}$ = low, Transmitting Interrupt Disabled.
0	1	$\overline{RTS}$ = low, Transmitting Interrupt Enabled.
1	0	$\overline{RTS}$ = high, Transmitting Interrupt Disabled.
1	1	$\overline{RTS}$ = low, Transmits a Break level on the Transmit Data Output. Transmitting Interrupt Disabled.

remote communication with other computers or peripheral devices. An external clock is required for the transmit and receive sections. This clock is generally 16 or 64 times the baud rate (software selection as noted in Table A-2).

Configuration details are summarized in Table A-2. To reset the ACIA, write the master reset word 03 to the control register. A typical serial word consists of 8 data bits, 1 stop bit, and an external clock rate that is 16 times the baud rate. From Table A-2 we see that a suitable configuration word is 0001 0101 (15 hex). This must be written to the control register following master reset. The ACIA does not have a hardware reset. To reset the ACIA, write 0000 0011 (03 hex) to its control register.

Sample System

An example system for use in this book is illustrated in Figure A-6.

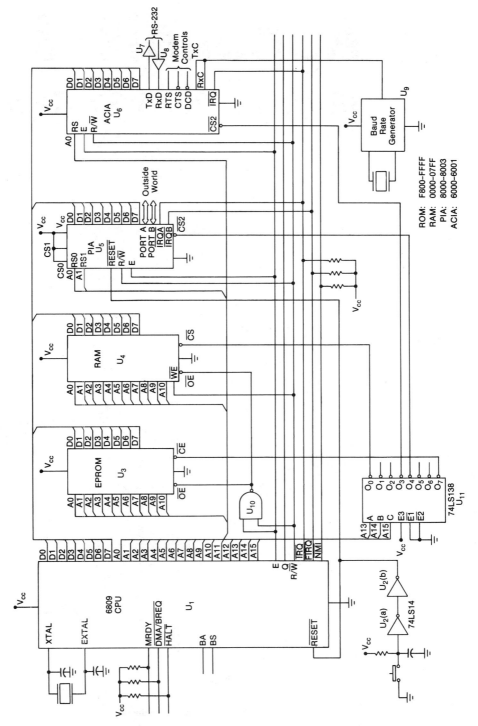

Figure A–6: Sample 6809 system for troubleshooting examples of this book.

ROM: F800–FFFF
RAM: 0000–07FF
PIA: 8000–8003
ACIA: 6000–6001

Appendix B
THE INTEL 8085 SYSTEM

THE 8085 CPU

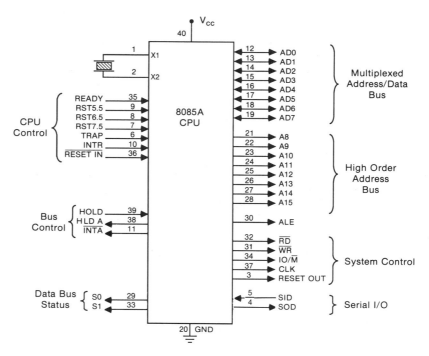

Figure B-1: 8085 pin assignments.

Address/data bus: low-order address lines, multiplexed with the data bus.

High-order address bus: high-order address bus lines, not multiplexed.

Address latch enable (ALE): the demultiplex signal. Its active (latching) edge is its falling edge.

Read ($\overline{RD}$): an active-low read control signal used by interface logic to gate data from memory or I/O devices onto the data bus during read transactions.

Write ($\overline{WR}$): an active-low write control signal used by external logic to gate data off the data bus during writes.

IO/$\overline{M}$: a signal output by the processor to tell external logic whether the transaction is a memory or an I/O transaction.

S0, S1: status lines that provide information about the bus state.

READY: an input used to insert wait states in the cycle.

TRAP: the nonmaskable (highest-priority) interrupt request input.

Interrupt request (INTR): a general-purpose (maskable) hardware interrupt.

Restart interrupts (RST 5.5, RST 6.5, and RST 7.5): maskable interrupt inputs.

Interrupt acknowledge ($\overline{INTA}$): acknowledges valid interrupt requests.

HOLD: permits devices to float the processor off the buses.

Hold acknowledge (HLDA): output by the processor to notify the requesting device when the buses become available.

$\overline{RESET\ IN}$: an active-low input used to initialize the CPU.

RESET OUT: active-high output which indicates that the CPU is in the process of being reset.

Serial input data (SID): a direct serial input.

Serial output data (SOD): a direct serial output.

X1, X2: connection for external crystal or RC network used to control internal clock oscillator.

CLK: clock output for use as a system clock. Derives its timing from the X1, X2 clock oscillator circuit.

TIMING WAVEFORMS

Figure B–2 shows the general nature of 8085 system timing. Addresses are guaranteed valid on the trailing edge of ALE—thus trailing edge logic must be used to demultiplex the bus. (For complete 8085 timing details, consult the manufacturer's data sheets.)

SOME FAMILY DEVICES

The 8085 family contains one of the richest sets of support chips of any of the 8-bit families. Included are a number of powerful chips, including serial and parallel I/O ports, a programmable interrupt controller, DMA controllers, communication interfaces, programmable interval timers, CRT controllers, and so on.

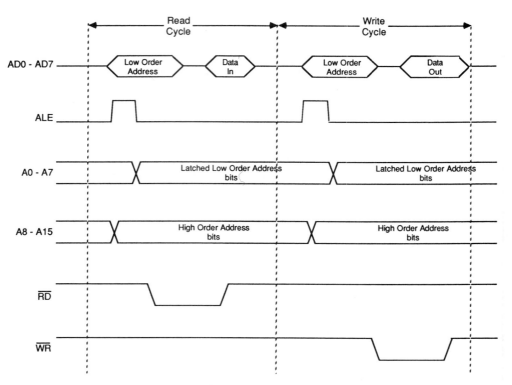

Figure B-2: General Read/Write timing relationships.

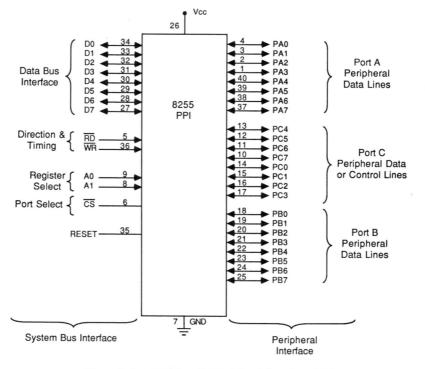

Figure B-3: 8255 Parallel Peripheral Interface (PPI).

Example B-1: The 8255A Parallel Peripheral Interface (PPI)

A universal, software-configurable, parallel I/O device, featuring two 8-bit ports designated A and B and one dual 4-bit port designated C (Figure B-3). From the software point of view, the PPI looks like three data registers and a control register, each with its own unique address (Figure B-4). The PPI has three basic modes of operation,

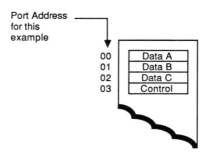

Figure B–4: From the programmer's viewpoint, the PPI looks like four registers.

designated mode 0, mode 1, and mode 2, respectively (Table B-1). The control register is used to select the desired mode.

Table B-1

Mode	Description
0	Simple input or output
1	Input or output with handshaking
2	Bidirectional I/O with handshaking

Mode 0: The basic mode. Provides simple input and output with no handshaking. Any port may be configured for input or output.[1] There are 16 different possibilities. To select a configuration, write the corresponding configuration byte to the control register. Figure B-5 illustrates some sample cases.

Example B-2: A Mode 0 Configuration

As an example, to configure ports A and C as output and port B as input, write the control byte 82 to the control register. A routine to configure the PPI for this case is indicated in Figure B-6(b).

SAMPLE SYSTEM

An example system for most of the 8085 examples in this book is illustrated in Figure B-7. It uses a memory-mapped design. I/O mapped designs differ slightly in that they use IO/$\overline{\text{M}}$ as a decoder conditioning signal.

---

[1]All lines in a given port must be input or all must be output—individual lines cannot be assigned separately.

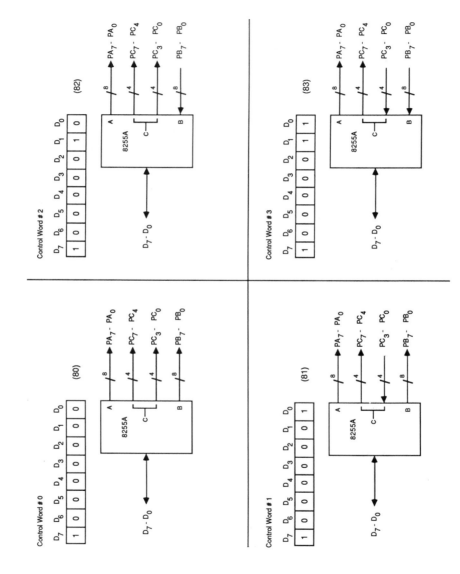

Figure B–5: Some example Mode 0 configurations. There are 16 variations. Copyright © 1986 by Intel Corporation. Used with permission.

274

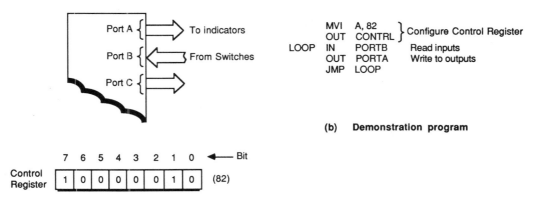

(b)   **Demonstration program**

(a)   **Port definition and
Control Register**

Figure B–6:   Illustrating configuration and usage of the 8255 PPI.

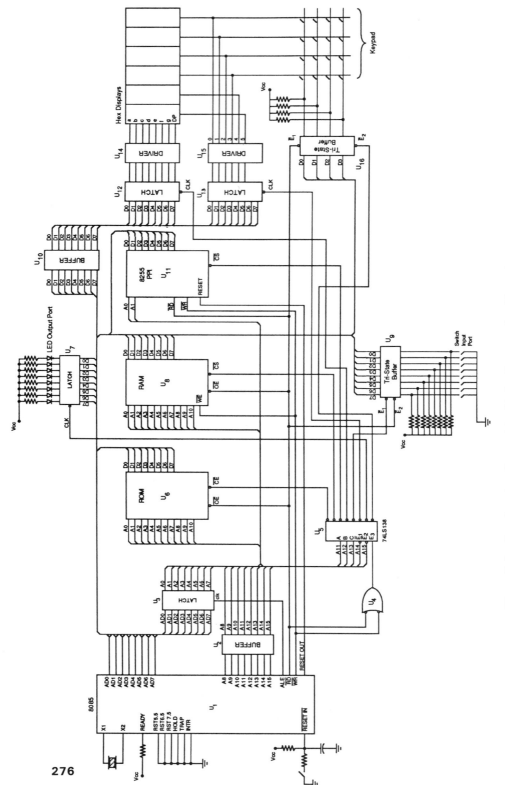

Figure B-7: Sample system for most troubleshooting examples. The system uses memory mapped I/O.

Appendix C
THE ZILOG Z80 SYSTEM

THE ZILOG PROCESSOR

The Zilog Z80 is an 8-bit I/O-mapped processor with pin assignments as indicated in Figure C-1.

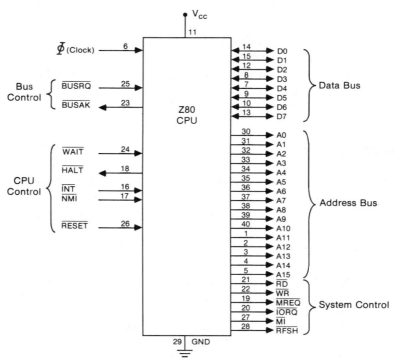

Figure C–1: Z80 pin assignments.

Address bus: a standard 16-bit, tri-stateable address bus able to access directly 64K bytes of memory space. The lower 8 bits are also used for I/O-mapped devices. During refresh, the lower 7 bits contain a valid refresh address.

Data bus: a standard 8-bit, bidirectional data bus.

Memory read ($\overline{RD}$): an active-low read control signal used by interface logic to gate data from memory or I/O devices onto the data bus during read transactions.

Memory write ($\overline{WR}$): an active-low write control signal used by external logic to gate data off the data bus during write transactions.

Memory request ($\overline{MREQ}$): an active-low output that indicates when a memory transaction is in progress.

Input/output request ($\overline{IORQ}$): an active-low output that indicates when an I/O transaction is in progress.

Machine cycle one ($\overline{M1}$): an active-low output that is asserted during the fetch portion of an instruction execution.

Halt state ($\overline{HALT}$): active-low output. Indicates that the CPU has executed a halt instruction and is armed, waiting for an interrupt.

$\overline{WAIT}$: a "Wait state" request input used to insert wait states into the cycle.

Nonmaskable interrupt ($\overline{NMI}$): the highest-priority interrupt request input.

Interrupt request ($\overline{INT}$): a general-purpose (maskable) hardware interrupt.

Bus request ($\overline{BUSRQ}$): an active-low input used to float the processor ff the buses.

Bus acknowledge ($\overline{BUSAK}$): an active-low output used to advise devices that the buses are floated.

$\overline{RESET}$: an active-low input used to initialize the CPU.

CPU clock (Φ): timing for the processor is supplied by a TTL-level clock input connected to this pin.

TIMING WAVEFORMS

Basic system timing is illustrated in Figure C-2. There are several variations on this basic waveform, depending on the transaction in progress and whether or not wait states are required. (For full details, consult the Z80 data book.)

SOME FAMILY DEVICES

The Z80 family contains a number of bus-compatible devices, including serial and parallel I/O ports, programmable interrupt controllers, DMA controllers, communication interfaces, programmable interval timers, CRT controllers, and so on. In addition, many Intel components are directly bus compatible with the Z80.

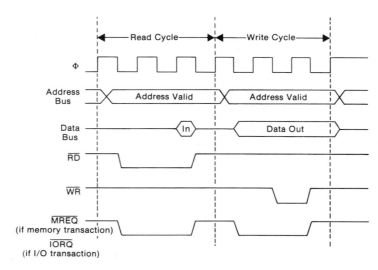

Figure C–2:   Basic Z80 timing waveforms.

Example C-1: The Z80-PIO Parallel I/O Interface (PIO)

The PIO is a universal, parallel I/O device featuring a pair of 8-bit ports with associated control lines as depicted in Figure C-3. Each port may be independently configured for

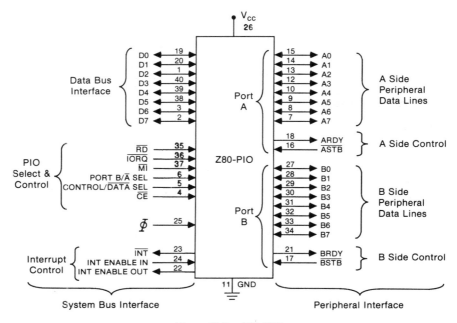

Figure C–3:   Z80 PIO

input, output, or control. When designated a control port, lines may be individually assigned to input or output. Port A may be configured as a bidirectional port. The PIO also implements a powerful interrupt capability.

From a software point of view, the PIO looks like four addressable registers (Figure C-4). The PIO has four basic modes, designated mode 0, mode 1, mode 2, and mode

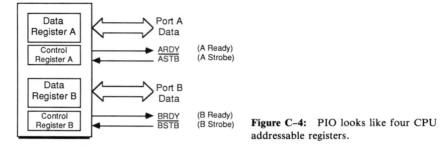

Figure C-4: PIO looks like four CPU addressable registers.

3 (Table C-1). The control registers are used to select the desired mode.

Table C-1

Mode	Operation
0	Output with handshaking
1	Input with handshaking
2	Bidirectional I/O with handshaking
3	Control mode

Check the Z80 data manual for further details.

Sample System

An example system for use in this book is illustrated in Figure C-5.

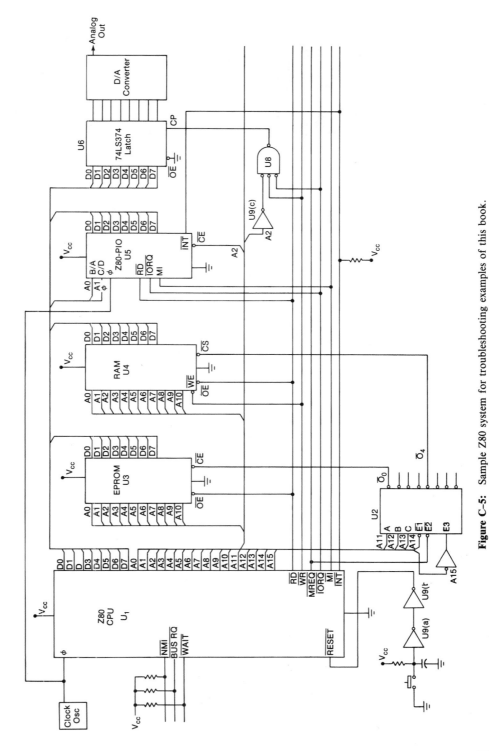

Figure C–5: Sample Z80 system for troubleshooting examples of this book.

Appendix D
AN EXAMPLE 68000 SYSTEM

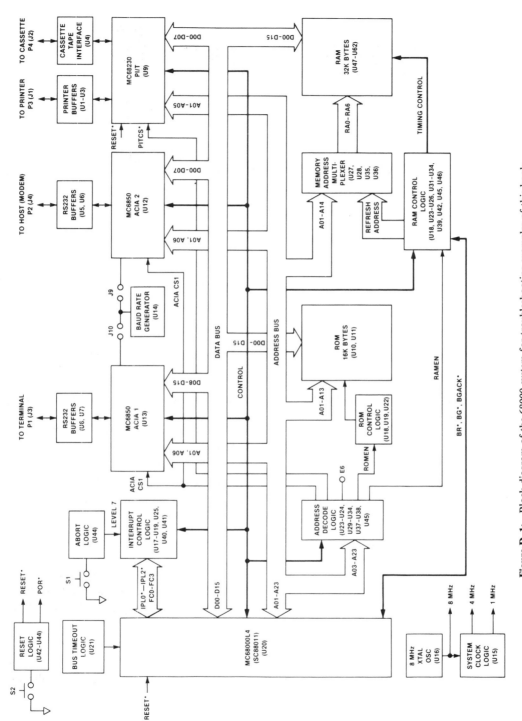

Figure D-1: Block diagram of the 68000 system for troubleshooting examples of this book. Copyright © Motorola Inc. Used with permission.

283

Appendix E

THE 9010A MICROSYSTEM TROUBLESHOOTER

Incorporates ten kilobytes of internal RAM that holds up to 100 programs with up to approximately 1000 total steps. Sixteen 32-bit registers are provided, nine of which are available for use by the programmer. (Details of register usage are contained in the Programmer's Manual.) Register E has a special usage. It is the intermediate register for I/O communication. A READ command copies data into the E register; a WRITE from the E register sends data back to the outside world. To illustrate, assume that address 8002 is an input port and address 8000 is an output port. The following routine reads input port data and writes it to the output port.

READ @ 8002   (input ⟶ register E)

WRITE @ 8000 = REGE   (register E ⟶ output)

PROGRAMMING OVERVIEW

Programs are constructed of sequences of the same 9010A tests, operations, and functions as those used for normal, hands-on troubleshooting plus a few additional steps—thus, if you know how to use the 9010A in the immediate mode, you already know most of what is required to program it.

Keys Unique to Programming

There are several keys unique to programmed operation. (These are the keys labeled "Test Sequencing" and "Arithmetic" in Figure 5–8.)

284

The display key (DISPL).   This key permits the user to create messages in programs to be used for operator prompts, display of computed or gathered data, and so on. Display outputs may be alphanumeric messages or numerical values (or a combination). Register contents may be displayed. Data may be displayed in decimal or hexadecimal format, depending on the display format control character used. For example, to display a register's content in decimal, precede the register number in the display statement by the decimal format control character @; to display in hexadecimal, use the format control character $.

Example E–1: Displaying Register Contents

Assume that register 5 contains the number 32 (hex). This is 50 in decimal. When executed, the command DPY-$5 outputs the contents of register 5 in hexadecimal (i.e., 32), whereas the command DPY-@5 outputs it in decimal (i.e., 50).

The label key (LABEL).   To control the flow of logic in a program, the programmer must be able to direct it to specified points, either unconditionally or as the result of some computational or logic step or as the result of some input stimulus. To define the desired destination point, a label is used. To create a label, press the LABEL key followed by the label number desired (i.e., LABEL 3).

The unconditional branch key (GOTO).   A GOTO statement in a program unconditionally directs operation to the label specified in the program statement.

Conditional branches (IF, >, and = keys).   These keys are used to create tests. The general form of the test is illustrated in Figure E–1. If the test is satisfied, the branch is taken. If it is not, the next instruction in sequence is executed.

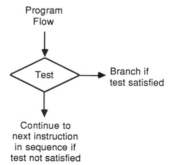

Figure E–1:   General form of a test.

SOME SAMPLE PROGRAMS

Following are two useful troubleshooting programs. Notice how the display command DPY is used to prompt the operator (DPY-POSITION PROBE-PRESS CONT) and how it provides feedback (DPY-ADDRESS @2). The latter statement displays the address captured in Register 2 on the console in decimal format.

```
         SYNC DATA
         DPY - POSITION PROBE-PRESS CONT
         STOP
      1: LABEL 1
         READ PROBE
         WRITE @ OOOO = OO            (See note below)
         READ PROBE
         IF REGO AND 1OOOOOO > O GOTO 4
         REG1 = 1
         REG2 = O
      2: LABEL 2
         READ PROBE
         WRITE @ OOOO = REG1          (See note below)
         READ PROBE
         IF REGO AND 1OOOOOO > O GOTO 3
         IF REG2 = 7  GOTO 4
         SHL REG1
         INC REG2
         GOTO 2
      3: LABEL 3
         DPY - DATA @2
         GOTO 5
      4: LABEL 4
         DPY - NOT A DATA LINE
      5: LABEL 5
         DPY - + PRESS CONT
         STOP
         DPY -
         GOTO 1
```

Figure E-2: Automatic Address Identification Program. (Adapted from 9010A Operator's Manual). Copyright © John Fluke Mfg Co Inc. Used with permission.

Example E-2: An Address Identification Program

The program shown in Figure E-2 makes use of the features described above. It automatically identifies address lines and displays them on the console readout. When using this program with multiplexed bus systems that use an external demultiplexing latch, care must be exercised, because the address may not be valid at the same time on opposite sides of the latch. As noted in Figure 5-12, the probe should be synchronized to ADDRESS for some measurement points, and to DATA for others.

The program works by successively writing a logic 1 to each address line in turn (Figure E-3), then via the READ PROBE instruction, detects when the "walking 1" arrives at the probe. A pair of registers keeps track of activity and determines on which line the probe was positioned when the 1 is detected. It then writes this address to the display. This program is used as discussed in Section 5-9.

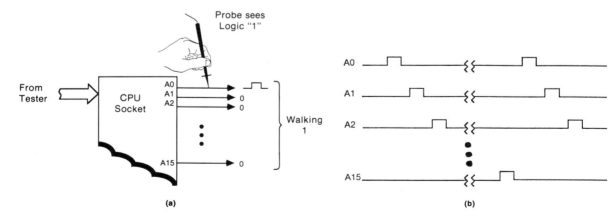

Figure E-3: "Walking 1" pattern on address bus for Automatic Address Identification Program.

Example E–3: A Data Bus Identification Program

This program (Figure E–4) is similar to the address identification program described above.

```
SYNC ADDRESS      (See Fig 5-12 for multiplexed buses)
DPY - POSITION PROBE-PRESS CONT
STOP
1: LABEL 1
READ PROBE
READ @ 0000
READ PROBE
IF REGO AND 1000000 > 0 GOTO 4
REG1 = 1
REG2 = 0
2: LABEL 2
READ PROBE
READ @ REG1
READ PROBE
IF REGO AND 1000000 > 0 GOTO 3
IF REG2 = F  GOTO 4
SHL REG1
INC REG2
GOTO 2
3: LABEL 3
DPY - ADDRESS @2
GOTO 5
4: LABEL 4
DPY - NOT AN ADDRESS
5: LABEL 5
DPY - + PRESS CONT
STOP
DPY -
GOTO 1
```

Figure E–4: Automatic Data Bus Identification Program.

Appendix F
STATIC STIMULUS TESTER
(MANUAL VERSION)

A simple manual tester can be constructed from switches, LEDs, and a few TTL devices, as indicated in Chapter 6. (Basic circuits are shown in Figure 6–4.) To construct a tester for any given processor, select and combine as many of these circuits as necessary.

AN EXAMPLE TESTER FOR THE 6809

A design for the 6809 is shown in Figure F–1.

> *Address simulation.* Address circuits use nondebounced switches, labeled A0 to A15. LED indicators display logic states on the address bus.
>
> *Clock signals.* The 6809 provides two clocks, denoted E and Q, respectively. These are generated using debounced switches as indicated.
>
> *R/$\overline{W}$.* R/$\overline{W}$ is used for direction control. It has two active states. For a read operation, R/$\overline{W}$ is set high; for a write operation, it is set low. For this signal, it is best to use a debounced switch.
>
> *Data bus simulation.* Because data bus operation is bidirectional, tri-state buffers are needed. Note that these buffers are controlled by the read/write line R/$\overline{W}$. For write operations, R/$\overline{W}$ = 0. This enables data switches D0 to D7 to pass their data to the bus and hence, to the device for which it is intended. For read operations, R/$\overline{W}$ = 1; this disables the tri-state buffers and hence disconnects data switches D0 to D7 from the bus. However, the displays are

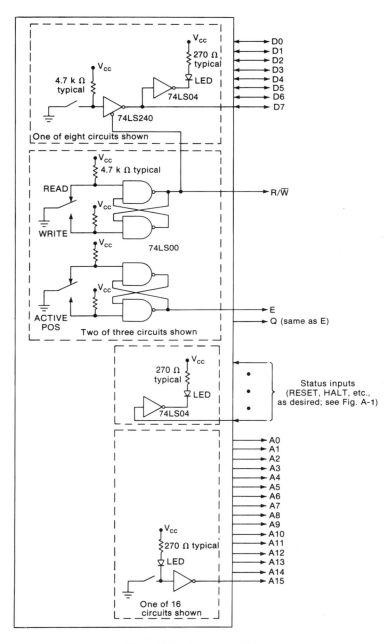

Figure F–1: Tester for 6809.

still connected. Since this is a read operation, the device accessed passes its data to the bus, where it is viewed on these displays.

Status lines. Since we only need to view status lines, simple indicators are used.

Testers for any processor with a nonmultiplexed bus may be constructed similarly. For testers using multiplexed buses, some additional considerations are in order. These are discussed below.

AN EXAMPLE TESTER FOR THE 8085

For multiplexed systems (such as the 8085), a scheme is needed that permits us to output addresses and data to the shared bus in the same logical order as does the actual 8085 (Figure B-2, Appendix B). Addresses are output early in the cycle, whereas data are output late. An appropriate circuit is shown in Figure F-2. Note that RD is used to enable and disable the data bus switches. Normally, they are enabled onto the bus. When a read transaction is in progress, RD floats them off the bus. However, the indicators remain. Thus data from the accessed device are displayed on bus indicators as required during reads.

Read and write procedures are summarized below. Ensure that all switches ($\overline{\text{RD}}$, $\overline{\text{WR}}$, ALE) are initially in the inactive position.

8085 Write Procedure

1. Set the address on AD0 to AD7 and A8 to A15.
2. Strobe ALE to latch low-order addresses.
3. Set the data on switches AD0 to AD7.
4. Set IO/$\overline{\text{M}}$ for memory or I/O as required.
5. Strobe $\overline{\text{WR}}$.

8085 Read Procedure

1. Set the address on AD0 to AD7 and A8 to A15.
2. Strobe ALE to latch low-order addresses.
3. Set IO/$\overline{\text{M}}$ for memory or I/O as required.
4. Hold $\overline{\text{RD}}$ in the active state to observe the input data on the data bus LEDS.

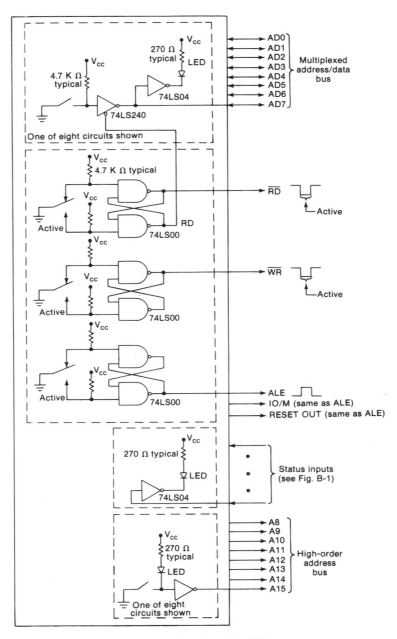

Figure F-2: Tester for 8085.

INDEX